The good (but cheap) Chicago Restaurant Book

This book is dedicated to
the late
Ronnie I. Yoshida, waiter at Wing Yee's
and a fine human being.

The good (but cheap) Chicago Restaurant Book

**Where to Find Great Meals
at Little Neighborhood Restaurants
From $1.50 to $4.95**

revised and enlarged edition

Jill Nathanson Rohde & Ron Rohde

THE SWALLOW PRESS INC.

CHICAGO

Published by
The Swallow Press Incorporated
811 West Junior Terrace
Chicago, Illinois 60613

First edition
First printing

This book is printed on recycled paper

LIBRARY OF CONGRESS CATALOG CARD NUMBER: 76-3133
ISBN 0-8040-0698-9

Special thanks to our parents, Don and Evelyn Nathanson and
Gertrude Rohde, for help, encouragement, and for starting us
out early on good food; to our publisher Mort Weisman; and to
our editor Donna Ippolito, not only for her work on the manu-
script, but for driving us around the city collecting last minute
changes. Thanks also to Larry Rosenberg who was willing to
go anywhere at any time, and to all the readers whose suggestions and kind words made all the eating seem worthwhile.

Table of Contents

Introduction

We've just spent the past two years re-eating our way through Chicago. Not only have we gone back to all the restaurants listed in our last book, gained and lost and regained several pounds, but we've also turned up over 65 new budget spots. Included too are several more nationalities: Colombian, Indonesian, Romanian, Vietnamese, and Cuban/Chinese.

To us, the beauty of Chicago continues to be its many distinctive neighborhoods and, of course, the people in them. The energy, diversity, and flavor of the streets remains very much alive. We've found that one of the best and easily the most pleasant ways to capture the feel and spirit of a neighborhood is to eat in it. Just take a stroll down Devon, Grand Avenue, or 18th Street, and nosh a knish, a ham-and-provolone-stacked sub, or drippy taco. The flavors, sights, sounds, and smells combine for one of the all-time sensory highs.

Even though franchises continue their rampage, we remain encouraged by the ability of the simple, Mom-and-Pop storefront to survive. Although the flowers on their tables might be plastic, the food is anything but. One can count on made-from-scratch soups, wholesome bread, and gravies that have never seen the inside of a package.

Many of "our" restaurants remain undiscovered by people from outside the neighborhood. Most have a cozy, almost-like-home feel to them. Some are even better than home. While wonderfully, ethnically diverse, all offer great food at bargain prices. Complete, filling dinners can be had for $4.95, and often much less. Even the smidgin-over-$3.00 roast duck, dumpling, kraut, soup, and strudel spread remains very much a reality. It just requires a jaunt to Berwyn or Riverside. In fact, we've done lots more driving, searching out the bargains in such spread-out locales as Palatine, Orland Park, Lakemoor, and Elgin.

We've kept in a splurge section, a small but diverse group of more expensive restaurants to visit when you feel the urge to really take off. These are places that stand out in terms of excellent food, unusual atmosphere, or both. The sections on lunches, Sunday brunches, and our favorite spots for snacks, sandwiches, street eats, and related goodies have also been expanded.

We've deleted several places from our earlier edition, either because they've closed (most regrettably, Little Czechoslovakia, Ana's, and Maharaja), jumped beyond our price range, or just weren't good enough anymore. We've kept a catch-all section to take care of restaurants that were either late discoveries, on the budget borderline, or else are notable for only a few special dishes.

To avoid special treatment we never tell any of the restaurant owners what we are up to, and generally try to be as inconspicuous as anyone copying a six-page menu under the table can be. We've got it down to being able to take notes and eat with chopsticks at the same time. Nobody really knows us yet (except at Ann Sather's and The French Kitchen), so we haven't had to resort to the subterfuge of bouffant wigs, dark shades, or plastic surgery.

This book naturally reflects our personal opinions, but we have tried to present a fair and honest evaluation. Our main criterion is, of course, the food: Does it taste good? Is a generous amount of loving attention and skill devoted to it? Is it of good quality, or at least prepared well enough to disguise the quality? Does it lift our spirits, linger fondly in our memory, and would we look forward to eating it again (maybe even the next day)?

For each restaurant included, we have sought to emphasize the best dishes and, if necessary, to point out the bummers. Keep in mind that restaurants may vary mightily in quality and service, especially the small, inexpensive ones. Also, menus are apt to change, due to the cook's inclination or seasonal bargains at the market. All prices were checked at press time, but don't be surprised by minor escalation.

What follows is a guide to Chicago's best budget restaurants —and there are some great ones. We hope that you will enjoy them as much as we have.

Jill Nathanson Rohde and Ron Rohde
December, 1976

Budget

Authors' Note

Liquor, or its absence, is noted in the following manner:

Full Bar: Restaurants that serve their own cocktails, beer, and wine.

B.Y.O.: No liquor service, but you are welcome to bring your own wine or beer.

No liquor: Abstain in these restaurants.

Also, the vast majority of our restaurants don't take credit cards. Luckily, they are inexpensive. In our "splurge" category, where you might need more cash than you care to tote in your pocket, we indicate which credit cards are accepted. Reservations are not necessary, unless noted.

El Criollo

1706 W. Fullerton
Phone: 549-3373
Parking: Street
Full bar

Tue.-Thur., Sun., 4:00 P.M.–Midnight
Fri., Sat., 4:00 P.M.–1:00 P.M.

The best and only Argentine restaurant in the city. El Criollo is located along a quiet stretch of factories and used to look like a typical workingman's bar. Now that it's been outfitted with travel posters, steerhorns, a bola, and tableclothes, it's moving toward a supper club ambiance.

The menu reflects the Argentine love affair with the cow. This passion is best in evidence with parillada, a kind of Argentine mixed grill ($6.25, can easily serve two). Sharing the plate are well-marinated, charcoal grilled short ribs, a smoothly flavored Argentine sausage, peppery blood sausage, and sauteed sweetbreads. It's also possible to dine on short ribs (asado, $4.50) alone. Both dishes come with a big bowl of salad, french bread, and a wonderful homemade salsa, fashioned from finely minced parsley, oil, vinegar, garlic, and crushed red pepper.

To eat more cheaply, it's necessary to switch to Mexican. Chicken, cheese, or beef enchiladas go for $3.50, tacos for $2.75 ($3.75 with rice and beans), and tostadas for $3.00. There are also several Mexican-style steaks priced at $4.50.

On weekends, be sure to sample empanadas (65¢), a golden-toned crescent-shaped turnover filled with a creative mix of ground beef, chopped eggs, raisins, green olives, and onions. Desserts (75¢-$1.00) can also be a treat. There's a delectable flan courting a rich topping of caramel sauce, and a gelatinous sweet potato pudding served with slices of mild white cheese. Wine, by the way, is pretty expensive.

Run by distinguished-looking Señor and Señora Porto, El Criollo comes alive on weekends when Sr. Porto takes to the piano and serenades with lush romantic tunes. Young Argentine couples applaud enthusiastically, and it's hard not to get wrapped up in the spirit. On other evenings, create your own by selecting some mellow Argentine tunes on the jukebox.

Blue Willow

3232 S. Harlem, Riverside Daily, 11:30 A.M.–8:00 P.M.
Phone: 442-7330
Parking: Street
No Liquor

The peaceful tone of a Czech mountain village translated on bustling Harlem Avenue. Walls are decorated with engraved walking sticks, woodburn-designed plates, and an expansive mountain landscape. Filmy white curtains cover the windows; meals are served on blue willow-patterned china. And the food is as easy to take as the decor, complete meals going for a dime or two over $3.00.

Soup starts things off smoothly. There's usually a placid but decent beef-noodle, and perhaps, a more defiant tripe, brimming with potatoes, carrots, and thin sliced meat in a semi-thick broth. The rye bread is a minor disappointment, as it's too soft and lacking in substance.

The menu includes a few variations on standard Bohemian restaurant fare. If pork California-style ($3.65) is around, by all means, go west. Three puff-crusted tenderloin patties come showered with sauteed onions and button mushrooms. Although fresh mushrooms would have made it even better, it's still a dish worthy of every bite. Pot roast ($3.15) is tender, slices varying from moist to slightly dry. There's also a crisp veal cutlet ($3.10), Bohemian-style steak (a Swiss cut, $3.15), pickled beef with sour cream gravy ($3.15), boiled beef with dill gravy ($3.15), and, of course, roast duck ($3.15).

Bohemians seem to specialize in light, smooth, near-perfect gravy, and that at Blue Willow is no exception. Try it on the bread dumplings; we were almost tempted to douse the kraut. Delicious kolacky for dessert, including one filled with a dense, almond-flavored poppy seed, and another with very pruney prunes.

Bratislava

2525 N. Clark
Phone: 348-6938
Parking: Street
Full bar

Wed.-Sat., 5:00 P.M.–11:00 P.M.
Sun., 4:00 P.M.–9:00 P.M.
Closed Monday, Tuesday

Bratislava has kept its charm intact, but not its prices, which are moving rapidly beyond our range. John, one of our favorite waiters, is no longer there, but the white billowing curtains, colorful print tablecloths, and Czech artifacts still combine to produce a cozy, very European flavor.

So does the food. One can always count on robust, vigorously seasoned soups (with the sauerkraut a standout) and a spirited seven-vegetable, slaw-like salad (95¢). The vegetables are shredded thin, marinated, and tossed with caraway. A dollop of sour cream makes it even better.

Goulashes, paprikashes, and several renditions of roast beef highlight the hearty Czech menu. Most successful is the homey-tasting beef goulash ($4.50); veal paprikash can range from eminently devourable to dull. Stuffed cabbage ($3.75) sports a creamy, dill-decorated sauce, and stuffed peppers are yet another tasty possibility ($3.95).

Plum dumplings covered with a sauce of melted butter and poppyseeds ($2.75 for 5) sometimes thump rather than float, and are just liable to come minus the poppyseeds. But the cheese strudel (85¢) never disappoints; it's light and feathery, subtly sparked with lemon and definitely one of the most seductive versions in town.

Czechoslovakia

6012 W. 26th St., Cicero
Phone: 656-9781
Parking: Street
Full bar

Tue.-Sun., Noon–8:00 P.M.
Closed Monday

Another good spot to put away a 3,000-calorie meal for under $3.00. The menu veers slightly in content from our other Bohemian places (no duck, no roast chicken), but certainly not in quantity. All meals encompass rolls and a robust rye, homemade soup, a choice of cole slaw, cucumber salad, pickled beets, or tossed lettuce, bread or potato dumplings, sauerkraut, and dessert.

We started auspiciously with goulash soup, heavy on meat, potatoes, and tiny firm dumplings. Mild chicken noodle offers fewer memories. The peppery marinated cucumbers, even with its slight perfume taste, is our salad preference, although the tossed salad isn't a bad one.

The women chefs reach their peak with stews. Evidence of long, slow simmering characterizes the oxtail ($2.65). Meat eagerly falls off the bone, and rich brown gravy can only be defined as mouth-wateringly succulent. The evenly tender karlsbad goulash ($2.75) is well-endowed with both beef and flavor, helped along by swirls of sour cream and a path of paprika. Bread dumplings are thick and substantial, and the kraut smooth and potent.

We also tried one evening special, the Bohemian burger ($2.15), and wished we hadn't strayed from the regular list. Not only was it cold, dry, and overcharred but accompanied by a strangely sour potato salad. Other choices from the "normal" lineup include roast pork loin ($3.10), meat loaf ($2.30), liver, bacon, and onions ($2.45), stuffed peppers ($2.45), and fruit dumplings ($2.40).

As at many Czech restaurants, there's a tiny bar off to one side of the room. Tables are covered in oilcloth, Hamm's beer signs hug the panelled walls, and the feel is sky blue waters rustic.

Olympic Restaurant

6139 W. Cermak, Cicero
Phone: 652-0101
Parking: Street
Full bar

Daily, 11:00 A.M.–8:00 P.M.
Closed Tuesday

With its carpeting, panelling, chandeliers, and bar, the Olympic looks fancier than other budget Bohemian restaurants. But there's no need to worry about fancy prices. Almost everything, other than steak, is $3.00 or less—which is really quite a bargain as dinners include soup, salad and dessert.

The daily offerings feature the usual beef, pork, and fowl. Their duck is as delicious as you would anticipate—moist, fleshy, crisp-skinned, and the $3.20 price never fails to amaze. Roast chicken ($3.00) is equally pleasing, especially since it comes with a tasty bread dressing. Roast pork ($3.00), breaded pork tenderloin ($3.00), and pickled beef ($3.20) are other choices. We found only the boiled beef ($3.00) disappointing. Its dill gravy sounded intriguing, but not only was it too thick and floury, there was also far too much of it.

Thursday's a good time to make it out to the Olympic as a host of specials is added to the menu. There are veal hearts with sour cream gravy ($2.50), pot roast and crisp potato pancakes ($3.00), meat loaf ($2.50), flicky (a ham-noodle combination, $2.10), and sometimes even rabbit ($4.00).

As for the meal's accessories, soups, in particular, are delicious. The vegetable soup is thick with white beans, barley, and noodles, the tripe soup is rich and peppery, and a light, pleasant taste characterizes the beef noodle. Sliced bread dumplings, which accompany most of the meat dishes, are fairly light and interestingly textured. They are the only ones we've had in which you can actually see chunks of bread. Both the sweet and sour cabbage and the sauerkraut have a gentle tang.

The Olympic is quiet and sedate. People here seem to be "dining out" rather than just "eating out." The motherly waitresses really take care of you and add a nice, friendly touch.

Pilsner

6725 W. Cermak, Berwyn   Daily, 11:00 A.M.–9:00 P.M.
Phone: 484-2294
Parking: Street
Full bar

Yet another well-balanced Czech. The Pilsner offers big, hearty soup-to-strudel meals, none of them over $3.20 (with the exception of the $5.50 T-bone steak). All is served in a brightly lit, somewhat impersonal dining room that is warmed considerably by friendly waitresses and the homey-tasting food.

Almost scandalous is their $3.20 duck dinner (only $2.99 on week-ends!). It's so big, crackly-skinned, and meaty that one would be hard pressed to prepare it any better or cheaper at home. Nearly as bountiful is the plump, juicy roast chicken ($3.00), and the tender, flavor-soaked roast pork ($3.20).

If none of these do it, there's Moravian sausage, boiled beef with dill, mushroom, or tomato sauce, svickova (pickled beef), pork "wienerschnitzel," and chicken paprika. All are accompanied by a stellar supporting cast: rye bread and rolls, soup, three delicate, spongy bread dumplings, sweet and sour white cabbage, or a mildly tingly kraut.

Better-than-average desserts too. The poppyseed strudel, actually more like a coffeecake or babka, is neatly laced with a moist filling of ground poppyseed. The marble cake is light, and Danish pudding, an unusual combo of vanilla pudding, strawberry jello, and whipped cream, tastes surprisingly more pleasant than it sounds.

Good Czech beer and European wine wash the meal down with ease.

Plaza Restaurant

7016 W. Cermak, Berwyn   Daily, 10:30 A.M.–8:00 P.M.
Phone: 795-6555   Sun., 10:30 A.M.–7:00 P.M.
Parking: Street
Full bar

The tiny Plaza Dining Room has gone big-time. Its former back-patting, table-sharing coziness have given way to an expansive, brightly lit modern dining area complete with bar. Prices are even up some, but at an average $3.25 per meal, we can't quibble. Fortunately the hearty, homecooked meals are still very much in evidence.

The Plaza is fruit dumpling paradise ($3.00, served every day except Sunday). Liable to be filled with either apricots or plums, they're light, chewy, and tennis ball sized. Tart pot cheese, sugar, and melted butter combine for a fine contrasting topping.

By far the most popular selection, however, is duck ($3.45). It's cooked to a golden crisp, tender, meaty perfection. Roast chicken ($3.20) or roast capon ($3.25), both accompanied by caraway-flecked dressing, are also succulent as are the thick, juicy roast pork ($3.30) and the plump, mild-mannered thueringer ($2.25). Other options include meat loaf ($2.20), roast beef ($3.30), pork tenderloin ($3.30), and smoked butt ($3.30).

Soups are substantial, particularly the thick chicken giblet or robust liver dumpling, but beef noodle is bland. The bread dumplings come across a little like paperweights, but the sauerkraut is just right. If you have any space left, there is usually a choice from among poppyseed cake or prune, apricot, or cheese kolacky.

The Restaurant (Binder's)

(one of our favorites)

7 E. Burlington Road, Riverside
Phone: 447-9730
Parking: Lot
No Liquor

Mon.-Sat., 11:00 A.M.–
8:00 P.M.
Closed Sunday

Our new favorite among the bevy of Bohemian bargains, The Restaurant is tiny and usually crowded with tables full of serious eaters. Prices are expectedly low (it's easy for two people to get away spending little over $6.00), and every course is a marvel.

Their roast chicken ($3.00) takes that humble version of the bird to new heights. The skin literally crackles and the flesh underneath is moist, tender perfection. A sliced, bread-pudding-like dressing, thick bread dumplings, expertly balanced kraut, and a mild gravy add weighty accompaniment. Nearly as tasty are the crisply-breaded, flap-jack-sized pork tenderloin patties ($3.25) or the fork-tender, homey-tasting roast pork ($3.00). Roast beef ($3.25), roast duck ($3.25), thueringer ($2.50), smoked butt ($3.00), and dumplings and eggs ($2.30) round out the menu.

If split pea soup is on hand, give it a try. It's smooth, mild, and nicely crunched with croutons. Other brews might include a spicy tripe, delicate beef-noodle, or potato. If a plum slice is on the agenda, luck is even more on your side. Served warm and festooned with fresh sliced plums and a dusting of powdered sugar, it is delicate, not too sweet, and delicious.

The Restaurant has only ten tables and is equally limited on decor. Food and its enjoyment are the chief concerns. Most of the staff and the patrons converse in Czech, but everyone is friendly and eager to please.

Walk off your meal by exploring the exceptionally lovely town of Riverside.

Ridgeland Restaurant

6408 W. Cermak, Berwyn
Phone: 749-1151
Parking: Street
B.Y.O.

Daily, 11:00 A.M.–7:30 P.M.
Sat., 11:00 A.M.–7:00 P.M.
Closed Sunday

Yet another Bohemian bargain on Cermak Road, the Ridge-land is right up there with the best. It's a big, gleaming store-front that can be recognized by apricot-colored curtains, green awning, and proximity to the Berwyn Movie Theater.

The offerings are "standard Bohemian restaurant," meaning hearty, uncomplicated meat and dumplings. Don't be con-fused by the three prices on the menu. They stand for "small portion," "regular portion," and "business lunch" (the same size, but 30¢ to 40¢ cheaper than the "regular" and served only between 11 A.M. and 2 P.M.).

The Ridgeland's highlight is, of course, the $3.25 duck dinner. The meat is super juicy, though sometimes slightly fatty, and the skin is crackly crisp. Other good choices are roast pork ($3.25), meat loaf ($2.40), ribs with sauerkraut ($2.90) and, if available, beef with a sour cream-dill gravy ($3.20). All of the meats, except the latter, are covered with a light, savory brown gravy which enhances rather than drowns out the flavor.

The accompanying bread dumplings are the lightest and airiest we've tasted, and the sauerkraut is just sour enough. Soups are excellent, particularly the rich, flavorful eggdrop (similar to chicken-dumpling).

As for desserts, if you visit the Ridgeland on Friday, its fruit dumpling day and you're in for a treat. They're won-drous things, plump and mildly sweet. The pot cheese, butter, cinnamon-sugar topping provide a pungent contrast to the mild dumpling. Split an order ($2.20) among two to four people.

As with other Bohemian restaurants, the Ridgeland closes and runs out of certain dishes early. You can call up ahead of time to reserve the selection you want (particularly if you're counting on duck.)

Stehlik's

4209 W. 26th
Phone: 762-3585
Parking: Street
No liquor

Mon.-Fri., 11:00 A.M.–8:00 P.M.
Sun., 11:00 A.M.–7:00 P.M.
Closed Saturday

If Archie Bunker lived in Chicago, Stehlik's would be his kind of restaurant. It's a small, homey, meat-and-potatoes place frequented primarily by people from this old Bohemian neighborhood. Most of the clientele are over forty, and lively conversation moves from counter to table and back again. As an outsider, you'll be looked over a bit, but not enough to make you feel uncomfortable.

The food at Stehlik's is good, plentiful, and cheap. All meals include a meat course, vegetable, dumpling, or potato, rye bread, and coffee. These complete meals average $2.40. A bowl of homemade soup is only 25¢ extra, and prices go up a bit on Sundays.

Simple, hearty foods make up the menu. There are short ribs ($2.60), roast pork ($2.50), meat loaf ($2.30), and bratwurst ($2.20). Roast chicken ($2.40), though a little dry, comes with a good, spicy bread dressing. Our favorite, however, is the breaded veal cutlet ($2.50); it's frisbee-sized, fresh-tasting, and meltingly crisp. Combine your meat with bread or potato dumplings and either sweet-and-sour white cabbage or a sauerkraut mild enough to convert an avowed sauerkraut-hater.

The robust soup puts Campbell's to shame. There might be a thick beef goulash soup, a light, sweet beef noodle, or a creamy cauliflower sporting big chunks of the vegetable.

The decor of Stehlik's is simple and pleasant, with its red-checked tablecloths and print wallpaper. Be sure to plan on an early dinner, as the crowd arrives at around 5:00, the waitress has her coat on at 7:00, and by 7:15, you might be spending the night.

Atlantic Fish & Chip

7115 W. Grand
Phone: 622-3259
Parking: Street
Full bar

Mon.-Thur., 4:00 P.M.–Midnight
Fri.-Sat., 4:00 P.M.–1:30 A.M.
Sun., 11:00 A.M.–Midnight
Reservations Friday & Saturday
Closed Tuesday

If you've always thought British food to be bland and boiled, check out the Atlantic Fish & Chip Restaurant. Only the cornbeef is boiled, and everything is well-seasoned. The menu features specialties from Wales, Scotland, and Ireland, as well as England, with several budget entrees for each category.

House specialties include Welsh beef stew ($3.25), several meat pies (around $3.25), flaky pasties (meat-filled turn-overs, $3.25), some great fish and chips ($2.50), and everyone's favorite, black pudding (similar to blood sausage.) A good choice is shepherd's pie ($3.75), a nicely flavored chopped steak topped with mashed potatoes and melted cheese. All meals come with buttered Irish soda bread, usually chips (french fries), and the inevitable canned peas.

Desserts include trifle (a jam-filled, whipped cream and sherry-doused cake), rice pudding, and chocolate eclairs, each for 75¢. There is also a good blueberry tart, served with homemade custard sauce (75¢).

To wash everything down, Atlantic has an extensive supply of English, Irish, Scottish and Welsh ales, beers, and stouts. A limited and fairly inexpensive wine list also bears perusing.

The Atlantic's owners, Emyr and Mair Morris, who are from Wales, have decorated their long dining room to resemble a lavish British pub. There's red flocked wall paper, black beams, and heavy chandeliers. On weekends, folksingers entertain, and the place takes on a lively, spirited air.

The Maggie

1447 W. Devon
Phone: 743-9251
Parking: Street
B.Y.O.

Mon.-Thur., 4:00 P.M.–9:00 P.M.
Fri., 4:00 P.M.–10:30 P.M.
Sat., 10:30 A.M.–10:30 P.M.
Sun., 10:30 A.M.–9:00 P.M.

The Maggie looks like it arrived intact from Scotland. The walls display a carnival of memorabilia: antique Scottish postcards, a clan map, coats of arms, paintings of ships; tables are covered in plastic-shielded tartans. Irish and Scottish newspapers hug a rack and the jukebox provides haven to the Irish Rovers, Dermot Henry, and Darby O'Gill.

The menu is as temptingly authentic—Scottish meat pie, Forfar bridie, cornish pastie, steak'n kidney pie, and black pudding. Everything's tasty, sometimes a bit oily, and very cheap. Making a choice is never easy, but most dishes can be ordered either as a complete meal (with peas, bread, and beverage) or as a side dish. So it's possible and enjoyable to order several things and share.

We're partial to the fish n' chips ($1.90), served lightly crusted, flaky-fleshed, and tongue-burning hot. Be sure to add a sprinkle or two of vinegar. Ground meat, potatoes, and onions encased in an ultra-rich and crisp, boat-shaped crust comprise the Cornish pastie ($1.80; $1.00). It's tasty, but slightly greasy. A softer, doughier crust cushions the ground sirloin-filled meat pie ($1.80; $1.00). Forfar bridie ($1.80; $1.00) and steak 'n kidney pie ($3.75) are variations on the meat and pastry theme.

Crustless possibilities include combinations of Irish sausage, bacon, and black pudding ($2.10; $2.95) or such standards as corned beef and cabbage ($3.75) and Irish stew ($3.75). Don't go away without tasting a crumpet (60¢). Halfway between an English muffin and fried farina, they taste heavenly when spread with butter and jelly (too bad it's plastic-wrapped). Join it with a cup of strong-brewed tea, and ghosts of Mary Poppins and Miss Marple appear.

St. Andrews Fish & Chips

4542 N. Western
Phone: 784-6200
Parking: Street
B.Y.O.

Daily, 4:00 P.M.–10:00 P.M.
Fri.-Sat., 4:00 P.M.–11:00 P.M.
Closed Monday

St. Andrews Fish & Chips is a tidy and cheerful tiny store-front. Walls are papered in tartan plaids and further deco-rated with pictures of the Scottish countryside, soldiers in full dress, and coats of arms.

The compact menu offers Scottish and English specialties, primarily fish dishes or offsprings of the meat pie and pastie. Everything is well prepared, neatly served, and tastily home-made. Dinners include bread or rolls, chips (french fries), and canned vegetables, and several cost under $2.00.

Their fish and chips ($1.95) should keep you out of the franchise outfits. The fish is dipped in a special batter, then quick-fried until golden-puffy outside, moist and flaky inside. It tastes fantastic, especially when sprinkled with a few drops of malt vinegar. Scallops ($2.95) and shrimp ($3.10) are two other deep-fried offerings. The salmon croquettes ($1.95) are delicious when feather-light, but at times have been gluey. Baked halibut or sole ($2.95) are appealingly served in a melted butter sauce and are both quite good.

For non-fish fanciers, one of the better selections is the Cornish pastie ($1.95), a savory mixture of well-seasoned ground chuck, chopped potatoes, and carrots wrapped in a rich flaky crust. Forfar bridie ($1.95) is a close relative but the ground meat is more strongly seasoned and the crust even crisper. Scotch pie, a similar pastry-meat combination ($1.95), steak and kidney pie ($3.15), or a pastry-enclosed sausage roll ($1.95) are other tasty options.

Portions at St. Andrews are not enormous, so if it's been a long time between meals, try ordering an a la carte side dish in addition to the regular dinner. Practically everything on the menu (meat pie, croquettes, etc.) is available on the side for 95¢. Dessert, too, is extra, but the creamy rice pud-ding (50¢) has a smooth, mellow taste, and the sherry trifle (55¢) is served with mounds of whipped cream.

Anything on the menu can be ordered to take out at con-siderably lower prices.

Ding Hoe

105 W. Division
Phone: 944-8433
Parking: Street
B.Y.O.

Daily, 4:00 P.M.–11:30 P.M.
Closed Tuesday

For many years Ding Hoe was a bleak little hole in the wall on Clark Street that enjoyed a devoted following for its fine, low-priced food. Since it moved around the corner, the food is still fine, and the place bigger and somewhat less drab. The menu is filled with over a hundred entrees, and not many Cantonese favorites are left out. Portions are quite generous, and prices are reasonable.

Everyone seems to begin their meal with egg rolls ($1.50), as Ding Hoe does them fine. The crackly shells are stuffed with crisp vegetables, shrimp, and pork. Fried wonton ($1.25) is also delicious. Vegetable soup (60¢) is a flavorful, nourishing broth filled with sliced fresh mushrooms, Chinese greens, pork, and tomatoes.

Choosing an entree calls for some heavy decision-making. Our favorite dish is kai ding ($3.65), a well-seasoned blend of chicken, black and button mushrooms, peapods, water chestnuts, and almonds. Not far behind are shrimp in lobster sauce ($3.50) and steamed beef with mushrooms, waterchestnuts, and peapods ($3.50). Buck toy tenderloin steak ($4.00) features tender beef and greens done up in oyster sauce, and a less expensive but just as tasty variation, buck toy cha shu ($3.25), substitutes barbecued pork for the steak. The sweet and sour dishes (pork, $2.90; chicken, $3.75) maintain their crispness and include an ample portion of meat. Fried rice ($1.95) is moist, and beef-mushroom chop suey ($2.85) is quite good, but the chow mein falls flat, primarily because the noodles are soggy. (They should switch to the super-thin, crisp ones.)

Service at Ding Hoe is prompt and courteous, and you are never hurried. There is generally seating as the restaurant is roomy. We think it's one of the best budget places to eat in the Division/Rush Street area.

Golden Crown

1951 Cherry Lane, Northbrook   Daily, 11:00 A.M.–8:30 P.M.
Phone: 272-1812   Fri., 11:00 A.M.–10:00 P.M.
Parking: Lot   Sun., 4:00 P.M.–8:30 P.M.
Full bar

For some excellent Chinese food in the northern suburbs, try the Golden Crown. The outstanding feature of this restaurant is owner Ray Wong's obvious emphasis on quality. He relies on crisp, fresh ingredients and uses plenty of them. If the menu states that a dish will have peapods and almonds, you don't have to conduct a search party.

There are well over sixty main dishes on the menu. An extra $1.40 will bring a dinner complete with soup, fried wonton, egg roll, fried rice, dessert, and tea!

Some entrees worth a try are the breast of chicken sub gum chow mein ($3.35), the sweet-and-sour pork with mandarin oranges ($3.45), and the char su sai foon ($3.55). The latter is an interesting blend of barbecued pork, peapods, water chestnuts, scrambled egg, and thin transparent noodles. Lichee nuts, candied ginger, and pineapple are included in the exotic sweet and sour beef ($3.55). Other possibilities are the breaded hong sue shrimp ($4.05) or the hong sue chicken kow with black mushrooms ($3.65).

For appetizers, the fried wonton ($1.50) and egg rolls ($1.65) are crisp and fresh-tasting. The meaty barbecued ribs ($2.75) sport a thick, gooey sauce but can occasionally be tough. They also make one of the best wonton soups we've ever tasted.

The setting at Golden Crown is an easy blend of oriental and modern. There are two medium-sized dining rooms which provide comfortable seating. The pace is relaxed, but be sure to plan on an early dinner as the restaurant closes at 8:30, except on Friday.

Directions: Take Edens Expressway north to Dundee. West on Dundee to Waukegan Road. South to Schmermer, then turn west to first stoplight. Turn left into shopping center and look for Golden Crown.

Wing Yee's

(one of our favorites)

2556 N. Clark   Daily, 3:00 P.M.–11:00 P.M.
Phone: 935-7380   Closed Monday
Parking: Street (difficult)
B.Y.O.

Although it has slipped a notch from its past glory, Wing Yee's remains our favorite place for Cantonese food. We have yet to taste better sweet and sour pork, pressed duck, or egg foo young. Soups are superb too, particularly the vegetable (85¢), a light broth filled with fresh mushrooms, spinach, tomatoes, celery, pork, etc.

Among the main dishes, several are recommended. All feature quality ingredients, are served hot and taste fresh. The almond-topped pressed duck ($3.80) is brilliant—a perfect contrast of crisp, greaseless skin and juicy meat. The sweet and sour pork or ribs ($3.50) have a light, crisp coating and come in a delicious gooey sauce. Chicken subgum chow mein Cantonese-style ($4.10) is excellent—a bounty of crunchy, fresh vegetables, white meat, almonds, and pan-fried noodles. A more unusual but equally delicious dish is sai foon ($3.70), a blend of glossy transparent noodles, pork, shrimp, and scallions in a soy-molasses sauce. Its cousin, chow foon ($2.90), is crisper, heavy on the bean sprouts, and equally good. Beef and vegetable dishes (beef and broccoli, beef and green beans, etc.) are also done up right, as is the moist, well-seasoned pork fried rice ($2.50).

Service at Wing Yee's can be slow. The wait for a table used to be long enough to get well into *War and Peace*, but lately the Classic Comic version is about all you'll have time for. Whatever the wait, we feel it's worth it.

Lantern Chinese Restaurant

1046½ W. Argyle   Daily, 11:00 A.M.–10:00 P.M.
Phone: 784-9487
Parking: Street
B.Y.O.

This fairly recent Argyle arrival has to be one of the all-time cheap Chinese restaurants. The food isn't fantastic, but if you're low on funds and crave a decent, filling Chinese meal, it would be hard to find a better bargain.

Restrain nibbling on the almond cookies, as main dishes come swiftly. The big, crisp eggroll ($1.00 for 2) are fully packed with shrimp, pork, a variety of greens, and probably, a hint of peanut butter. (As we enjoyed ours, a man sat in the back of the dining room carefully wrapping the next day's supply.) The crackly fried wonton ($1.00) are piled so high they defy finishing.

Easily the best entree is the Chinese-style fried chicken ($2.25), very plump, juicy, and crisp-crusted. Only the scallion, lemon, and tomato-chunk garnish and oddly-cut portions give away its non-Southern origins.

Angular slices of broccoli, waterchestnuts, and flat, tender strips of beef ($2.45) combine for a tasty dish, but the sweet and sour shrimp ($2.65) suffers from overcooked vegetables, soggy batter, and an overenthusiastic sprinkle of vinegar.

There are several amazing dinner deals. For instance, for only $10.50, four can feast on eggrolls, wonton soup, fried chicken, shrimp lo mein, beef and peapods, chicken fried rice, tea, and almond cookies.

Decoration is limited to fake panelling, a scattering of hanging lanterns, and handwritten announcements of the various dinner combos. The crowd is diverse: spunky older women, young Latino, Black, and Chinese couples, and a few families. And there's always enough action on Argyle to liven up the evening.

Tai Sam Yon

1318 E. 53rd St.
Phone: 484-1062
Parking: Street
B.Y.O. (discreetly)

Tue.-Sat., 11:00 A.M.–8:30 P.M.
Sun., Noon–8:30 P.M.
Closed Monday

Very few people from outside the south side know about Tai Sam Yon. The faded, eerily-lit dining room has all the cheer of a bus station in Kansas, but somehow this makes the food seem even better by comparison. Many believe it's the best Cantonese restaurant in the city, and although we're not true believers, there's plenty of goodness to be found.

Fat eggroll ($1.35) come stuffed with a variety of finely chopped goodies—cabbage, bok choy, bean sprouts, and pork, but the barbecued ribs ($2.30) taste tough and too greasy. The wonton soup (55¢) has also slipped, the wonton being doughy and the broth drab and under-seasoned.

Entrees make a comeback. One of the restaurant's major attractions is their generosity with quality ingredients like water chestnuts, peapods, and, especially, black mushrooms. A fine example of abundance can be found in abalone with vegetables ($4.15). Joining the chewy shellfish in a mild sauce are loads of crisp cooked vegetables and nearly a sackful of mushrooms.

Another favorite, barbecued pork with cashews ($3.50), features a bountiful, well-flavored mix of crunchy nuts, tender meat, and finely cut vegetables. The candy-crisp sweet and sour pork ($3.10) or shrimp ($3.95) bask in an evenly balanced sauce. Shrimp in lobster sauce ($4.00) would have been a standout had there been more shrimp and less salt.

If any of these dishes fail to turn you on, there are plenty more, including a good pressed duck ($3.50), chicken sub-gum chow mein ($2.90), and pork fritters ($3.15). An extra $1.35 buys a complete soup, eggroll, ribs, rice, tea, and almond cookie dinner.

Orchid Room

5951 N. Broadway
Phone: 878-1155
Parking: Street
B.Y.O.

Mon.-Thur., 4:30 P.M.–10:30 P.M.
Fri., 4:30 P.M.–11:00 P.M.
Sat., 11:30 A.M.–11:00 P.M.
Sun., 11:30 A.M.–10:30 P.M.

One of the first good Mandarin restaurants that's not in the splurge category. No dish on the menu is over $4.95, and most are under $4.00. Yet an impressive variety of popular Northern offerings are available.

Be sure to start your meal with a soup and/or appetizer. Shrimp toast ($1.45) is a worthy beginning, even though its quality varies. When it's good, it's very, very good—crisp and buttery-tasting. Steamer bo-bo ($1.55) are delicate, meat-filled dumplings, but are so tiny that you're liable to ask "Is that all there is?" Kwo-teh (fried pork-filled dumplings, $1.55) and fried wonton ($1.25) are both quite good.

Some main dishes are chicken with cashews ($3.75), Mongolian beef (a glazed combination of thin beef slices, scallions, and hot pepper, $4.15), and beef with seasonal vegetables ($3.95). Moo shu pork ($3.95), which is generally our favorite Mandarin dish, lives up to expectations. Razor-thin pancakes are accompanied by a crunchy mixture of finely-shredded pork, scallions, bamboo shoots, and egg. An unusual and excellent dish is crab meat soong ($4.25), a delicate blending of thin, crisp noodles, minced crab, scallions, carrots, and waterchestnuts, also served with pancakes.

Finish your meal with glazed apples or bananas ($1.95 for six pieces), as sensuous a dessert as there is. Working at your table, the waitress dips the hot, syrup-coated fruit into ice water until the coating reaches a brittle, candy-like hardness. It's sticky, sweet, and delightful, only to be avoided if you've recently visited the dentist.

Northern China

(one of our favorites)

5601 N. Clark   Mon.-Thur., 11:30 A.M.–10:00 P.M.
Phone: 334-8194   Fri., Sat., 11:30 A.M.–11:00 P.M.
Parking: Street   Sun., Noon–9:00 P.M.
B.Y.O.

One of Chicago's newer Northern Chinese entries, this attractive storefront is not only eminently affordable, its food is memorably edible. Food is artistically styled and gracefully served by a smiling, helpful young waitress.

The comprehensive menu ranges from the "everyday" (moo shu pork, Mongolian beef, almond chicken) to the exotic (jellyfish salad, and braised sea cucumbers). Prices hover around $3.50, which is very lenient for a Mandarin restaurant.

We started nicely with a delicately balanced hot and sour soup ($1.95, serves 2), brimming with shrimp, pork, bean curd, cloud ears, and mushrooms. Lovely, crisp-shelled spring rolls ($1.50) contain a slightly oily but flavorful blend of pork, beancurd slivers, and sprouts.

Entrees are equally compelling. It's hard to find anyone who doesn't like moo shu pork ($3.25), and that served at the Northern China will make even more converts. Although the pancake is a little too thick, one easily forgets after biting into the crunchy, beautifully-flavored filling. Garlic chicken ($3.25) is another standout, filled with shimmering bits of chicken, mushrooms, and waterchestnuts. The ginger beef ($3.75) carries several matchsticks of fresh ginger which enhance rather than obliterate the delicate quality of the beef.

Sizzling rice shrimp ($4.00), garnished with carrots cut in the shape of fish, offers the brittle crunch of toasted rice against the softly batter-coated shrimp. All is held together by a gentle sweet and sour sauce. Providing further textural thrills is snow peas and black mushrooms ($3.75), a contrast of crisp-to-the-bite peas and earthy, soft mushrooms.

La Colombianita

2903 W. Diversey   Daily, 2:00 P.M.–10:00 P.M.
Phone: 278-3432   Sat., Sun., 2:00 P.M.–Midnight
Parking: Street   Closed Monday
Beer only

La Colombianita opened not too long ago, and its genial owner assured us that he had not yet begun to decorate. As is, it looks like a glorified snack shop with a small, panelled rear dining room. The food is far more decorous, and, in fact very tasty, even though it may take awhile making it to your table. However, everyone is so friendly, the music good, and the beer so plentiful, that one scarcely notices.

Begin with an order of empanadas (30¢ each), as the crisp chartreuse turnovers come quickly and taste smooth and soothing. The owner suggested we bite off a corner, sprinkle on hot sauce, and proceed. We followed his advice, and he treated us to another round on the house.

The entrees center primarily upon variously prepared beef and pork dishes. Most carry along an avocado-graced salad and at least two starchy side kicks: rice, red beans, yucca, or patacones (thick salted discs of mashed plantain, a close kin to the banana).

One of the more flavorful entrees is bistec a la criolla ($3.25), fall-apart tender beef showered with onions and tomatoes. Two fried eggs add even more garnish and flavor to a similar cut in bistec a caballo ($3.75). Sobrebarriga ($3.25), a stringier, beer-marinated beef comes crackly on the outside, and soft and chewy inside.

In addition to beer, pop, and coffee, several homemade beverages are offered, including cinnamon-sprinkled avena (40¢), which is made from milk and ground oatmeal, tastes like liquid rice pudding, and is actually quite good.

La Creperie
(one of our favorites)

2845 N. Clark
Phone: 528-9050
Parking: Street (difficult)
B.Y.O.

Daily, 5:00 P.M.–11:00 P.M.
Closed Tuesday
No reservations accepted

Dining at La Crêperie is always enjoyable. The food is delicious and the price pleasingly low. Crêpes range from 40¢ for a plain crêpe with butter up to $3.25 for a seafood crêpe. Most cost under $2.00. The restaurant is small, cozy, and tastefully decorated. The young owner hails from Brittany, home of the crêpe, and really knows his trade.

The chalked-up menu features 12 buckwheat dinner crêpes. The chicken crêpe ($2.50) is remarkably soothing—large pieces of white meat in a delicate cream sauce garnished with parmesan-sprinkled, sauteed mushrooms. Another favorite is the ham, cheese and tomato crêpe ($2.10). The flavors blend nicely and come out something like a mild pizza. The ham and cheese ($1.65) and ham and egg ($1.65) are variations on the same theme. Both are tasty, as is the spinach creme crêpe ($1.65).

The crêpes, folded envelope style, are not tea-room size. One, along with a dessert crêpe or salad (85¢) makes a meal. The crouton and parmesan-topped tossed greens are fresh and the dressing tart and flavorful.

The whole wheat dessert crêpes are almost more pleasure than the dinner crêpes. The crêpe with jam ($1.00) is a melting mouthful and the banana, strawberry, or apple whipped cream crêpes ($1.60 each) contain a fresh fruit filling and are topped with whipped cream and powdered sugar.

An appealing bargain, if you'd like a taste of everything, is the chicken crêpe dinner. The $4.50 price includes a dinner crêpe, salad, dessert crêpe, and beverage. Most people bring their own wine, but the hot cider mulled with cinnamon sticks is delicious and tranquilizing.

Expect a wait at La Crêperie as seating is limited, and there's always a patiently waiting crowd.

Les Ouefs

163 E. Walton St.   Daily, 10:00 A.M.–Midnight
Phone: 337-7330   Closed Monday
Parking: Street (difficult)
Full bar

In the move from its former Clark Street storefront location to a berth inside the Playboy building, Les Ouefs remains filled with funky furniture and knickknacks, but eggs are still the come-on.

The menu is exceedingly mouthwatering. Omelets swell with such voluptuous enclosures as spinach, mushrooms, and mornay sauce; zucchini, eggplant, green pepper, tomato, onions, and garlic; or "tender nuggets of chicken enveloped in wine sauce and sweet white grapes." Most cost $4.25, and include in the price a basket of cake-textured blueberry muffins, breadsticks, and powdered sugar-dusted "snowflakes" as well as a salad or soup bar. The soups we have yet to try, but the salad fixings are super-varied and fresh.

For omelet scoffers, Les Ouefs makes such concessions as an elaborate hamburger, steak sandwich, and several daily specials. We generally stick to the eggs. Among our favorites are the previously mentioned spinach-inspired Florentine ($4.25), the Divan, ballooned with chicken, broccoli, and mornay sauce ($4.25), and, if the chicken livers are good, the omelet Bolgique ($3.95), further enhanced by onions and tarragon.

Also tasty is the Bauer Fruhstuck ($4.25), an oversized scrambled egg "pancake" filled with chunks of ham and potatoes, nestled under a melt of Monterey Jack cheese. Not as together is the omelet Manchu ($4.25), as stir-fried, soy-sauced chicken and vegetables somehow taste better among Chinese lanterns or minus the eggs.

Beguilingly fattening and expensive beverages, including a fresh strawberry milkshake ($1.50), coffee spiced with cinnamon and brown sugar (80¢), and goggle moggle, a whipped hot milk, egg, and honey concoction ($1.00). Service can vary from sensitive to scattered.

La Poele D'or

1121 S. Arlington Heights Rd., Tue.-Thur., Sun., 11:30 A.M.–
  Arlington Heights   8:30 P.M.
Phone: 593-9148 Fri., Sat., 11:30 A.M.–
Parking: Lot   8:30 P.M.
B.Y.O. Closed Monday

Wickedly rich crepes and omelets abound in this pleasant Normandy farmhouse-like restaurant. If you've always thought crepes were strictly the dainty stuff of bridal showers and bridge luncheons, a surprise awaits. Not only are La Poêle's versions abundantly filled, but amazingly filling. In fact the thin pancake almost loses its identity under its lush contents. And omelets are equally luxurious.

A broiler-browned top gives the crepe Duchesse ($3.25) a particularly mouth-watering visage. Stocked with chicken, asparagus, and mushrooms in a gruyere and wine-laced cheese sauce, its good looks don't deceive. Equally seductive is the crepe Princesse ($3.45), chicken livers, ham, and mushrooms enfolded in a madeira sauce. For seafood lovers, there's either the Cardenal, filled with scallops, shrimp, crab, and mussels ($4.65) or the Imperial, lobster and crab sharing a sherry-rich sauce.

Omelets are primarily variations on the crepe theme, as there's one with brandy-spiked chicken livers and mushrooms (Chasseur, $3.45), one with chicken and asparagus plus corn (Lyonnaise, $3.25), and another with sherried crab and lobster (Merveille, $4.25). Of particular appeal is the Forestière ($3.25), honey-toned, garlic-tinged, and generously plied with mushrooms, potatoes, and gruyere cheese.

A good salad, pleasantly shrouded with a mustardy vinaigrette, is included as is a basket of french bread. If you don't suffer from gout, split the croute mignonne appetizer ($1.95), a feathery puff pastry filled with madeira-spiked chicken livers, ham, and mushrooms. There's also a filmy, chocolate-sprinkled cheesecake (85¢) that's a bit too insubstantial for us, but others swear by it.

Liborio

4005 N. Broadway   Mon.-Fri., Sun., 11:00 A.M.–Midnight
Phone: 549-8723   Sat., 11:00 A.M.–2:00 A.M.
Parking: Street
Full bar

Liborio has something of the flavor of old Havana mixed in with present-day Chicago. The dining room is spacious and modern—a blend of Latin, early American, and western frontier. Cuban businessmen pore over their papers, attractive young couples dine here along with a suave-looking man or two who would be perfect for casting in a remake of Boston Blackie. It all makes for an interesting atmosphere, especially at night, when an elaborately coiffed blond unexpectedly begins a medley of show tunes on the piano.

The menu, comprised of several Cuban specialties, is fascinating in its own right. There's the traditional arroz con pollo (chicken and rice, $4.75), a relatively inexpensive, but out-of-our-budget paella ($6.50; call ahead to order), and a delicious, thick black bean soup. Sweet, sauteed ripe plantains (bananas) or deep-fried plantain chips (90¢) make excellent appetizers.

There are a dozen dinner possibilities which average $4.25 and include a basket of hot crusty french bread, salad, rice, usually a soup, and coffee. The roast chicken, Cuban-style ($4.25), is served with a light tomato sauce, rice, and black bean soup, which tastes delicious ladled over the rice. The lightly sauteed pork cutlet ($4.45) and the tender, marinated carne asada (roast beef, $4.35) are both well-prepared. There are also several interesting, inexpensive seafood dishes.

The menu features no less than fifteen egg dishes. The unusual ripe plantain omelet ($3.25) tastes slightly sweet. There is also a selection of Cuban sandwiches and several desserts including refreshing guava or papaya with cream cheese, bread pudding, an excellent flan (95¢), and an even better, though also overpriced, creamy pudding called natilla (95¢).

La Primera Lechonera #2

5653 N. Clark
Phone: 769-4545
Parking: Street
B.Y.O.

Daily, 11:00 A.M.–10:00 P.M.
Saturday, 11:00 A.M.–11:00 P.M.

A down home Cuban diner that doesn't attempt to cater to norteamericano tastes. The result is well-prepared, easy-to-take food that wouldn't alarm a visiting aunt from Altoona. Seasoning is understated, and meals center around a menage of meat, black beans, and rice.

A basket of tasty, hot, buttered french bread precedes everything. Follow it, perhaps, with Cuban roast beef (boliche asada, $3.00), a tender Swiss steak-like cut, slightly dry but well-shot with flavor. Another good bet is the combo. $3.20 buys a stomach-stretching array—lechon (roast pork), tamale, croqueta, salad, rice, and beans. The lechon is properly juicy, the yellow-orange tinted tamale hides bits of pork, and the croqueta tastes something like french fried mashed potatoes. A deep purple glow sets off the subtle-tasting mix of rice and beans.

If a soup called ajiaco is on tap, don't pass it by. Brimming with potatoes, beef, corn on the cob, yucca, and bananas, it exudes a homey goodness.

Expand further by ordering a few extras, particularly the soft, thick, deliciously sweet fried bananas (platanos maduros). Sip a batido, a foamy shake blended from milk and tropical fruit (we like the mamey flavor), and maybe toss in a few more calories by sampling the dense, smooth flan.

The platinum panelled restaurant is minimally decorated but super-spotless. Even better, it is steeped in a loose, free-flowing camaraderie. The owner's good-humored teenage daughter often waits on tables, and the cooks look like emigrés from a Hemingway story. Attractive young customers trade local gossip and will happily aid a first-time visitor through any language hassles.

There's another La Primera Lechonera at 2318 N. Milwaukee (772-6266).

Mandarin

3516 W. North Avenue,
   Stone Park
Phone: 865-9770
Parking: Lot
B.Y.O.

Mon.-Thur., Sun., 11:00 A.M.–
   9:00 P.M.
Fri., Sat., 11:00 A.M.–11:00 P.M.

The Mandarin looks like a combination Montana truck stop and Chinese gift shop, is run by a gracious, elderly Chinese couple who speak Spanish, and features Cuban and Chinese food, with a veal cutlet and hamburger thrown in too.

The menu lists no fewer than 177 items, plus several daily specials. A pleasant gastronomic schizophrenia ensues. There's everything from arroz con pollo to chicken fried rice, eggrolls and egg foo young to huevos con platanos, wonton soup and black bean soup. For dessert one can neatly combine fortune cookies with flan.

It's hard to make any kind of dent in the menu, but a good place to start is with the Cuban-fried plantain (60¢), a soft, fleshy relative of the banana, that is sauteed to a caramelly sweetness. Cantonese fried shrimp ($2.00) is less exciting, being submerged in a far too heavy batter.

For entrees, attempt the Mandarin chow mein ($3.75), a glossy mass of sauteed pork, shrimp, black and button mushrooms, peapods, waterchestnuts, and onions all piled onto soft pan-fried noodles. More potently flavored is chicken with garlic sauce ($3.95), chunks of white meat nicely offset by a limpid sauce. The moist ham fried rice is served in a voluptuous portion, and an order of Cuban roast pork ($2.60) contains not only tender slices of meat but a delicious black bean soup, white rice, and the wondrously inedible yucca.

By all means save room for flan (60¢), as creamy and satiny a version as we've ever tasted. The fortune cookies are good too.

French Restaurants

French restaurants can't really fit into a $4.95 budget anymore. However we don't feel it necessary to totally deprive ourselves, so we've included three that we feel offer a fine meal for the money.

FRENCH

La Bouillabaisse

1418 W. Fullerton	Tue.-Fri., 11:00 A.M.–2:30 P.M.;
Phone: 281-5688	5:30 P.M.–11:00 P.M.
Parking: Street	Sat., Sun., 5:30 P.M.–11:00 P.M.
Full bar	

One of Chicago's newer French arrivals and a most welcome one. The cavernous dining room, festooned with heavy oils of ships at sea, a saxophone, and hanging wooden spoon, is reminiscent of a suburban rec room. However, friendly service and a relaxed unpretentiousness make up for any scarcity of atmospheric points.

The succinct menu offers everything from filet mignon to coq au vin, and of course, bouillabaisse. Meals include Toscana bread, a salad of crunchy romaine, hard-cooked eggs, and tomatoes bathed in a too oily vinaigrette, deftly prepared vegetables, and a starch (either rice, scalloped potatoes, or french fries.)

Easily the pièce de résistance is the bouillabaisse ($11.95 for one, or two.) Not a big bowl of fish soup as we had expected, it is served, according to our waitress and Julia Child, à la Marseilles. First a platter of lobster, mussels, shrimp, whiting, and red snapper arrive, joined with a bowl of fish broth and a potent garlic sauce. All fish is purchased fresh each day and tastes it.

Those who'd rather not get into the swim can enjoy daube ($5.50), a carefully simmered beef stew, or a pleasant coq au vin ($5.50). The tender duck ($8.50) is marred by an over-zealous splash of orange sauce.

Appetizers and desserts can run up the bill, but if you're in the mood to splurge, the garlicky, butter-bathed escargots ($2.50) are intensely aromatic, and the onion soup ($1.50) carries a sturdy melted cheese topping. Desserts are homemade, and there's often a great cheesecake.

FRENCH

Cafe Bernard

2100 N. Halsted
Phone: 871-2100
  (reservations)
Parking: Street
Full bar

Lunch: Tue.-Fri., 11:00 A.M.–2:00 P.M.
Dinner: Tue.-Thur., Sun., 5:00 P.M.–
  10:30 P.M.
Fri.-Sat., 5:00 P.M.–11:30 P.M.
Closed Monday

Cafe Bernard offers a cozy setting for some generally well prepared French food. It's possible to dine on entree, salad, and bread for a gentle $5.00.

All meals begin with a basket of chunky French bread and fresh velvety greens tossed with a smooth, mustard-inspired dressing. Appetizers are a la carte, and include a splendid, but not spectacular, baked onion soup ($1.00), a smooth paté ($1.75) that tastes far better than it looks, and an airy quiche ($1.50).

Entrees range from a bouyant boeuf bourguignon ($4.95) to tenderly sauteed, caper-garnished calf's brains ($3.95). If you've always been squeamish about the latter, this is the place to take the plunge as it is an excellent dish. Braised sweetbreads ($4.95) intertwine with mushrooms and onions in a convincingly seasoned wine sauce, and the trout amandine ($5.25) has a flaky richness.

Duck ($5.50) is a tasty, crisp-skinned version subtly doused with orange sauce, but easily our favorite fowl is poulet moutarde ($5.00). Half of a plump, meaty chicken comes invitingly topped by a buttery, bread crumb coating, artfully seasoned with Dijon mustard. It's delicious.

Not as consistent are the mussels ($5.00), which arrive attractively submerged in a creamy, onion-spiked broth. They can vary from outstanding to out and out strong. Several daily specials, mostly seafood, are listed on blackboards, placed somewhat beyond eyesight range, around the room. Accompanying the meal are rice or parslied potatoes, and a fresh vegetable.

The setting offers an intimate, bistro-like charm. Natural pine-panelled walls, hanging funnel lamps, checked tablecloths, and line drawings of cooking utensils help create the mood. A few drawbacks: service ranges from helpful to harried, and when there's a crowd (which there usually is), noise approaches sonic boom level and seating becomes close enough to feel tempted to grab a mouthful of your neighbor's mousse.

The French Kitchen

(one of our favorites)

3437 W. 63rd
Phone: 778-9476
   (reservations)
Parking: Street
B.Y.O. (25¢ per person
   glass charge)

Tue.-Sat., 5:00 P.M.–11:00 P.M.
Sun., 3:00 P.M.–10:00 P.M.
Closed Monday

We feel The French Kitchen's the best low-priced French restaurant in Chicago. It is run by Lorraine Hooker who, armed with French cooking lessons but no previous restaurant experience, decided to open up her own place. Working on a shoestring budget, she and her kids turned an empty storefront into a charming replica of a French country inn, replete with lush hanging plants, colorful print tablecloths, and a beamed ceiling.

The menu features five regular entrees and one or two daily specials. They're priced between $6.00 and $7.50 and include a salad tossed with a very sweet, basil-tarragon-flavored vinaigrette dressing, rice, French bread, and beverage.

The five main entrees are a not quite classic coq au vin (the sauce is redder, almost barbecue-like, $6.00); beef Wellington, striding a bed of plump, sweet raisins ($7.50); a meltingly tender sole, garnished with mushrooms and shrimp and baked in a paper sack ($6.25); a rich, creamy crab mornay ($6.25); and jambon en croûte, excellent, flavorful ham enveloped in pastry and served with scalloped pineapple ($6.00).

Also noteworthy are the creatively prepared daily specials, such as estouffade, a delicate French country stew which blends beef, onions, potatoes, and green olives, or citriade, which combines sole and scallops in a light wine sauce, subtly flavored with orange peel. There also might be fresh dill-dotted salmon baked in a crust or whole trout stuffed with spinach, mushrooms, tomatoes, and tiny shrimp.

Whatever happens, don't forgo the soups, especially if the dill and cucumber-flecked cold crab ($1.00) is on ice. Stocked with enough firm chunks of crab to make you forget it's expensive, it's a delightfully refreshing marvel. The hearty, superbly seasoned beef and barley soup (50¢) is another standout. We also recommend a dessert, particularly the poached pear lavished with brandy-sparked, freshly whipped cream (75¢), the chocolate mousse (75¢) or the lemon souffle crêpe ($1.50).

Berghoff

(one of our favorites)

17 W. Adams
Phone: 427-3170
Parking: Impossible
Full bar

Main dining room:
  Daily, 11:30 A.M.–9:30 P.M.
  Closed Sunday
Annex:
  Daily, 11:00 A.M.–8.00 P.M.
  Closed 2:00 P.M.–5:00 P.M.

Berghoff has everything: good food, varied menu, comfortable setting (provided you're not rushed), serious waiters, and maybe even a famous face or two, especially if they're being indicted. (Berghoff is next door to the Federal Building.) While it's not the only good budget restaurant downtown, it is the best.

The menu varies daily and tilts toward the German. There's wiener schnitzel ($3.85), kassler ribchen (smoked young pork loin, $3.60), sauerbraten ($3.65), roulade of beef ($3.75), and Alpen ragout, a savory blend of veal slices and fresh mushrooms in wine sauce ($3.60). In addition, there's a very interesting selection of fish and seafood, including fresh Boston scrod ($3.75), broiled white fish ($4.25), fried oysters ($3.10), and a great combination that features a small lobster tail as well as sole, shrimp, and scallops that's priced slightly over our heads at $5.25. There's also an ample sampling of steaks and chops.

Most dinners, other than steaks, run under $3.85 and include a really good rye bread and two side dishes, perhaps German fried potatoes, spaetzel, creamed spinach, glazed carrots, or fresh corn on the cob. Dessert, soup, and beverage are extra. Soups (45¢) are generally delicious and run the gamut from cream of asparagus to oxtail. In summer there's a lovely cold fruit soup filled with strawberries and cherries. Standouts among desserts are lemon meringue pie (55¢), German chocolate cake (75¢), and Black Forest cake (90¢).

Europa House

2125 W. Roscoe
Phone: 528-2562
Parking: Street
Full bar

Daily, 10:30 A.M.–12:30 A.M.
Sat., 10:30 A.M.–2:00 A.M.
Closed Monday

A well-kept neighborhood secret that maybe we shouldn't be telling about (but it's a big, well-staffed place). Europa House serves belt-loosening meals at non-uptight prices, especially for German food. Dinners feature soup, bread, salad, potatoes, and vegetable and most cost under $4.95.

Bread can bring on instant gluttony, if you're not careful. There's a black bread, thick cut rye, and rye, white, and pumpernickel rolls. Providing them company are sturdy soups. The well-supplied chicken noodle has a light, fresh taste, and the liver dumpling, though on the delicate side, is definitely not ashamed of its origins. The shredded carrot, "baco"-topped salad tastes of too many hours spent in the refrigerator.

Entrees rev up interest. Several stalwart specials line the menu: sauerbraten, beef rouladen, roast duck, wiener schnitzel, pork tenderloin tips and noodles, and smoked thueringer.

Duck ($4.50) is everything it should be—crisp skin, moist flesh, and plenty of both. Joining it are bread dressing and too much brown gravy (request it on the side). Chicken livers ($3.25) come mild, gently textured, and sauced by a wine-inspired gravy. The crackly, juicy pork tenderloin ($3.75) can also do no wrong.

Vegetables (red cabbage, canned string beans) taste dull and waterlogged, but the hash browns are properly crisp, and spaetzle are fat, firm, and slightly browned. Powdered sugar-sprinkled apple strudel (50¢) is not flaky or delicate enough to be a great version, but if you're in the mood, try it.

Europa House has a convivial, small town ambiance. One gets the feeling that everyone has just spent the day fishing, canning, or panelling the basement. Waitresses are concerned, and on weekends a woman organist lifts spirits further from her platform perch inside the horseshoe bar.

Germania Inn

1540 N. Clark
Phone: 642-9349
Parking: Street
Full bar

Mon.-Fri., Noon–2:30 P.M.
5:00 P.M.–10:00 P.M.
Sat., Noon–10:00 P.M.
Closed Sunday

A snug, cottage-like setting replete with pine-panelled walls and checked tablecloths, where one can be just as sure of reliable, well-prepared food as of a Democratic victory in the 1st Ward. The succinct menu is accented by daily specials such as Monday's kassler ribs, Wednesday's lamb shank, and Thursday's spare ribs and kraut (each costs $3.75). Included in all dinners are soup, bread, and a salad or vegetable. Not bad for a German restaurant, particularly one in such posh environs.

Exceptionally savory is the smoky, cohesive navy bean soup. Thin, grainy pumpernickel and hefty rye help it along. Salad is a cucumber, tomato, and beet above average, but it could be colder.

Outstanding among the entrees are the broiled pork chops ($4.95). Two incredibly juicy, meaty, and well-seasoned chops come to an order, and we still remember them fondly. Wiener schnitzel ($4.75) would have been wonderful had it been less bountifully breaded. The sausages—bratwurst, knackwurst, and thueringer (each, $3.75)—are appropriately juicy and robust.

The menu also embraces smoked pork chops ($4.95), beef rouladen ($4.75), pot roast ($4.75), and a pork shank ($4.25). If possible, try for the tender, crisp German fries and spunky red cabbage as side dishes.

Good imported German beer smoothes dinner down and spirits up. The well-dressed crowd is somewhat clubby, wave to each other, and are undoubtedly Bear fans and, probably, Republicans.

Hogen's

4560 N. Lincoln
Phone: 334-9406
Parking: Lot
Full bar

Daily, 9:00 A.M.–2:00 A.M.
Sat., 9:00 A.M.–3:00 A.M.
Sun., 12 Noon–2:00 A.M.

Hogen's was selected by some Hollywood producers as the archtypical Polish neighborhood restaurant-bar, and was used as the setting for a Polish "Walton Family" TV pilot, titled "Mama Kovack." This has caused a few chuckles at Hogen's, which is actually your typical German neighborhood restaurant-bar, a fixture at Wilson and Lincoln since 1890.

However, one thing at Hogen's stands out as hardly typical —the prices. It is easily the cheapest German restaurant we've found. You have to look hard to find anything over $3.00 on the menu, which rotates daily. Six to ten entrees are featured, with roast pork ($2.65), roast beef ($2.50), and bratwurst ($2.50) being everyday standbys.

Weekends are your best bet, as the menu is the fullest and the choices are most traditionally German. On Saturdays, there's sauerbraten and dumplings ($2.50), beef rouladen ($2.65), smoked butt and red cabbage ($2.65), and the most inexpensive roast duck ($3.10) we've found this side of Cicero. Sunday features more of the same plus a bargain-priced wiener schnitzel ($2.95). On weekdays, the moist meatloaf ($2.10) on Monday is a good bet as are the braised oxtails ($2.25) on Thursdays. On all dishes, ask them to go easy on the gravy. All entrees come with two side dishes (try for the red cabbage) plus rye bread.

Portions will fill you, especially if you begin a meal with homemade soup (45¢). The pea soup on Monday is exceptionally well-made. Dessert's available too, for an extra tab. The strudel's tasty (50¢), but we suggest avoiding the cardboard-like crusted pies.

Hogen's dining patrons sit in a panelled backroom, secluded by a partition from the rowdier drinkers in the bar up front. Everything about the place—food, patrons, and people who work there—seems hearty and robust.

Treffpunkt

4743 N. Lincoln	Mon., Wed.-Fri., 5:00 P.M.–2:00 A.M.
Phone: 784-9296	Sat., 11:00 A.M.–3:00 A.M.
Parking: Street	Sun., Noon–2:00 A.M.
Full bar	Closed Tuesday

Very authentic, very lively (especially on weekends), and very neighborhoody, the Treffpunckt caters mostly to middle-aged German couples from the surrounding area. The long, tunnel-like dining room has a bar on one side, tables on the other, a profusion of ornate beer steins, and efficient, no-nonsense waitresses.

The menu is gently priced, and includes a gemeitlich gathering: wiener schnitzel, pork shank, beef rouladen, kassler ribs and kraut, and smoked thueringer. Meals all feature a sturdy rye, homemade soup (usually a lively liver dumpling), salad, vegetable, and potato.

Check out the schnitzel ($4.95), juicy, tender veal basking under a bubbly hot crust. It is accompanied by terrific fried potatoes for which Germans seem to have a particular knack.

Rouladen's ($4.95) heavier fare, as the gravy-bathed, tender beef is wrapped around finely chopped pickles, bacon, and a soaked hunk of rye. It comes with tart red cabbage and two potato dumplings that could easily pass for billiard balls.

Filling out the menu are fried pork chops ($3.95), a "farmer's breakfast" of eggs, ham and fried potatoes ($2.50), and steak tartar with egg yolk, anchovy, onion, and caper trimmings ($3.25).

Portions are typically teutonic, but if you're still hungry, sink into the good and hot apple strudel, amply punctuated with nuts and raisins.

In April there's a Bock Beer Festival which features such additional goodies as buffalo burgers, buffalo goulash, and venison roast. And on most nights, a spirited, accordian-led combo helps to create a free-floating conviviality.

Grecian Restaurant Psistaria

2412-14 W. Lawrence   Daily, 11:30 A.M.–4:00 A.M.
Phone: 728-6308
Parking: Street
Full bar

The Grecian Psistaria reflects the Greek zest for living. A Greek electric combo plays lively tunes up front while casting lingering glances at tables of unescorted young women. Waiters burst into song at unexpected moments, and from time to time people are moved to dance. It's spirited, noisy, and fun. The food also happens to be among the best Greek cooking in town.

The dining room is mammoth, with murals of Greek seaside villages and a grotto-like effect on one wall. Waiters, dressed in the traditional white shirt and black tie, refuse to neglect you. They fill your bread basket at least three times and your water glass, four. The menu is comprehensive, and most entrees cost $2.95 and under.

Try starting off your meal with a bowl of avgolemono, egg-lemon soup (75¢). It's smooth and nicely tart. The eggplant salad (95¢) is creamy and heavy with garlic. The huge portion of fish roe (90¢) is smooth-textured, not overly fishy and goes beautifully with the soft Greek bread.

The menu is weighted with baked or braised lamb dishes (average $2.95), served with a side-dish of either cauliflower, green beans, eggplant, rice, or potatoes. The excellent moussaka ($2.75) is at least three inches high and features a potato layer in addition to the usual eggplant and ground meat. The dolmades (rolled grape leaves stuffed with ground lamb) are bathed in a tangy egg-lemon sauce, with just the slightest hint of mint. If you're after something more unusual, a well-prepared octopus with macaroni (Fridays only, $2.95) and fried squid ($2.75) are available.

For dessert there is a wonderfully smooth creamy rice pudding (75¢) in addition to the usual pastries.

When the band plays, drinks go up astronomically; for instance, a $4.00 bottle of wine will cost you $7.00. There is no band on Mondays, so drinks are lower and the place is much quieter.

Greek Islands

766 W. Jackson
Phone: 782-9855
Parking: Street
Full bar

Mon.-Thur., 11:00 A.M.–Midnight
Fri.-Sat., 11:00 A.M.–1:00 A.M.
Sun., Noon–Midnight

You could say that when you've eaten in one Greek restaurant you've eaten in them all. However we've found subtle nuances to distinguish one Greek eatery from another. For instance, Greek Islands makes what has to be the best saganaki in town, their menu is more adventurous than most (snails, octopus in wine sauce, plus unusual daily specials), and their waiters wear light blue jackets rather than the usual black and white outfit. Their prices, happily enough, are not distinguishable from any other Greek restaurant—they're the same good old cheap.

Reliable entrees include fresh tasting dolmades ($2.50), braised lamb with vegetables or rice ($2.95), and gyros ($2.95). The combination plate ($3.50) generally includes lamb, moussaka, dolmades, potatoes, rice, and vegetables as well as a sampling of one of the day's specials. There's also a nice variety of fish—fried smelts ($2.95), whole snapper and sea bass (prices fluctuate), and fried cod (bakalao) in garlic sauce.

From among the daily specials we favor lamb and artichokes with egg-lemon sauce ($3.25), stewed lima beans ($1.00) and shrimp Greek-style, which are served in their shell over rice in a light tomato-egg sauce ($4.25).

Soft, sesame-sprinkled Greek bread comes with each entree. An extra $1.50 buys a complete meal, which includes egg-lemon soup, a good-sized Greek salad, dessert, and coffee. Don't overlook the saganaki (flaming cheese). Each bite combines the lacy crispness of the coating with the incredibly rich melted cheese.

The interior of Greek Islands bears evidence of a visit by the mysterious muralist whose specialty seems to be creating bland turquoise seascapes on Greek restaurant walls. However, there's nothing dull about the atmosphere. It's lively and friendly.

Parthenon

314 S. Halsted   Daily, 11 A.M.–2:00 A.M.
Phone: 726-2407
Parking: Street, and a free lot
      (evenings only)
Full bar

The Parthenon is unquestionably Chicago's most popular Greek restaurant, though we don't feel the cuisine necessarily surpasses that of a number of other Greek eateries. The service is generally swift, and the waiters move about with considerable energy and grace. The two large dining rooms are usually filled to capacity.

The menu features several standout dishes, all very reasonably priced. The generous portion of saganaki ($1.50) is done up beautifully here and served with pizzazz. The gyros (grilled lamb and beef, $3.00) is perfectly prepared—thin-sliced and crusty. The sharp-flavored spinach pie is served in an unusually large portion. Roast leg of lamb is excellent, and the braised lamb ($3.00) is both mild-flavored and tender. Try your lamb with either stewed eggplant or zucchini.

The two casseroles fare less well. Moussaka ($2.50) tastes more like a heavily salted meat loaf than a subtly spiced lamb and eggplant combination. The meat seems to be hiding altogether in the noodle-dominated pastitsio ($2.50).

Desserts, however, are expertly prepared. The fresh, flaky baklava lives up to its reputation, and the galactobouriko is smooth, mildly sweet, and not too soggy. At 50¢, they are sold at a price more like that of a bakery than a restaurant.

Roditys

(one of our favorites)

222 S. Halsted   Daily, 11:00 A.M.–1:00 A.M.
Phone: 454-0800   Sat., 11:00 A.M.–2:00 A.M.
Parking: Lot
Full bar

One of old Greek Town's better and lesser known restaurants. There may not be as much hoopla and opaa as at some of the other places, but we always notice lots of Greeks eating here. There's good reason, as the food's consistently well-prepared, portions are plentiful, and the service is officious without being overbearing.

There's no necessity to go on the lamb. Joining the predictable braised lamb and vegetable duos are chicken shish kebab, Greek sausage, fried smelts, squid, and octopus. There's also a handful of innovative daily specials, perhaps rice and ground lamb-stuffed tomatoes, a cheese-smothered vegetable casserole, or shrimp in a sauce of tomato and feta cheese. Most everything sneaks in under $3.00, and includes soft, sesame-coated Greek bread.

We're especially partial to the smelt ($2.50). Served in a portion close to a good night's catch, they're sweet, delicate, and nearly greaseless. The more oily squid ($2.50) possess a genial flavor and texture, and an unusual spiciness lends interest to the tiny, crackly Greek sausage ($2.75). There's also gyros ($2.75), broiled Greek meatballs ($2.50), and the usual combo of moussaka, pastitsio, dolmades, roast lamb, and vegetables ($3.50).

Side dishes well worth some extra bites include the Greek salad, an herb-smothered mass of tomatoes, onions, radishes, cukes, olives, banana peppers, and feta cheese (serves 2, $1.35). The cool, thick, almost too fishy taramosalata (fish roe, $1.00) or the cucumber and garlic-outfitted yogurt (tzatziki, $1.50) bear attention. They also prepare dandelion greens ($1.25) with such finesse that you'll never scoff at one again. Creamy, cloud-like rice pudding (75¢) plus the proverbial pastries for dessert.

Guatemala Restaurant

1027 W. Wilson
Phone: 271-2761
Parking: Street
B.Y.O.

Daily, 11:30 A.M.–11:00 P.M.
Closed Tuesday

Next time you're hit by an uncontrollable craving for Guatemalan food, try the Guatemala Restaurant on Wilson Avenue. Squeezed in between the Habana Barber Shop and an East Indian grocery on one of Chicago's livelier streets, the Guatemala is the place to go for food from south of the Mexican border.

It's a little family-run place that offers cuisine quite similar to Mexican. Posted on the wall, the brief menu is weighted with beef dishes, averaging $2.50. There's bistek with fried potatoes, beef with spicy ranchero sauce, and a very tender and flavorful carne guisada (beef stew), served with rice and beans. For contrast, try the large bowl of shrimp soup. Though it's priced somewhat high at $3.00, the tomato-based broth is tasty and loaded with shrimp.

Specials vary each day and might include chile rellenos, homemade tamales or sauteed pork chops. Excellent as a snack or light lunch are the refried beans, served with a side dish of sweet fried bananas ($1.50). A plateful of napkin-covered warm tortillas accompanies all meals.

Each table in the small, paneled restaurant is set with a lovely embroidered Guatemalan tablecloth. Service is friendly, though there may be a slight, but not insurmountable, language barrier. Food is made to order, the pace is relaxed, and the cook can often be heard singing in the kitchen.

The Herbanite

2050 N. Halsted   Tue.-Sun., 6:00 P.M.–10:00 P.M.
Phone: 871-9216   Closed Monday
Parking: Street
B.Y.O.
No smoking

A laid-back, herb-tea-pottery shop that serves terrific food. The style is gourmet-"natural" with soul overtones. Seasoning is done with a magical touch, making good use of their huge stock of herbs. Everything tastes crisp and fresh, and is picturesquely (and very slowly) served. Plan on spending a lengthy evening, but the place is so mellow you probably won't care.

The menu concentrates on fish, fowl, and vegetables. All come with a basket of fried cornjacks (flat, gritty, cornmeal "flapjacks" studded with scallions) and honey.

For openers, they do up a perfect vegetable and brown rice at a very nice price ($3.00). Deftly seasoned and showered with alfalfa sprouts, it includes a mix of mushrooms, carrots, greens, red cabbage, green beans, almonds, and sunflower seeds. There's also a delicious chicken ($3.75), marinated in wine, tamari (a natural soy sauce), and herbs, and sprinkled with a crisp, beautifully-seasoned bouquet of almonds, tomatoes, and onions. The tamari and wine-basted whole Cornish hen ($5.50), stuffed with rice, almonds, apples, and sunflower seeds, can easily feed two.

Moving into fish, there's a distinctive curried rice and shrimp (not overly heavy with shrimp, $3.75) and rainbow trout stuffed with crab, apples, coconut, and almonds ($5.50). Brown rice and stir-fried vegetables usually accompany most dishes. Salads (75¢; $1.75) are expectedly fresh and topped by a lovely, multi-herbed dressing.

Portions are so big they dwarf the plate; service is loose and friendly. The decor is a casual mix of chairs, laminated tables, plants, pottery, and glass jars filled with every herb, spice, and tea imaginable. A thoroughly nice place.

Bread Shop Kitchen

3411 N. Halsted
Phone: 871-3831
Parking: Street
No liquor
No smoking

Tue.-Sat., Noon–9:00 P.M.
Closed Sunday and Monday

Finally, an honest vegetarian restaurant in Chicago. At the Bread Shop Kitchen, eggs are fertile, oils are unprocessed, grains are whole, and milk and cheese are raw. No sugar and very little butter is used, and dishes which eschew dairy products altogether are marked with an asterisk.

It's a friendly, informal, unpretentious place. Diners wait on themselves. Each evening's menu is chalked on a blackboard, and items are erased as soon as the kitchen runs out. Appearing most evenings are two soups, a few salads, sandwiches, and one or two "main dishes." Prices are salutary for even the most withering wallet. Just about everything is under $2.00, and, when you consider that the food's really good for you, it's an extra bargain.

A dense, crisp-crusted whole wheat bread, baked in their own bakery across the street, comes gratis, and it's much better than any commercial rival. We kept it good company with a vegetable melange of steamed kale, carrots, zucchini, potatoes, and onions, tossed with a thin, lemon-flavored cheese sauce ($1.75).

Less inspiring is green pepper rice, a big bowl of gummy brown rice hiding only a few pepper chunks. Bean and barley soup (65¢) is both flavorful and nutritious, thick with three kinds of beans. Equally nice is the crisp vegetable salad (75¢) brightened with grated carrots and red cabbage.

Try the thick, sticky, apricot-topped cheesecake (75¢) which is usually around for dessert.

Bon Ton

1153 N. State	Mon.-Thur., 11:00 A.M.–
Phone: 943-0538	10:00 P.M.
Parking: Street (difficult)	Fri., Sat., 11:00 A.M.–11:00 P.M.
B.Y.O.	Closed Sunday

Located in the midst of the Rush Street glitter, Bon Ton offers a welcome relief from the splashy tourist places that dominate the area. It has a genteel tea room aura that feels distinctly European. The food is beautifully served, the pastry is fabulous, and the prices a pleasant surprise. All entrees, including salad and bread, cost $3.50 or less. Service, however, tends to be abrupt and snooty.

The most popular selection on the brief menu is shish kebab (a half order, at $3.50, is ample). The meat is well-marinated, plump and tender. Tons of rice pilaf accompany it. Chicken paprika ($3.50) is fork tender and tastes great with the buttery spaetzle that accompanies it. If you're a stuffed-pepper freak, Bon Ton has some of the tastiest we've ever eaten. The peppers are cooked until just tender and their flavor mixes smoothly with the ground meat filling and mild tomato sauce ($3.50). Stuffed cabbage ($3.50), Hungarian goulash ($3.50), and meat-filled bliny ($2.25) are three other interesting possibilities.

Share a piroshkee (65¢) to start off your meal. The peppery, ground-meat-filled pastry is superb. There are also several soups, the most tasty being the beef soup with wonton-like meat dumplings (80¢) or the bean with smoked meat and dumpling (40¢ a cup; 60¢ a bowl).

Try to save room for dessert, or take some home with you. Bon Ton specializes in delicious pastries, ranging in price from 35¢ to 55¢. The variety is tantalizing: rich, stick-to-the-roof-of-your-mouth cheesecake-meringue squares, napoleons, dobosh tortes, custard-filled chocolate eclairs, hazelnut rolls, linzer tortes, and more.

Bon Ton is generally crowded and a wait can be expected. Time passes rather quickly as both the pastries and the patrons merit observation.

Hungarian Restaurant

4146 N. Lincoln
Phone: 248-1003
Parking: Street
B.Y.O.

Wed.-Sat., 5:00 P.M.–10:00 P.M.
Sun., Noon–10:00 P.M.
Closed Monday and Tuesday

The Hungarian is the archtypical ethnic restaurant. It's an inviting, cozy little storefront with a marked eastern European flavor. The walls are covered in flowered paper over which hang woven mats and paintings of farmers at work in the fields. Bunches of plastic flowers and grapes hang about, and gypsy music plays in the background. Recently under new ownership, the Hungarian's menu has changed very little, though the food can be erratic.

Portions are generally good-sized, and an entree plus salad and bread averages $3.75. The most consistently good dish is the moist, flavorful stuffed cabbage ($3.50), which rests upon a pile of sauerkraut and is swathed with sour cream. Both the tender, burnt umber-toned beef goulash ($3.50), and the mushroom-garnished Burgundy goulash ($4.50) can be delicious. The szekely goulash ($3.50), a beef-sauerkraut-sour cream affair is also great, if you have a tart tooth. Not as appetizing is the overcooked, salty chicken paprikash ($3.25). Tasty, nicely browned spaetzle usually comes along, and maybe, some canned vegetables.

The sesame-coated bread is fresh and soft, but the salad is unfortunately drowned in a pool of dressing. Soups (50¢) are homemade and hearty. There's a particularly good cream of chicken soup, studded with neat little chewy dumplings. If you're up for dessert, there's strudel (70¢) and delicate, jam-filled palascinta, a Hungarian crêpe (90¢).

Service is very personable, but expect a long, leisurely evening if they're shorthanded.

Magyar Czarda

3724 W. Montrose
Phone: 588-9219
Parking: Street
Full bar

Daily, 3:00 P.M.–7:00 P.M.
Sat., Sun., Noon–7:00 P.M.

This local bar is probably the closest thing we have in Chicago to a neighborhood Budapest bar. Lights are dim, passionate gypsy music holds sway, and if anything, conversations (in Hungarian) are even more passionate. The swarthy, bearded, cigar-chomping bartender looks like he's stopped and started a few fights in his day, but now seems content to oversee the gathered throng.

When we alerted the hostess to our dining interest, she roused an older woman who had been nursing a beer at the next table. As the woman slowly made her way into the kitchen, we had the feeling it wouldn't be a routine evening.

Although there's no formal menu, two to four entrees are generally served each night. Meals average between $2.50 and $3.00. No added frills like soup or dessert, but there's a fine honest character to the food. From the evening's beef guylas, fried pork chops, stuffed cabbage, and chicken paprikas, we selected the latter two. But first comes a teeth-teasing rye bread and either a cucumber or tossed green salad. The cukes could have been sliced thinner, but are complemented by a slightly salty, paprika-spiced marinade. A tart sweetness characterizes the well-dressed greens, scallions, peppers, and cucumbers.

Chicken paprikas arrives steaming hot. Meat is firm, tender, and deftly seasoned by a rosy sauce that owes its bloom to a healthy dose of paprika. The accompanying rice does a beautiful job of soaking up the juices. Three rotund cabbage rolls, rippled with sour cream, rest on a pile of tangy sauerkraut. Mouth-puckering to be sure, but not inordinately so, they are quieted down by the non-aggressive rice.

Gateway to India

(one of our favorites)

1543 N. Wells	Tue.-Sun., 11:30 A.M.–2:00 P.M.;
Phone: 642-7755	5:00 P.M.–11:00 P.M.
Parking: Street	Closed Monday
Full bar	

Fragrant odors nearly knock you over upon entering the posh, high-ceilinged mansion that houses this charming Indian restaurant. The feeling is at once intimate and friendly, heightened by subdued Indian music and soft-spoken waiters. They'll ask how hot you'd like your food: Be brave enough to specify at least medium-hot, as nothing's really over-powering.

Brittle, red pepper-spiked papadum (a kind of Indian cracker) get the meal off to a lively start. Accompany them with thick, well-seasoned mulligatawany soup or a wonderfully spicy, ginger-spiked cream of tomato.

We've found the curries to share an equally subtle touch. Our special favorite is the gentle ghobi masala, or cauliflower curry ($1.75). Almost as delicate is the chicken shaki korma ($2.75), caressed by a velvety sauce, sweetened with dried fruit and almonds. A more prominent yogurt flavor characterizes lamb tikka ($2.75) and peppers combine beautifully with tender chunks of lamb in the stewlike lamb jhal frezi ($2.75).

Two other tasty dishes are nicely charcoaled and moist tandoori chicken ($2.75 for half a chicken) and mattar paneer ($1.75), a vegetarian mix of peas and spongy squares of ricotta cheese. Vegetarians can also find solace in a mixed vegetable curry ($1.75), mushroom curry ($1.75), or alu raita, a potato and yogurt combination ($1.00).

The breads are not only delicious, but perfect for soaking up excess gravy. Try the earthy-tasting whole wheat paratha (50¢) or the blistery, chewy nan (60¢). A frothy mango shake (75¢) not only refreshes but will cool off anything that needs it.

Reservations are helpful on weekends.

Gaylord

678 N. Clark	Mon.-Thur., 11:00 A.M.–2:00 P.M.;
Phone: 664-1700	5:30 P.M.–10:30 P.M.
Parking: Lot,	Fri.-Sat., 11:00 A.M.–2:00 P.M.;
across street	5:30 P.M.–11:00 P.M.
Full bar	Sun., 5:30 P.M.–10:30 P.M.

The attractive Gaylord serves a wide range of carefully prepared Indian dishes. If in doubt, ask the waiters. They are courteous, knowledgeable, and happy to explain the complexities of the menu.

Most everything is a la carte. Going over our $4.95 budget is easy, as the menu is loaded with delicacies that are too good to miss. One dish we especially recommend is tandoori chicken (½ chicken, $2.75; whole, $5.00). It is marinated, then grilled over charcoal in a special clay oven. The result is one of the tenderest and most full-flavored chickens we've ever eaten. Two other excellent tandoori style dishes are boti kabab (small chunks of skewered lamb, $3.50) and seikh kabab (mixed ground lamb, onions, and herbs, $3.75).

Curries are also delicious, particularly the vegetarian alu bengan (eggplant and potato, $2.50) and the subtly-flavored roghan josh (lamb curry, $3.95). There's also a mellow chicken jaipuri (cooked in a yogurt sauce and topped with hard boiled egg slices, $2.75) and shajahni (a stew-like dish of chicken, mushrooms, nuts, and herbs, $3.00).

Rice is the perfect complement to the curries, and one order of rice and peas pullau ($1.50) is plenty for three people. Try a side dish of vegetable samosa (40¢), a light, deep-fried mix of vegetables and potatoes, something like a knish. The good breads include bubbly-surfaced, pancake-sized nan (70¢) and the keema nan, filled with minced lamb, which is even better ($1.00).

Desserts are sweet and distinctive. We particularly like ras malai ($1.00), a refreshing, spongy-textured pudding fashioned from milk and cheese. The unusual candy-like jalabi, made of ground chick pea flour, is much sweeter and tastes like deep-fried perfume.

Fifteen percent service is automatically added to the bill.

August Moon

225 W. 26th
Phone: 842-2951
Parking: Lot
B.Y.O.

Sun.-Thur., 11:30 A.M.–9:00 P.M.
Fri., Sat., 11:30 A.M.–10:00 P.M.
Closed Monday

Chicago's only Indonesian restaurant also spreads out to embrace Mandarin, Cantonese, and Fukian dishes. But stick with the Indonesian, as it's not only unusual, but unusually good and decently-priced. Portions aren't huge, so be sure to order at least one dish per person.

By far the most unusual offering is gado gado ($2.50), an Indonesian salad of crisp pink, green, and yellow shrimp chips dotting a bed of cold noodles, bean sprouts, green beans, potatoes, and cucumbers. Flavored with peanut butter and brilliant with textures, it is far more palatable than it sounds.

There's delicious bakmi goreng ($3.50), an Indonesian chow mein piled with soft noodles, shrimp, beef, onion strips, and bok choy, all permeated by a mild sweetness. Even more ingredient-stocked is tjap tjai ($3.75), a sauteed meat-vegetable melange featuring shrimp, beef, carrots, cabbage, string beans, and both shrimp and rice cakes. Chicken with coconut milk ($3.25) is intensely aromatic and looks innocent enough, but is fired up by a splash of red pepper.

Make one foray into the Chinese by ordering the crackly-skinned Fukian fried chicken ($2.50) which is so good it should make the Colonel envious. Smoky-tasting tea and plain rice come with all meals. Augment the meal a bit further by ordering an appetizer of pork satay ($2.50), skewers of juicy pork joined by a creamy peanut sauce, pickled cucumbers, and thick, bland rice cakes.

The decor at August Moon is more stark brown panelling than Marlon Brando teahouse, and service can be incredibly slow. But the owner's kids, who are usually engrossed in coloring books, add a nice, homey touch.

Ouzi's

6740 N. California
Phone: 465-5616
Parking: Street
No liquor

Mon.-Thur., and Sun., 11:00 A.M.–
  8:45 P.M.
Fri., 11:00 A.M.–2:00 P.M.
Sat., 10:00 A.M.–1:00 A.M.

It's easy to feel at home at Ouzi's. The place is big on families and warmth, lots of people know each other, and kids play on the floor next to the tables. This casualness carries over to the food display and service, which is easy-going, do-it-yourself. The style is Israeli kosher, and strictly meat, potatoes, and vegetables. No dairy products of any kind are used, and all dishes are permeated by a tasty, homemade, though not exactly delicate, character.

Heading the offerings are a variety of stuffed vegetables: zucchini, peppers, cabbage, and eggplant. The eggplant ($2.10) is particularly savory, a layered, moussaka-like affair featuring juicy ground meat, eggplant, potatoes, celery, onions, mushrooms, tomatoes, and even cabbage. Flavors blend beautifully, and the taste is more Jewish sweet and sour than straight Mediterranean.

If the roast chicken ($2.75) is around, it's nicely browned and moist, and even better if courting a side helping of baked farfel (crumbled matzoh) and mushrooms. Sweet and sour fish ($2.50) and some very tasty and cheap falafel (deep fried balls of spiced ground chickpeas wrapped in pita bread, 40¢ and 90¢) are two other options.

Supplement the main course with a side snack chosen from a display above the counter. The deep-fried cauliflower puffs (50¢) and mixed vegetable fritters (50¢) taste particularly lively. There are also eggrolls (50¢) and triangular meat knishes (50¢), but avoid the meat and potato knish (75¢) as it's greasy and oddly flavored.

If you can handle dessert, there's a syrupy baklava and some strong Turkish coffee (40¢) to wash it down.

Sabra Kosher Restaurant

2712 W. Pratt   Daily, Noon–10:00 P.M.
Phone: 764-3563   Closed Friday at sundown until Saturday
Parking: Street   at sundown.
No liquor

Whether you have a taste for exotic Middle Eastern cooking or more earthy eastern European fare, you'll find either at Sabra. It's an Israeli-kosher restaurant that combines the best of both. Shish kabob and musaka share the menu with brisket and goulash. There's pita bread and soft, fluffy rolls, rice pilaf, and potatoes. The restaurant is strictly meat only, meaning no dairy products are permitted either in the cooking or at the table.

However this shouldn't cramp anyone too much. There are several exciting things on the menu. We recommend you start by sharing a combination plate ($2.50) of Middle Eastern appetizers—homos, tehina (sesame spread) and deep fried felafel balls. The plate is attractively served and all three are delicious. It comes with pita bread for dipping. You might also consider the Israeli salad—tomato, cucumber, green pepper, oil, and lemon ($1.00) or the eggplant salad ($1.50). Soups are good too, particularly the gusty tomato-based lima bean soup (75¢).

Middle Eastern dinners include shish kabob made from either beef, lamb, or a combination ($4.95), pashtida (a noodle-meat casserole similar to Greek pastitsio, $2.95), and a decent musaka ($2.95). However, we generally prefer their non-Middle Eastern entrees—goulash ($3.50), brisket ($3.50), and baked chicken ($3.50). Goulash is particularly tasty, as it's made of tender brisket chunks simmered in a light, green-pepper-flavored tomato sauce. Entrees are accompanied by rice pilaf, vegetable (usually canned peas and carrots), and excellent soft rolls.

Desserts we could do without. The baklava (60¢) is too soggy, and the ice cream cake (60¢) made of non-dairy ice cream tastes like it. However the rest of the meal is both filling and tasty, making dessert somewhat superfluous anyway.

Tel Aviv

6349 N. California
Phone: 764-3776
Parking: Street
No liquor

Mon.-Thur. & Sun.,
 11:30 A.M.–8:00 P.M.
Fri., 11:30 A.M.–Sundown
Closed Saturday

Step inside the Tel Aviv, and it's as if you're no longer in Chicago. Hebrew is the prevailing language, men and boys wear yalmulkes, and Israeli flags and posters decorate the walls. Tel Aviv is a dairy restaurant (no meat is served), and primarily offers vegetable variations and fish.

The menu is partly Middle Eastern specialties: falafel (deep fried balls of ground chick peas and spices), chomos (a ground chick pea spread), and eggplant salad. The other half is cut between vegetarian plates and typical deli offerings —gefilte fish, apple blintz, and beet borscht. There's even Kosher pizza!

Food is serve-yourself, with several dishes displayed on a steam table. Falafel (50¢; 90¢) is superb. It's crisp, dripping with salad and tahini (sesame) sauce and practically overflows its pouch of middle eastern bread. The vegetable plate ($1.50) provides a variety of preparations and colors. There's stewed zucchini, roast potatoes, boiled carrots, and gluey but tasty rice with mushrooms. An equally appealing vegie is the french fried cauliflower (65¢ for 4). Big flowerettes come lightly breaded, midway between soft and resilient, and nearly greaseless.

Baked fish ($2.80), smothered in a celery-mushroom-studded tomato sauce, provides yet another possibility. And don't forget the pizza. It's 50¢ a slice, very garlicky and not bad at all.

Bimbo's

Routes 12 & 68, Palatine
Phone: 359-6171
Parking: Lot
Full bar

Daily, 4:00 P.M.–11:00 P.M.
Fri., Sat., 4:00 P.M.–Midnight
Closed Sunday

Bimbo's has the aura of a fifties roadhouse—pine-panelled, smoky, gruff. It's the kind of place where you'd expect to find Keely Smith torching a song and Robert Mitchum lounging coolly at a rear table. What you actually do encounter are tables filled with normal-looking suburban couples, a loud TV, and loads to eat. The food's not spectacular, but it's certainly substantial and more tasty than not.

Meals begin with a nice, non-show biz salad bar: pickled beets, slaw, marinated garbanzo beans, macaroni salad, kidney bean salad, raw vegetables, and a cheddar cheese spread and crackers. It does its job, as everything tastes fresh and skillfully seasoned.

Soup comes next. We enjoyed the well-packed bean soup far more than the ordinary onion. Salad is basic shredded iceberg and dressing; save a few garbanzos from the salad bar for spice.

The entrees range from pasta to seafood to veal, with the latter priced beyond our reach. We chose the boneless chicken parmesan ($4.50) which had been flattened, crisp-fried, and covered with melted cheese and a judiciously applied tomato sauce. There's also lightly spicy, deep fried chicken Florentine ($4.75) and a nicely priced chicken Vesuvio ($4.75).

Not as successful is shrimp marinara ($4.50), as the heavy tomato sauce fights rather than comforts the shrimp. Small dishes of mostaccioli add pleasant company. It's also possible to dine on pasta alone, with such options as tortellini ($3.50), linguini with red or white clam sauce ($3.50), and gnocchi ($3.50).

ITALIAN

Bruna's

2424 S. Oakley
Phone: 847-8875
Parking: Street
Full bar

Mon., Thur.-Sat., 5:00 P.M.–Midnight
Sun., 3:00 P.M.–Midnight
Closed Tuesday and Wednesday

Bruna's is almost more like a neighborhood tap than a restaurant. It's the kind of place where, elbows resting on the counter, people hang around for hours to shoot the breeze. One enters the eating area through the bar, and it's not unusual for several customers to turn around and nod hello.

The dining room, with its faded pastel murals, looks like it hasn't changed in forty years. This adds a comforting, time-worn quality which hopefully won't ever be panelled and mirrored into oblivion.

Served in abundant quantities by a domineering, no-nonsense waitress, the food too exudes a simple homeyness.

Pastas are a good bet, particularly the feathery, non-sticky ravioli ($2.75). Although its sauce bears evidence of long hours of cooking, it could benefit from slightly more oomph! Not so for the spaghetti al accughi (anchovy, $2.50), as it packs an unusual wallop which requires some easing into. It gets better with each bite.

Linguini with clam sauce ($3.50) is abundantly showered with clams and flavor, and mostaccioli with butter and cheese ($2.25) comes across as light and soothing. Other pastas, including spaghetti marinara and green noodles, range from $2.00 to $2.75.

Non-noodle fanciers will do well with the amply-sauced chicken cacciatore ($4.75) or the not-so-Italian calf's liver with onions and bacon ($3.95). A steamy, beany minestrone, thick-cut bread, routine iceberg salad, and dessert, including a creamier than usual spumoni, accompany all meat entrees. Pastas play host to salad and bread only.

Cas and Lou's

3457 W. Irving Park
Phone: 588-8445
Parking: Street
Full bar

Mon.-Thur., 11:00 A.M.–Midnight
Fri., 11:00 A.M.–2:00 A.M.
Sat., 4:00 P.M.–2:00 A.M.
Sun., 4:00 P.M.–10:00 P.M.

Cas and Lou's began about 12 years ago as a corner deli. Customers would spot the Aiello family munching something good in the back room and ask for a sample. Instead of continuing to give their dinner away, the Aiellos gradually eliminated selling groceries and took to cooking them. They have spiffied their place up even further by adding a tri-level dining room steeped in rustic charm and a new, much more expensive menu.

The food is still fine, and the kitchen continues to dish up several pastas, a selection of beef and pork entrees, and have recently added seafood. The pastas are the least pricey, and range from $2.25 for noodles and tomato sauce up to $4.25 for pasta paesano, topped with ricotta and meat sauce. Meat dinners other than breaded pork Sicilian-style ($4.95) and meatballs covered with tomato sauce and romano cheese ($4.95) are priced beyond our reach.

Sauces come with a choice of noodles: mostaccioli, spaghetti, linguini, or fettuce (a flat and fairly thin variety). A standout is fettuce a la Cas and Lou, pasta held together by a rich butter, egg, and ricotta cheese mixture, spiced with threads of proscuittini. Linguini with clam sauce ($3.50) is also done up well (lots of clams), the lasagna ($3.95) is big and cheesy, and there's a nice pasta burro and aglie (butter and garlic, $3.50) or a blander pasta burro and uova (butter and eggs, $3.50).

For a bit of ruffage, split an antipasto due ($3.50), an impressive conglomerate of prosciutto, mortadella, salami, olive salad, provolone cheese, and anchovies. And no matter how much you've eaten, try to save a bit of space for the freshest, most ambrosiac cannoli around (75¢). The crunchy shell, smooth, rich ricotta filling, and healthy sprinkling of pistachios and powdered sugar make it irresistible.

Febo's

(one of our favorites)

2501 S. Western
Phone: 523-0839
Parking: Lot, on
    Western Avenue
Full bar

Daily, 11:00 A.M.–Midnight
Fri.-Sat., 11:00 A.M.–1:00 A.M.
Closed Sunday
Reservations suggested

The search for an inexpensive Italian restaurant that goes beyond the usual pasta dishes need not take you to Florence or Bologna. There's one right here on Chicago's near southwest side. Febo's prices are slightly higher than our other budget Italian eateries, but dinners include appetizer and soup as well as dessert.

Most meals are priced from $4.25 to $5.25, other than higher-priced steak and veal dishes. We suggest you begin your meal with an antipasto plate—it's attractively arranged and each person gets his own. Fresh, chewy Fontana bread goes along nicely. Soup's next, and minestrone (available Wednesday, Friday, and Saturday only) is the standout. The salad sports more ingredients than usual and a welcome gathering of herbs.

However, the entrees are what Febo's is all about. The linguine Alfredo ($4.75) with its garlicky, butter-cheese sauce is both delicate and potent. Baked green noodles ($4.25), tortellini a la Bolognese ($4.50), and super rich cannelloni ($4.75) are also far from ordinary.

Our favorite dish at Febo's, which you'll have to spend a bit more for, is their chicken Alfredo ($5.50). The juicy, sauteed chicken is smothered with mushrooms and served in a lemon-herb seasoned wine sauce along with artichoke hearts and crisp, whole new potatoes. The exquisite sister dish, chicken Vesuvio ($5.25), comes minus the mushrooms and artichokes but with some equally tantalizing long, crisp potatoes.

Dessert choices include a disappointing cannoli (it's been frozen), spumoni, and an excellent tortoni crowned with whipped cream.

Febo's is a huge, permanently crowded place that is laid out in a series of small dining rooms. In one of the rooms seating can be had in old, high-back wooden booths that look like they were lifted out of a European train.

La Fontanella
(one of our favorites)

2414 S. Oakley
Phone: 927-5249
(reservations)
Parking: Street
Full bar

Daily, 11:00 A.M.–11:00 P.M.
Sat.-Sun., 4:30 P.M.–Midnight
Closed Monday

La Fontanella is the perfect movie-set neighborhood Italian restaurant. It could easily be in Brooklyn, but luckily it's in Chicago. The feeling is friendly, warm, and storefront cozy. Franca Desideri cooks, her husband Guido minds bar and helps attend tables, and daughter Isabella is the waitress. Food is made to order, so plan on relaxing. The prices will relax you even further as they are comfortably low.

Their menu is ambitious for such a small operation. Not only are there the usual pastas (ranging from $2.00 to $2.50), but also saltimbocca, chicken vesuvio, and frittata, an Italian omelette. One of our favorite dishes is chicken a la Franca ($5.00), a specialty of the house. Each piece is lightly fried and bursts with a filling of butter, herbs, and parmesan cheese. Pan-fried potatoes and artichokes make an unbeatable accompaniment.

Don't overlook the frittata ($2.50), a puffy golden disc that is more extra ingredients than egg. And what extras—juicy sausage, wonderfully soft, sweet-tasting potatoes, green peppers, and mushrooms. There's also an interesting Sicilian dish called arancini, deep fried balls of rice stuffed with marble-sized meatballs ($2.50). It is served with a rich meat sauce on the side, plus a small antipasto. Rich meat sauce also blankets the giant serving of lasagna ($2.50), but somehow the buttery cheese and cream sauce surrounding the green noodles ($2.50) tastes even more extravagant.

They also do a great pizza (medium cheese and sausage, $3.50). It wears a truly seductive smothering of cheese, is quite garlicky, and nicely crisp-crusted. To round you out a little more, the crackly shelled, creamy filled cannoli is superb.

Gennaro's

1352 W. Taylor
Phone: 243-1035
        733-8790
Parking: Street
Full bar

Daily, 5:00 P.M.–9:00 P.M.
Fri.-Sat., 5:00 P.M.–10:00 P.M.
Closed Monday

Gennaro's retains some of the flavor of the speakeasy days. The front door is often locked, and you usually have to knock solidly to gain admittance. But once you enter, it's all pretty straight. The TV is on, and most people are thoroughly engaged in scarfing down big platesful of spaghetti. The walls are covered with glossy panelling, fish trophies, and photographs.

The compact menu centers on its homemade pasta and pizza. All of the noodle dishes cost under $3.00. Standouts are the gnocchi (chewy, potato noodles) with tomato sauce ($2.65) and the cheese-filled ravioli ($2.65). A meatball or sausage addition costs 60¢ more. The linguine isn't mixed and rolled in Gennaro's kitchen, but you can have it topped by an unusual anchovy, garlic, and oil sauce ($3.00).

The term "small" pizza ($3.90) is a misnomer. The one we received practically covered the table. It can easily serve four when combined with a pasta dish or two. The crust is thin and crunchy, while the topping is spicy and well-laden with cheese. We found the sausage pizzas to be a bit sparse on the meat, though.

Accompany your starch with a gigantic antipasto ($1.75 per person). They're so enormous that the meats are served on one plate and the vegetables on another.

Desserts are available, including spumoni, tortoni, or homemade cannoli with either a chocolate or vanilla filling. There are several Italian wines to wash it all down.

Mategrano's

1321 W. Taylor
Phone: 243-8441
Parking: Rear lot
  and street
Full bar

Mon.-Fri., 11:15 A.M.–2:30 P.M.;
  5:00 P.M.–9:00 P.M.
Sat., 4:00 P.M.–10:00 P.M.
Thur. and Sat. buffet,
  6:00 P.M.–9:00 P.M.
Sun., 3:00 P.M.–8:00 P.M.

If you've never attended an Italian wedding feast, Mategrano's offers a good substitute. On Thursday and Saturday nights they present an all-you-can-eat buffet for $3.95 that will challenge the most gargantuan appetite. The buffet is made up of eighteen or so Italian specialties, many of them unusual.

A typical spread includes various pastas, perhaps a lasagna, mostaccioli, and macaroni pie. There's herb-seasoned baked chicken, homemade Italian sausage, and a savory beef and green bean stew. The thick, meaty eggplant parmigiana is delicious and so are the ricotta cheese puffs.

Vegetables aren't neglected. There are batter-fried zucchini strips, cold marinated zucchini slices, an escarole and white bean combination, green bean salad, and marinated whole sweet peppers. Don't skip the pizza bread, but go light on the limp and soggy tossed salad.

Each trip to the buffet will bring a new surprise, so use restraint and keep an eye on the waitresses bearing platters from the kitchen. Better things may be yet to come! There are also small pitchers of light red wine, but they're priced a little high at $2.00.

Be sure to call in for reservations on buffet nights because Mategrano's is packed with people—all eating like there's no tomorrow. And it's a good place to be, just in case there isn't.

On non-buffet nights the menu includes a wide variety of interesting pasta dishes all priced under $3.95.

Toscano's

2439 S. Oakley
Phone: 376-4841
Parking: Street
Full bar

Daily, 11:00 A.M.–Midnight
Fri., 11:00 A.M.–1:00 A.M.
Sat., 11:00 A.M.–2:00 A.M.
Sun., Noon–10:00 P.M.
Closed Monday

Tucked away on a southwest side residential street is Toscano's, an unpretentious, neighborhood kind of place. It's crowded, but not too crowded, and very efficiently and smoothly run. It's best to come here with a ravenous appetite.

Complete dinners, which are served from 5:00 to 10:00 P.M., consist of a chewy Italian bread from nearby Fontana's bakery, an above-average minestrone, fresh salad, entree, beverage, and dessert.

The menu is loaded with pastas, and includes a choice of six tomato-based sauces, the more interesting being the Italian sausage, chicken liver, or the house specialty, chicken liver and mushroom. The lasagna ($3.55), as the menu suggests, is "truly a treat." The broad noodles are prepared al dente, layered between a subtle meat sauce, and topped by a thick, sizzling layer of melted mozzarella.

There is also a selection of chicken and veal dishes, most priced higher than our $4.50 budget. Try the chicken, Toscano-style ($3.50). Resembling cacciatiore, the meat is cooked tender in a flavorful, wine-spiked tomato-mushroom sauce. It's very tasty, though the sauce could have more mushrooms.

Portions are large at Toscano's, but try to save room for dessert. Rather than spumoni or tortoni, spend 20¢ extra for some excellent cannoli. The shell is fresh and crunchy and the ricotta filling is scrumptiously rich.

ITALIAN

Traverso's

15601 S. Harlem, Orland Park   Daily 4:00 P.M.–2:00 A.M.
Phone: 532-2220
Parking: Lot
Full bar

A sprawling place, on weekends it looks like the gathering spot for every south suburbanite between 15 and 50. The decor is typically Italian restaurant-modern—lots of red and black, bare brick and wood, a few somber oil paintings, and cushy leatherette chairs. The young, uniformed waitresses move about quickly and efficiently as if tracked on a pre-destined course.

Pizza ($3.50 for a medium cheese and onion) highlights the succinct menu. Crisp of crust, with a fresh, mild, if not overly distinctive flavor, it comes uniquely served upon a grill. A real detraction is the use of what tasted like dehydrated onions in place of the real thing.

More memorable are the soft, airy pillows of homemade ravioli ($3.65). Lasagna ($3.95) is generously proportioned and creamy, but the overall flavor lacks a necessary richness. Other menu choices include fried chicken, boneless lake perch, and several sandwiches.

Minestrone (50¢) starts the meal off right, as it's loaded with ingredients, including barley, and tastes terrific when chunks of French bread are dunked into it. The hefty, crunchy salad is well complemented by a spirited, herb-flickered Italian vinaigrette.

However, the meal's real highlight comes last, as their cheesecake could rival any in Orland Park, and most in Chicago. It's creamy, dense, slightly tart, and just rich enough. Even the graham cracker crust packs more personality than usual. After we finished our first piece, we couldn't resist asking for another.

Villa Marconi

2358 S. Oakley
Phone: 847-3168
Parking: Street
Full bar

Mon.-Thur., 11:00 A.M.–10:00 P.M.
Fri., 11:00 A.M.–Midnight
Sat., 5:00 P.M.–Midnight
Closed Sunday

Villa Marconi has a distinct air of middle class dignity about it. Last time here, we were seated next to a huge family gathering, celebrating with subdued aplomb the 75th birthday of the family patriarch. Platters of herb-sprinkled chicken, salads, and oven-roasted potatoes appeared with the regularity of a Roman feast. We were so obviously envious that our waitress slipped us a few potatoes.

Fortunately the regular menu is not too hard to take either, and prices are amazingly inexpensive. Even the veal dishes at $3.75, are affordable.

Although good Fontana bread, a tasty vegetable soup, and a no-special-thrills salad are included in the dinner, start off with an appetizer of grostini (75¢). It's crisp-toasted bread gently piled with caper-anchovy-scented chopped liver, and very flavorful.

An excellent pasta is the tortellini ($3.00), tiny, ripple-edged dumplings embedded with finely ground meat and blanketed with a deep rich tomato sauce. Other pasta possibilities include gnocchi ($3.00), ravioli ($2.50), mostaccioli ($2.50), and spaghetti ($2.50).

If you've a taste for something less starchy, try the chicken cacciatore ($3.50), as it's tender and munificently mushroomed. Veal scallopini ($3.75) benefits from a heady wine sauce, but lacks tenderness and an overall delicacy of flavor.

For dessert choose spumoni (50¢) as the cannoli's (75¢) limp exterior bears evidence of time spent in the freezer.

A warm, festive place where the waitresses will undoubtedly call you "dolly."

Iroha

3346 N. Clark   Daily, 1:00 P.M.–9:00 P.M.
Phone: 549-9465   Closed Tuesday
Parking: Street
B.Y.O.

From the outside, Iroha looks like any of the handful of
Oriental groceries dotting Clark Street, but a peek inside
reveals a substantial, cozy little restaurant. Huge goldfish loll
lazily in tanks, crocheted doilies cover the counter stools, and
blue and white banners hide the windows. If WLS didn't vie
with the "el" for background "music," you could swear to
being in Tokyo.

The bi-lingual menu is small, but innovative. Heading the
appetizers are two that are rarely found elsewhere. The first
is gyoza (85¢), lightly sauteed dumplings that are filled with
a spicy mix of ground pork. The other, motoyaki ($1.25),
consists of three gently sauteed shrimp covered with a smooth
egg yolk sauce. Both provide an excellent overture to the main
course.

In this area, we're partial to the tender, artfully seasoned
pork teriyaki ($2.75) and any of the fresh fish, if available.
The sweet, moist striped bass is particularly pleasing as is the
charcoal broiled mackerel ($3.00).

For a greater variety of taste and textures, try yakisoba
($2.50), a stir-fried liaison of pork, cabbage, carrots, onions,
peppers, carrots, and buckwheat noodles, doused with a semi-
sweet garlic-soy sauce.

Tempura ($3.25), unfortunately, doesn't achieve the status
of the other dishes. Although its coating is properly greaseless and feathery, the overall taste is bland. Not so with the
soup, salad, or tea, included with each meal. If the marinated
cauliflower salad is available, it's an especially delicious blend
of crisp raw flowerettes, herbs, oil, and vinegar.

Matsuya

(one of our favorites)

3469 N. Clark   Daily, 5:00 P.M.–10:00 P.M.
Phone: 248-2677   Sat., Sun., Noon–10:00 P.M.
Parking: Street
B.Y.O.

A spritely, spacious, greenery-filled restaurant that does fantastic things with fresh fish. Look for a handwritten paper posted on the wall, headlined "Today's Fish," and take a plunge.

Possibilities often include a broiled, crisp-edged mackerel ($2.75) that possesses incredibly flaky flesh and a sweet taste; a less intense, mild butterfish ($2.85); or a rich, more oily tuna ($2.85), aromatically imbued with teriyaki sauce.

Matsuya also serves its tuna raw in one of the better renditions of sashimi ($3.75, but can also be ordered in half-portions) we've ever tasted. The tender tuna slices can be sparked with either of two sauces, one of mint green wasabi (Japanese horseradish paste) and the other, fresh-grated white horseradish. Both can be toned down with generous splashes of soy. The too-heavily-battered tempura ($2.95) doesn't come off quite as well.

Matsuya also does a plump, perfectly-charcoaled chicken teriyaki ($2.75) that has no peer for the price, except perhaps that served at the Old Town Art Fair.

A flavorful clear soup and small dish of pucker-inducing vegetables proceed each meal, but we suggest ordering an extra appetizer or two. Especially refreshing is goma-ae, sesame seed and soy-sauce cold spinach (75¢) and kani-sunomono ($1.25), crab flakes and tissue-thin cucumber slices bathed in a sweetened vinegar sauce.

Miyako

3242 N. Clark
Phone: 549-1085
Parking: Street
B.Y.O.

Daily, Noon–10:00 P.M.
Thur., 4:00 P.M.–10:00 P.M.
Closed Wednesday

Miyako is probably Chicago's cheapest Japanese restaurant. All entrees cost under $3.00, and several are below $2.00. Its setting is nothing to write home about, but it's a clean place, and the food is both delicious and authentic.

There is a wide selection of entrees ranging from everpopular tempura and teriyaki to more rare kayaku (eel) udon ($2.35) and abalone sashimi ($3.50). All meals include a clear but filling broth, a small dish of pickled vegetables, and a pot of mild brewed tea. Rice is 25¢ extra per person. Appetizers of pickled gomaye (spinach, 75¢) and sunomono (cucumber, 75¢) are excellent.

The sukiyaki at $3.50 is the most expensive item on the menu, but it is served in a portion big enough for two. Tender, thin-sliced beef, nappa (cabbage), fresh mushrooms, scallions, and thin transparent saifun noodles share a slightly sweet broth. The sukiyaki is well-made and flavorful, as are the udon dishes. These are basically large bowls of soup containing long, somewhat thick noodles to which a variety of ingredients may be added. Try the tempura udon ($3.00) which features batter-fried shrimp, and green beans, or nabeyaki udon ($2.70), a blend of chicken, egg, and vegetables. The donburi or rice-based dishes are not only tasty, but put your skill with chopsticks to the test. (Silverware is served only upon request.)

The expertly-prepared tempura ($3.50) has a crisp, light batter. The three large butterfly shrimp are firm and freshtasting and come with equally delicate batter-fried sweet potato, eggplant, and green beans. Beef teriyaki ($2.65) is the lowest-priced around, the portion is generous, and the meat well-marinated and tender.

As characteristic of most Japanese restaurants, service at Miyako's is both unobtrusive and efficient. Portions are large, and it's easy for two people to enjoy a satisfying dinner for under $7.00.

Naniwa

923 W. Belmont
Phone: 348-9027
Parking: Street
B.Y.O.

Daily, 4:00 P.M.–10:00 P.M.
Sat.-Sun., Noon–10:00 P.M.
Closed Wednesday

Naniwa's setting is plain storefront, and service can occasionally be disinterested. However, it features some fine Japanese cooking at very pleasing prices. Located next door to Ann Sather's, Naniwa's offers an altogether different atmosphere. The room is somewhat somber and bare of decoration, but a taste of beef teriyaki or shrimp tempura will immediately dissolve any temporary blahs.

The menu is lengthy and features several Japanese specialties, most of which are $3.00 or under. All entrees include a small dish of pickled vegetables, a large covered bowl of rice, and a pot of brewed tea. There are a variety of udon (noodle dishes), nabe (soups), and donburi (meat, vegetables, and rice), as well as the more usual but well-prepared teriyaki and tempura.

Try oyako donburi ($2.00), bits of chicken, scrambled egg, bamboo shoots, and onions seasoned with a saki-sugar-soy sauce mixture and served on a bed of rice. The portion is large, and the combination of flavors is delicious. Pork or beef nabe ($3.00) is a healthful, flavorsome soup featuring thin noodles, meat, soy curd, and assorted vegetables, including fresh mushrooms. It is served in a black iron pot and acts as a restorative, especially on an icy winter day. There is also a more unusual ika (squid) nabe ($3.00). They prepare beef teriyaki ($3.00) with finesse here. Thinly sliced meat is served in a light, not too sweet teriyaki sauce that tastes marvelous with the rice. Tempura and sashimi (marinated raw fish) are slightly more expensive at $3.50, but both are quite good.

New Japan

45 W. Division
Phone: 787-4248
Parking: Street
B.Y.O.

Mon.-Thur., 11:45 A.M.–2:30 P.M.;
5:00 P.M.–10:00 P.M.
Fri., Sat., 11:45 A.M.–2:30 P.M.;
5:00 P.M.–11:00 P.M.
Closed Sunday

A fine little hideaway for Japanese food located amidst the Division/Rush Street hustle. The brief menu comes up with several bargains, and it's not difficult for two people to pack away a crate of food for under $7.00.

For starters, try the crunchy, sprout-filled eggroll (39¢), maybe a crisp-coated chicken wing or two (39¢ each), and an order of gyoza ($1.05), wonton-like dumplings stuffed with minced pork, scallions, cabbage, and a hint of garlic.

Bean sprouts, cabbage, soft noodles, and pork practically engulf the plate in yakisoba, a Japanese version of chow mein. The dish is not only well-packed with crunch and flavor, but politely priced. A small order, which really isn't small, goes for $1.65 and a large, for $2.25.

Equally kind is the tempura dinner ($2.75) which features a scallion and noodle-flecked soup, pickled vegetables, rice, and green tea in addition to the light, lacy shrimp and vegetables. Nestled under the batter can be found three firm shrimp, eggplant, mushrooms, onions, and sweet potatoes.

Finishing up the menu are a $3.25 beef teriyaki dinner, ramein, a kind of meal-in-one soup ($1.90; $2.30), and misoramein ($2.15; $2.50), which is the same basic soup to which soybean paste has been added.

The New Japan's setting is as clean and clear as its menu. Seven hot melon tables and chairs plus a small counter are squeezed into the narrow storefront. Rice paper lanterns, mirrors, and lattice work help create a semblance of openness.

Tenkatsu

3365 N. Clark
Phone: 549-8697
Parking: Street
B.Y.O.

Mon.-Fri., 5:00 P.M.–10:00 P.M.
Sat., Sun., 12 Noon–10:00 P.M.
Closed Monday

A simpler and more unpretentious place than Tenkatsu would be hard to find. Recent remodeling has spruced it up a bit, though the food has never needed any redoing. Most dishes cost well under $4.00 and portions are generous. All meals include a small dish of spicy pickled cabbage, a soup containing soybean curd and scallions, and tea. Teriyaki and tempura are served with rice.

One of our favorites is beef yasai ($3.50), an impressive mound of thin, tender beef slices, fresh bean sprouts, bamboo shoots, fried onions, scallions, and transparent noodles in a semisweet soy broth. It's a cozy blend of flavors and textures, and is quite delicious. The udon (noodle soup, $2.30) has a slightly smoky taste, is very filling, and makes a terrific bargain meal, especially with a tempura addition (called "tempura udon").

Another great dish is the donburi ($2.75). It is prepared several ways, two of the best being oyako (chicken and egg) and niku (beef and egg). These ingredients plus fresh mushrooms, bamboo shoots, fried onions, scallions, and transparent noodles are piled atop a bed of rice. This dish always gets better and better while you eat it, as the rice keeps soaking in more of the juice. Beef teriyaki ($3.50) and shrimp tempura ($3.75) are both reliable and well-prepared.

Sukiyaki Tei

2916½ W. Devon
Phone: 262-4181
Parking: Street
B.Y.O.

Mon.-Thur., Noon–3:00 P.M.;
    5:00 P.M.–10:00 P.M.
Fri., Sat., Noon–3:00 P.M.;
    5:00 P.M.–11:00 P.M.
Sun., 5:00 P.M.–10:00 P.M.

A serene little restaurant located on Devon's knish row. Probably the only Japanese/Hawaiian restaurant in the city, one flick of your Bik, and you'd miss it. Don't! It has an interesting, if limited, menu of very inexpensive and filling dishes. Included are three appetizers, shrimp tempura ($2.85) and steak teriyaki ($3.50) dinners, and three a la carte choices—Hawaiian-style sukiyaki ($1.85), Hawaiian-style tempura (basically, tempura served over rice, $1.85), and a noodle, dumpling, and pork-studded soup called saimin ($1.75).

The appetizers, known as pupus, are a real plus. Our special favorite is okole, a tender, fluted, steamed dumpling filled with minced pork, shrimp, and vegetables (four for $1.00, or 30¢ each). Its taste is at once subtle, substantial, and sweet, and is easily one of the better treats we've had in a long time. The crunchy, golden brown shell of the eggroll (50¢) hides a filling somewhat oily and lacking in spunk. Pep it up a bit with a dunk into the refreshing, chunky apricot sauce. The sauce also does beautiful things for the plump, moist, sesame-fried chicken wings (40¢ each).

The tempura falls a little flat, mainly because the batter does. Although the coating misses having that necessary light crispness, it does envelop a variety of nice things, including shrimp, sweet potatoes, mushrooms, onions, green beans, and even cucumbers.

However, sukiyaki Hawaiian-style is a cheap eats dream. Served in a large bowl, its white rice base soaks up the flavor of a semi-sweet, soy sauce-tossed melange of sauteed beef, onions, scallions, bean sprouts, and egg. It's as flavorful as it is filling, and along with an appetizer or two, makes a perfect just-over-$2.00-dinner.

The Bagel
(one of our favorites)

4806 N. Kedzie   Daily, 5:00 A.M.–9:00 P.M.
Phone: 463-7141   Sun., 5:00 A.M.–2:00 P.M.
Parking: Street
No liquor

You don't have to be Jewish to enjoy The Bagel. It's for anyone with an urge to feast on healthy portions of good, Jewish "soul food," served up with a bit of mothering. The Bagel is a simple store front located in the old Jewish neighborhood around Lawrence and Kedzie. There's a warm familiarity in the place, and lots of kibbitzing between the crowd and the waitresses.

However, the main business of the establishment is its food, and there's plenty of it. Dinners run between $3.75 and $4.50 and include appetizer or soup, apple sauce, cole slaw or salad, meat, potato, vegetables, dessert, and beverage.

As soon as you sit down, the waitress places a plate of crisp, kosher dills on your table. This is soon followed by a basket filled with pumpernickel bread and thick slices of challe (egg bread), which keeps getting refilled.

There are some beautiful starters: fresh pickled herring, moist chopped liver, matzoh ball soup on Friday, kreplach on Wednesday, and, frequently, mushroom-barley.

Main courses vary. There might be a Polish-style white fish stuffed with gefilte fish ($3.95) or a cold, pickled sweet and sour white fish ($3.50). Rich, juicy baked veal breast ($4.50) is served in a football-sized portion while baked brisket ($4.50) is somewhat smaller. Along with the meat you may luck upon a crisp potato or noodle kugel (pudding). Vegetables are not the high point of Jewish cooking, and the canned peas and carrots at The Bagel are no exception, though your waitress will keep urging you to try some. If you still can make it, there's a nice custard-like rice pudding for dessert.

Nothing is cooked fancy at The Bagel. It's just good, stick-to-your-ribs-forever fare.

For Sunday breakfast, fried herring and great, enormous scrambled omelettes are served. Try the Spanish or the Denver.

Frances'

2453 N. Clark
Phone: 525-9675
Parking: Street (difficult)
No liquor

Tue.-Sun., 6:00 A.M.–11:30 P.M.
Closed Monday

Where would Clark Street be without Frances' to feed its broke but hungry citizens? The place has a passionate following for good reason. There is always something warm and nourishing to be had at prices that rival those of the Bohemian restaurants on the southwest side. An onion-smothered hamburger the size of a 16″ softball, plus three side dishes will cost you $1.95. A duck dinner is only $3.35. And there's a wide variety in between: beef stew ($2.95), meat loaf ($2.35), veal cutlet ($3.45), turkey leg ($2.95), roast chicken ($2.55), and more.

The side dishes vary in type and appeal. Among the best are the kishke and the noodles. The cole slaw has a nice flavor, though it tends to be soupy, and most of the vegetables are best forgotten unless you're partial to food straight from the can. There's always a good supply of excellent, chewy rye bread.

Food is displayed steam table fashion. You make your selection, choose a seat, and wait for the waitress to bring the order. It all looks surprisingly more appealing on your plate, and most meals not only fill you up but are downright tasty.

Frances' makes no attempt at decoration, other than a few signs touting grilled reubens or fried matzoh. If you're a strict adherent of the "cleanliness is next to godliness" maxim, don't look too hard. The place gets a little raunchy as the evening winds down. But if you're after an inexpensive hot meal, try Frances'.

Cho Sun O.K.

4200 N. Lincoln   Wed.-Mon., 10:00 A.M.–11:00 P.M.
Phone: 348-9409   Closed Tuesday
Parking: Street
B.Y.O.

A Korean restaurant located in Teutonic territory along Lincoln Avenue. It's actually a glorified grill, somewhat dim and grim, but run by a friendly young husband and wife team. Their menu includes several Korean standards, plus a T-bone steak, tuna salad, and standard Chinese dishes. We concentrated on the Korean.

Koreans do beautiful things with marinated, charcoal grilled meats, and those at Cho Sun are more than O.K. Especially flavorful is the juicy, well-charred galbi (flattened short ribs, $3.50), though parts of it can be a bit tough. Fried mandoo ($2.10), similar to fried wonton, have coarse-ground sausage encased in each honey-toned, flaky shell.

Chop chae ($2.65), a glimmering stir-fried mass of onions, carrots, broccoli, celery, cellophane noodles, black mushrooms, and beef, packs several textural contrasts. Also on hand is dahk bokum ($2.75), a glazed gathering of fat chicken chunks, carrot discs, onions, and green peppers. Eat carefully, because tiny bones present a hazard.

The menu includes a few taste bud stretchers such as chi gae, a soup featuring both fish cakes and bean cakes ($3.00) and sliced raw abalone ($3.80). A dull salad or its antithesis, kimchee, a fiery Korean pickled vegetable dish, come with all meals.

Several Korean couples were here the night of our visit, all obviously enjoying themselves. The only distraction was the insistent tone of an all-news radio station.

Dae Ho

2741 W. Devon   Sun.-Fri., 11:30 A.M.–11:00 P.M.
Phone: 274-8499   Sat., 11:30 A.M.–1:00 A.M.
Parking: Street   Closed Tuesday
Beer only

Prices are higher than at the Korean grills, but Dae Ho's
setting is appropriately more plush. It's the perfect place to
go when you want to combine Korean food with a little
"atmosphere." Cushiony booths bring on instant comfort, and
curtains, rug, tablecloths, and even the lights are a study in
scarlet. Fortunately the food doesn't fade out, as whatever
we've tasted has been artfully prepared and carefully seasoned. However portions are small, so be sure to order at
least three dishes for two people.

Try any of the grilled meats. The charcoal edge combines
beautifully with the semi-sweet marinade. San juck, skewered
pieces of tender beef and vegetables ($3.95), is particularly
appealing but then so is the galbi (short ribs, $3.50) and
bul-ko-gi (wafer-thin slices of beef or pork, $3.50).

We generally complement a grilled meat with chop che
($4.50) because we enjoy its variety and crisp texture. Dae
Ho's version, though inexplicably high-priced, combines transparent noodles, carrots, onions, scallions, sprouts, mushrooms,
spinach, and beef in a particularly well-flavored meld. Bee-
beem-bob ($3.50) is as fun to eat as to say. Marinated beef
strips, vegetables, and a fried egg top a pile of rice, and when
stirred together, comes out rich and satisfying.

All meals include a big bowl of tasty eggdrop soup and
good tea. There's also an exquisite, satiny flan for dessert.
Plaintive Korean ballads add a romantic backdrop. There is,
however, one waitress who comes on compulsive and de-
manding, but hopefully she's undergone EST or isn't there
anymore.

Seoul House

5346 N. Clark
Phone: 728-6756
Parking: Street
B.Y.O.

Daily, 11:00 A.M.–11:00 P.M.
Closed Tuesday

For a different kind of Seoul food, this is the place. A popular restaurant with local Koreans, everything here is fresh, flavorful, and carefully cooked to order.

All meals come with individual, covered silver bowls of hot steamed rice, pickled vegetables (quite spicy), and tea. Chopsticks, rather than silverware, are placed at each setting. A good opportunity to put them to work is with an appetizer of fried mahndoo (45¢ for 2 pieces), puffy meat-filled turnovers that are a cross between won ton and egg roll.

A charcoaled meat dish is worth ordering for its aroma alone. You have your choice from among fire meat—thin-sliced grilled beef that is not a mouth-burner as its name might imply ($3.35), gahlbee, charcoaled short ribs ($3.30), and sanjuk, a blend of charcoaled sirloin cubes, mushrooms, green peppers, tomatoes, and scallions ($3.50). In each dish, the meat is given a lengthy marinating before actual grilling.

Some other dishes that have special appeal are chop chae, a sauteed mixture of beef, mushrooms, shredded carrots, scallions, and glossy noodles ($3.15), tahng suyuck, a close relative of sweet and sour pork but with a more pungent vinegar sauce ($3.15), and dalhk bokem, plump juicy chunks of chicken stir-fried with green peppers, onions, carrots, and fungus in a sweet salty sauce ($3.15). Perhaps our favorite dish, however, is the beef, shrimp, and abalone with fresh, crisp vegetables ($3.95). It's a feast of textures and tastes. Last time we tried it, the abalone were among the best we've ever eaten and had just the right slightly chewy (but not rubbery) texture.

The Korean Grill

Korean grills are a "cheap eats" paradise. They're simple, unadorned coffee shops that serve (in addition to such typical Americana as a bowl of chili, Campbell's, or Special K) a small Korean repertoire of standards like galbi, fried mahn doo, and bibim bop. All of it's inexpensive and exceedingly tasty; no dish costs more than $3.50, and most average a dollar less. The following are a brief sampling:

Chop Chae

5661 N. Clark	Daily, 10:00 A.M.–10:00 P.M.
Phone: 784-1381	Sat., 8:00 A.M.–10:00 P.M.
	Closed Wednesday

Probably our favorite, if we had to make a choice. Portions are big, and quality is excellent. A special bonus is the Korean pizza, listed in Korean at the top of the menu, and tasting like a butter-flaky quiche with Oriental overtones. Black mushrooms give added character to the glossy chop chae (a stir-fried vegetable mix), the won ton-like mahn doo are just crisp enough, and the galbi (short ribs) are well-marinated, nicely blackened, and very chewy. Only the san juck (skewered meat and vegetables) is a rather tasteless disappointment.

KOREAN GRILLS

Han's Grill

1833 W. Wilson	Daily, 7:30 A.M.–7:00 P.M.
Phone: 784-9483	Closed Sunday

A slightly run down but clean little place that serves only four Korean dishes, none of them priced over $2.20. Check out the grilled meats (san juck, galbi, pool gogi); they're tender, well-marinated, a little fatty, but bursting with flavor. Served atop a bed of shredded lettuce, and accompanied, perhaps, by a bowl of rice, they make a fine budget meal.

Kim's Galbi House

1902 W. Foster   Daily, 6:00 A.M.–9:00 P.M.
Phone: 275-8722

As unpretentious a place as one could find, but the food is great. The shish kabob-like san juk is laced with cubes of tender, flavor-packed beef and still-crisp vegetables. Broccoli, carrots, scallions, mushrooms, onions, transparent noodles, and thin strips of beef combine beautifully for a colorful, crunchy chop chae. Mahn doo is greasy but good. Big bowls of nourishing eggdrop soup and rice come with all meals.

KOREAN GRILLS

Lantern

3422 N. Sheffield   Mon.-Sat., 10:30 A.M.–9:30 P.M.
Phone: 528-2160   Sun., 10:30 A.M.–8:00 P.M.
                           Closed Tuesday

They do an excellent chop chae (very fresh, lots of crunch) and some nicely spicy mahn doo, which owes its extra kick to a filling of finely minced kimchee, a hot pickled vegetable. Galbi is invitingly charred, a bit greasy, but well shot with a spritely marinade. Several filling soups too.

Lee's Mongolian Steak House

3434 W. Irving
Phone: 539-2250

Mon.-Thur., 10:00 A.M.–9:00 P.M.
Fri. & Sat., 10:00 A.M.–10:00 P.M.
Sun., Noon–9:00 P.M.

A friendly, cheerful place with equally pleasant food. The charcoaled meats are uniformly tasty and thin fingers of green pepper, broccoli, and bamboo shoots make the chop chae extra lively. Mounds of over-moist rice and an excellent, if incongruous, cole slaw add company to each meal. If you'd like a breather from Korean, there are also ten different omelettes and even a chopped liver sandwich.

Pool Gogi

6928 N. Glenwood
Phone: 761-1366

Daily, 8:00 A.M.–9:00 P.M.

A popular Rogers Park hangout that has already won a large following. Two tempting offerings are dalhk bokem, a glazed combine of chicken chunks, peppers, carrots, and onions, and bibim bop, a mildly spicy vegetable, shredded beef, fried egg conglomerate bedded atop a mound of rice. Chop chae is too soupy, the kimchee is pure dragon fire, and the mahn doo, crisp and crackly.

Healthy Food Restaurant

3236 S. Halsted   Daily, 7:00 A.M.–8:00 P.M.
Phone: 326-2724   Sun., 8:00 A.M.–8:00 P.M.
Parking: Street
No liquor

Located in Mayor Daley's Bridgeport community, this isn't an organic food spot as its name might imply. Rather, it's a simple neighborhood restaurant featuring healthy portions of good, Lithuanian home-cooking. The interior is somewhat dark and gloomy, looking a bit like a lost relative of the old Marquis Lunches. The menu will pep you up considerably, as practically all meals, including dessert, cost between $1.85 and $3.75. A large bowl of soup is 50¢ extra.

The breads are a tour through the rye: black rye, light rye, and a marvelous, spongy-textured buttermilk rye. Every day there are two robust soups: perhaps a sauerkraut, chicken noodle, vegetable, barley, or hot beet. In the summer, don't miss the fantastic cold beet borscht garnished with sour cream and fresh dill.

Dinner specials vary each day, and feature such basics as short ribs ($3.20), chicken livers ($2.55), thin-sliced, tender beef liver with either onions or bacon ($2.55), pork chops ($3.55), and a strangely spiced meat loaf ($2.25). Vegetables, potatoes, and salad are included. Be sure to request the pan-fried potatoes, as they're golden crisp on the outside and soft and tender inside. Also, we suggest asking them to go easy on the gravy.

If you're in the mood for something lighter, Healthy Food makes some great blynas: rich, eggy pancakes folded envelope-style around cheese, blueberry, or apple filling ($2.05-$2.15). They're dusted with powdered sugar, served with sour cream, and are unbelievably good.

Neringa

2632 W. 71st
Phone: 925-5777
Parking: Street
No liquor

Daily, 8:00 A.M.–8:00 P.M.
Closed Wednesday

Located at the corner of an orderly row of houses in insular Marquette Park, the Neringa is another fine Lithuanian restaurant. Superficially the restaurant looks no different from any other corner coffee shop in the city, though one look at the menu will dispel any desire to order a BLT on toast. The Neringa boasts an expansive yet inexpensive list of Lithuanian specialties. Complete meals, including salad and a light dessert, are priced between $2.10 and $3.00.

There's a fine selection of breads: raisin, a chewy anise-flavored rye, and a regular rye. Soups are about 65¢ extra, but the cold beet borscht is worth it. It's loaded with chopped cucumbers, hard boiled egg, chives, and sour cream as well as beets. And it comes with a boiled potato served on the side. The sauerkraut soup is reliable, but we recommend skipping the beef and barley.

Choosing a main course can be traumatic, for there are just too many tempters. Meat blintzes ($2.75), stuffed cabbage ($2.80), cepelinai (meat-filled potato dumplings, $2.75), mushroom dumplings ($1.95), thueringer with kraut ($2.75), roast duck ($3.00), and more. The meat blintzes ($2.20) are exceptionally tasty, but the real highlight are the rolled pancakes filled with a perfect cranberry sauce ($2.10) that is neither too sweet nor too tart. Top them with sour cream, and you're in heaven.

The Neringa is big, clean, and usually bustling. Most of your fellow diners are from the neighborhood, and all of them seem to know a good bargain when they see one.

Ramune

2547 W. 69th   Daily, 8:00 A.M.–8:00 P.M.
Phone: 925-4254
Parking: Street
No liquor

A sparkling, tidy neighborhood deli that does a cozy little restaurant business on the side. A small dining area is just beyond the rye bread-loaded counter. The ambitious menu gets into tradition with such favorites as kugelis, potato pancakes, cepelinai, stuffed cabbage, kotletai, and meat, cheese, or mushroom-filled blintzes and dumplings.

Soups precede everything. Particularly refreshing is the scallion, cucumber, and sour cream-studded cold beet borscht (15¢ extra). If you'd rather hold onto your change, there might be a sauerkraut, barley, or chicken soup, any of which come gratis. Salad arrives next, and be sure to top it with sour cream, rather than a bottled dressing.

Entrees are typically brawny. Kotletai ($2.50), a well-seasoned cross between meatballs and meatloaf manages to capture the best of both. Don't be alarmed by the torpedo-shaped, doughy-looking cepelinai ($2.50). They're ground meat-filled potato dumplings, and while not the thing one would encounter at a gourmet dinner, they have an appealing buoyancy and flavor.

The chewy cheese dumplings ($2.50) would be a dairy farmer's delight. Not only do they enclose a creamy cheese filling and drip with melted butter, but come with a side dish of sour cream. Kugelis ($2.50) consists of six golden-fried, bacon-dotted slices of potato pudding. Greasiness is kept to a minimum and so is the knock-out flavor of bacon.

The Ramune has a wondrously old-fashioned neighborhood feel to it. There are all kinds of sights to delight the eye and stomach, from racks filled with hazelnuts to glass jars glistening with colorfully-wrapped candy.

Ruta

6812 S. Western
Phone: 778-3493
Parking: Street
No liquor

Mon.-Fri., 10:30 A.M.–7:00 P.M.
Closed Saturday & Sunday

A pleasant, freshly-painted, plastic flower-decorated place where seating can be had at a double horseshoe counter, tables, or booths. The latter offer a tight squeeze so try to sit across from someone with whom you'd like to get better acquainted. Middle-aged couples form the main dining cadre and most seem to be regulars. Waitresses know their business and move about with proficient ease.

The food is typically low-priced, with few of the entrees being over $3.00. Included in the bargain are tasty homemade soups (perhaps lima bean, chicken rice, or a fairly tame sauerkraut), delicious Latvian sour rye and pumpernickel, beverage, and dessert.

Our favorite meals are, unfortunately, the most fattening. Their apple pancakes ($2.50) are a true delight. Crisp, blistered, fritter-like puffs, they come embedded with fresh apple slices and sprinkled with powdered sugar. Fried to a perfect honey tone, maybe a bit greasy, they taste even better with sour cream, apple sauce, or preferably, both. Almost as difficult to resist are the cheese blintzes ($2.50), two eggy crepes enveloped around a creamy filling of tart pot cheese.

Less guilt-inducing are the sauteed liver ($2.50), smoky homemade pork sausage ($2.70) and Lithuanian schnitzel with smetana sauce ($2.70). The latter is a tender patty of breaded veal, covered with sour cream (smetana) and fried onions. It tastes great, and our only regret is that there wasn't more of it.

The usual Lithuanian desserts—canned peaches, jello, vanilla pudding—come with the meal. But the best way to go about the Ruta is for everyone to order a meat entree, and then split an apple pancake or blintz for dessert.

LITHUANIAN

Tulpe (Tulip)

2447 W. 69th   Mon.-Fri. & Sun., 10:00 A.M.–7:00 P.M.
Phone: 925-1123   Sat., 8:00 A.M.–8:00 P.M.
Parking: Street
No liquor

Walking into the Tulpe, you get a flash of how a stranger must have felt upon entering a bar in Tombstone. The cooks stare, the waitresses stare, and customers stare because this is essentially a tight, neighborhood place that sees few outsiders. It's also very tiny, so if the three tables and minute counter are filled, you have to stand inside the doorway looking about as inconspicuous as Alice Cooper at a DAR convention. However, once you settle in, no one is really unsocial, and the food and prices are friendly as can be.

Complete meals, which include soup, salad, dessert, and beverage, run between $1.90 and $2.80. It's easy to devour the basketful of Latvian sour rye. But move easily. Next there's a big bowl of sauerkraut soup (or something equally delicate!) served with a boiled potato on the side. Main dishes vary, and some worth sampling are the kotletai patties (a cross between meatballs and meatloaf), roast pork with sauerkraut, liver and onions, beef stew, and fabulous Lithuanian pancakes filled with cranberry, cheese, or apple.

Dessert is usually something unexciting, like a dish of canned fruit. However, it's about all you can eat anyway.

La Choza

7630 N. Paulina
Phone: 465-9401
Parking: Street
B.Y.O.

Tue.-Fri., Noon–11:30 P.M.
Sat., Noon–Midnight
Sun., Noon–10:30 P.M.
Closed Monday

La Choza's expanded, but the feeling remains cozy even though the crowd is still wall-to-wall. Food quality has suffered during this growth, but hopefully it will pick up again. By all means start your meal with their cheesy kamoosh (deep-fried tortillas with melted cheese, $1.30 for 2 people; $2.00 for 4), easily one of the most luscious dishes around. It takes restraint not to grab all the pieces yourself. The rich, mild guacamole ($1.40) is good too.

Beside the standard taco-tostada circuit, La Choza prepares steak eleven different ways. You can have it with ranchero (spicy tomato) sauce ($4.75), sauteed with green peppers, tomatoes, and onions ($4.75), or stuffed into a flour tortilla along with avocado sauce and a covering of piquant Indian sauce ("burrochoza," $5.00). We particularly like Steak Oaxaca ($5.00), in which strips of sirloin steak are topped by a harmonious blend of finely chopped onions, tomatoes, parsley, and melted white Mexican cheese. The whole thing is piled on a tortilla and tastes scrumptious. If you'd like it fiery, request an addition of hot peppers.

The Choza combination plate ($3.25) is a good one and includes a cheese enchilada, beef taco, and mild chile relleno. Avocado tostadas ($2.80) are delicious as are the flautas, three soft tortillas filled with chicken, beef, or sausage and enveloped in an avocado and sour cream topping ($2.85). All meals include rice and beans and begin with crisp tortillas and hot sauce.

We recommend closing your meal with mango pudding (65¢). It's creamy, very fruity-tasting, and very sweet.

La Cocina Mexicana

(one of our favorites)

948 W. Webster
Phone: 525-9793
Parking: Street
B.Y.O.

Daily, 3:00 P.M.–10:00 P.M.
Closed Tuesday

One of our favorite Mexican restaurants is tucked behind a hanging sign that simply states, "Mexican Food." Although long popular with young neighborhood residents, it's the kind of place you could walk by five times a day without noticing. However, don't let its nondescript appearance keep you from entering and sampling some delicious, fairly inexpensive Mexican food.

Their tostadas ($2.40) are artfully made—a perfect balance of crisp tortilla, beans, meat, lettuce, and cheese. It's possible to sample three different kinds from among chicken, ground beef, chorizo, and avocado. The latter are particularly scrumptious. Flautas ($3.25) are another attraction. They're fat with chicken and doused with a smooth avocado-sour cream sauce. The delicately spiced Mexican beef stew ($4.00) is quite good—tender chunks of meat simmered in a subtle, tomato-inspired sauce. The stew comes with a salad, beans, rice, and a basket of warm tortillas. The combination plate ($3.75) is the usual offering of taco, tostada, enchilada, rice, and beans. The fresh-tasting beans are exceptionally well made, and the rice is tasty. For the more adventurous, breaded tongue and menudo (tripe) are on the menu.

The swiftness of the service depends upon the size of the crowd. If there are more than three or four tables filled, expect a wait. The atmosphere is friendly and similar to a Mexican home where nothing is rushed.

El Jarocho

61 N. Bothwell, Palatine
Phone: 358-4148
Parking: Street
Wine & Beer

Daily, 5:00 P.M.–9:00 P.M.
Closed Sunday

Food takes second place at El Jarocho, as its owner, Nellie Tejeda, is a bona fide mind-blower. She'll yell, cajole, intimidate, and maybe even end up liking you. No sooner than you're seated and before being handed a menu, she'll demand, "Have you ordered yet?" Don't blink an eye, just calmly ask for the El Jarocho Deluxe Mexican Dinner ($7.00 for two) and settle back to await a most pleasant culinary assault.

First come huge, crisp, saucer-shaped tortilla chips accompanied by a tongue-numbing salsa verde (green sauce). A creamy, cheese-and-tomato-studded guacamole follows quickly. Next, a bucket of steaming soft tortillas and a soupy, mild-tempered chili. Then come the ever faithful rice and beans. The latter are particularly good, dense of texture and subtly flavored with pork, onions, and garlic. You'll even be offered seconds, but move cautiously, as the meal's only half-over.

Entrees follow: first tomato-bathed enchiladas stuffed with an easy-going blend of ground meat and spices and a nearly identical filling encased in crunchy taco shells. Adding further variety is fork-tender chicken sauced with a chocolate-tinged, sesame-studded mole and a small serving of slightly over-chewy, but pleasantly flavored spareribs. Plenty to stuff even the most insatiable of appetites.

Nellie's dining room is a hodgepodge of memorabilia. Family photos, antiques, Mexican-style knickknacks, a colorful medley of tablecloths, and big orange couch lend a homey air. But don't let that fool you—home was never like this!

Mini Max Tacos n' Things

1119 W. Webster   Daily, 9:00 A.M.–9:00 P.M.
Phone: 358-3493   Closed Monday
Parking: Street
No liquor

A tiny restaurant squeezed into the rear of a Latino grocery. The eating area, only six small tables, sits on an attractive, brick-floored area where a perfect view can be had of the shoppers. Watching is almost as fun as eating.

Cooking is done out in the open, and a surprising assortment of dishes are offered for such cramped kitchen quarters. But things run smoothly, and meals are a bargain. Most dishes are prepared to order, other than the long-simmering stews (guisados) and taco fillings, and include good, thick-set beans and rice.

This is no place to resist tacos (60¢ for a warm tortilla shell; 70¢ for soft-fried). Filling choices abound: ground beef, pepper steak, flank steak, tongue, pork, chicken, and chicharron (crisp pork skin).

Chicken flautas ($2.25) are equally satisfying. Two brittle, peashooter-like shells come tightly packed with tender, flavorsome chicken, and frosted with sour cream-blended avocado sauce. Mole-doused enchiladas ($2.50) are for those in search of the feisty, as the spicy sauce definitely tingles. Huevos rancheros ($1.50) make for a filling, inexpensive meal, and, in deference to the Cuban-born owner, there's a special dinner of Cuban steak, black beans, rice, and fried banana chips ($3.25). His attractive, friendly wife often waits on tables, and both have teamed up to produce an altogether charming mini-restaurant.

El Nuevo Leon

1515 W. 18th
Phone: 421-1517
Parking: Street
No liquor

Sun.-Thur., 8:00 A.M.–3:00 A.M.
Fri.-Sat., 8:00 A.M.–6:00 A.M.

El Nuevo Leon is a bustling neighborhood restaurant filled with Mexican-American families and young couples. It seems to be the most popular place on 18th Street. There are several reasons for its success. The food is good, the prices moderate, and the service is some of the fastest this side of MacDonald's.

The menu contains most standard items, plus a few not so standard, like tacos with brains, and chilaquiles (a fried tortilla, scrambled egg, and tomato mixture, $2.10). Tacos ($1.70) aren't extraordinary, but the tacos barbacoa with steamed, shredded beef are chewy and good. The combination plate ($2.75)—taco, tostada, enchilada, and tamale—offers a diverse sampling at a low price. The tamale, with its shredded beef filling, is quite tasty, and the chicken-filled enchilada is bathed in mild, melted cheese. Rice and beans aren't included, so if you can't do without, it will cost you 50¢ more. The ground beef and potato-filled chile relleno ($2.50) is the real thing—very hot and spicy. It is available weekends only.

The thick and stew-like beef soup contains good-sized chunks of beef and often a fresh piece of corn on the cob ($1.75). Guacamole ($1.50 for a small order) is priced a bit high for its Lilliputian size.

The decor at El Nuevo Leon is standard Mexican restaurant: velvet paintings on paneled walls, salmon-colored vinyl booths, and a big day-glo jukebox. It's a friendly, lively place, and if you're ever hit by those "wish I were in Mexico blues," it offers a good substitute.

El Tipico

1836 W. Foster
Phone: 878-0839
Parking: Lot in rear
Full bar

Mon., 11:30 A.M.–12:30 P.M.
Tue.–Sun., 11:30 A.M.–2:00 A.M.

From the outside, El Tipico looks more expensive than it is. Though it isn't as cheap as our other Mexican restaurants, it offers by far the most handsome setting, with its stuccoed white walls, beamed, bi-level dining area, and comfortable wood and leather basket chairs. While the menu includes several higher-priced beef entrees, there are many dishes for under $3.25.

Enchiladas are a specialty here, with five different varieties being offered. The best bet is the Tri-Color Combination ($3.25)—one filled with chicken and topped with green sauce, another with beef covered in melted white cheese, and the third filled with yellow cheese and topped with tomato sauce. The dish also includes beans and too-mushy rice.

Tacos ($2.50) are moist, and offer a choice of ground beef, avocado, chicken, or pork filling. In addition to some standard combination plates, there are several chicken dinners, including one with a tomato-based ranchero sauce and another with an excellent green sauce.

El Tipico also features an interesting sampling of appetizers. Besides the always reliable nachos (yet another name for crisp tortillas with melted cheese, $1.20) and guacamole, there are quesadillas (melted cheese-filled soft tortillas, 50¢) and rolled burritos (50¢) filled with mildly spiced sausage. Both taste great, though they're slightly greasy.

Everything is cooked to order here, so it's best to enjoy the wait by downing the bowlful of hot, crispy tortilla chips, along with some Mexican beer.

El Zarape

9 N. State, Elgin
Phone: 741-2825
Parking: Street
No liquor

Mon.-Sat., 11:00 A.M.–9:30 P.M.
Sun., 11:00 A.M.–4:00 P.M.

Elgin's answer to 18th Street. A bright, familial place that serves real-tasting but mildly seasoned Mexican meals. The menu is comprehensive, everything from enchiladas suizas to shrimp soup to cheese-topped sirloin steak. Very little costs more than $2.95.

Appetizers are especially delicious. Try quesadillas (60¢), crisp, slightly oily miniature tortillas wrapped around either a guacamole or cheese and onion filling. Nachos ($1.00), crisp tortilla chips smothered with bubbly cheese, avocados, and hot peppers, are equally sublime. We've been tempted to make a meal of them, but then, the entrees aren't too hard to take either.

Try enchiladas entomatadas ($2.80), tortilla-enveloped ground beef hosting a tomato sauce, melted cheese topping. More unusual are chilaquiles ($2.10), a semi-spicy meatless casserole of tortilla strips, cheese, tomato sauce, and sour cream. Sopes ($2.50), fat, hand-patted cornmeal discs piled with ground beef, tomatoes, shredded lettuce, and cheese, are also unusual and good. Be sure to specify Mexican cheese on all these dishes, or you're liable to be zapped with melted velveeta.

Good avocado tacos ($2.25), plate-hugging burritos ($2.10), and flautas ($2.50). The light, runny refried beans are fine, but even the addition of corn, celery, tomatoes, and onions doesn't do much to liven up the flat-tasting rice.

Waitresses are young and soft-spoken, customers come mostly from Elgin's sizable Chicano population, and the mood is easy and informal. It's the place to go if you're in Elgin, especially if you have an urge for an enchilada.

Mediterranean House

3910 Dempster, Skokie
Phone: 679-7222
Parking: Lot
B.Y.O.

Daily, 11:00 A.M.–1:00 A.M.

Located in Skokie on Dempster's franchise row and looking much like a franchise operation itself, Mediterranean House will fool you. Within its glossy setting is served some far from ordinary, authentic Middle Eastern food. Although Mediterranean House is a serve-yourself place, most of the food is freshly prepared, and prices are low enough so that you can sample several of the excellent exotic entrees and side dishes.

Be sure to try the falafil sandwich ($1.35), as All-Middle Eastern as the hotdog is All-American. Ground chick peas and spices are shaped into balls, crisply deep fried and placed into a pocket of pita bread along with lettuce, tomatoes, and a tahini (sesame) based dressing. The whole thing tastes great, is far healthier than a hotdog and could easily become a habit. Kibbi (75¢), a deep-fried mixture of cracked wheat stuffed with juicy ground beef, onions, and pine nuts, is delicious too. Shawirma is similar to Greek gyros, and is served with rice pilaf and pita for $3.15 or as a sandwich for $1.90.

The most expensive item on the menu is the combination plate ($3.25), containing shish kabab, shawirma, kifta kabab (spicy, fresh-tasting meatballs), pilaf, lettuce, tomato, and pita. You can make several mix and match sandwiches from this variety.

There are two extraordinary dips: hommos (65¢), a delicious blend of ground chick peas, tahini sauce, onion, and oil, and baba ghanooj (75¢), a mixture of chopped eggplant, tahini, lemon juice, parsley, and garlic. Both go beautifully with pita.

Desserts are seductively displayed. It's best just to look and point. You can always be safe with baklava (60¢), but the katayef (60¢), a pancake stuffed with walnuts and sugar syrup or Harisa (60¢), a semolina-based cake imbedded with pistachios, walnuts, and pine nuts and soaked in a sugar syrup, are both unusual and interesting. Accompany dessert with sweet, grainy Turkish coffee (40¢).

Middle East Restaurant

5444 S. Damen   Daily, Noon–Midnight
Phone: 471-5433
Parking: Lot and street
B.Y.O.

Adjoining a smoke-filled Arab men's social club is the quiet
and subdued Middle East Restaurant. Because it's not on most
people's regular route, the Middle East remains largely unknown to non-Arabs. Although the cooking is authentic, the
rustic, glazed, knotty pine walls give the place the feeling of
a north woods hunting lodge, so you may want to play the
jukebox or peek into the clubroom next door for a bit of
atmosphere.

The Middle East's cook is talented, and it seems as though
everything he prepares is both unusual and delicious. The
menu lists standard entrees plus several rotating daily specials. However, don't be surprised if your waiter recites a
list of specials which in no way coincides with those printed
on the menu.

One thing you can always count on is a superb bargain-
priced shish kebab ($3.50) and various lamb or beef and
vegetable combinations. For instance, there might be a cauliflower, meat, and yogurt trio ($3.00), zucchini and lamb
($3.00), stuffed cabbage ($3.50), and Kefta. One evening
we sampled a marvelous vegetable stew, thick with chunks of
tender beef, potatoes, green beans, and cauliflower ($2.00).
The food here is most similar to Greek, but we find it to be
more subtly seasoned, less oily, and having fewer overcooked
vegetables.

Rice pilaf costs extra with the stew-like dishes (50¢-75¢).
The salads are extra too, but they're definitely worth it. There
are two sizes and prices (75¢ and $1.25), with the smaller
being just right for two people. Especially tasty is the Arabian
salad, a lively combination of finely chopped tomato, lettuce,
cucumber, and parsley, tossed with tahini sauce.

For dessert they sometimes have kenafa (50¢), syrupy
shredded wheat filled with sweet cheese. Accompany it with
rich thick coffee (25¢).

94

Inti-Raimi

5846 N. Glenwood   Fri., Sat., Sun., only,
Phone: 334-9099   3:00 P.M.–11:00 P.M.
Parking: Street
B.Y.O.

Dining at this quiet Peruvian restaurant is truly an experience. It's as non-commercial and authentic a place as one could find and still be in Chicago. The posted menu is written in Spanish, without benefit of translation or prices. The owners speak almost no English, so if your Spanish is rusty or non-existent, expect a little confusion. Choosing a meal can be hit or miss, but that's part of the fun. You're best off ordering several things and sharing.

Particularly enjoyable, but a bit expensive, is papa la huancaina ($1.50 for one), a firm-textured boiled potato topped with a spicy cheese sauce, mild white cheese slices, feathers of fresh cilantro (coriander), and marinated olives. The sweet pepper punctuated tamale ($1.00) tastes interestingly grainy, and comes with a garnish of pickled onion rings.

The gyros look-alike, bistec apanado ($3.00), is smoothly marinated, thin-sliced, and attractively crisp-edged. Offering more of a challenge, churrasco ($3.00) is a tough but tasty breakfast steak. But by far the best dish is coliflor saltado ($2.50; it was a special the night of our visit), a stir-fried, carefully seasoned mass of cauliflower, potato strips, beef, onions, and tomatoes.

Ceviche ($3.00) calls for more intrepid taste buds, as a mix of raw octopus, onions, and jalapeño peppers sharing a tangy lime-sparked marinade is admittedly not for everyone. Boiled sweet potatoes provide a pleasant foil. Two dishes we'd avoid next time are escabeche, cold marinated boiled chicken ($2.50) and the oversalted and battered pescado frito (fried fish, $3.50).

Inti-Raimi offers a good chance to sample indigenous Peruvian dishes at affordable prices. Just don't expect the gourmet quality and polish of the higher-priced Peruvian restaurants.

Mabuhay

5101 N. Clark   Daily, 11:00 A.M.–2:00 A.M.
Phone: 275-3688
Parking: Street
Full bar

Mabuhay provides a good, not too expensive place to experiment with Philippine food. Although more than half the menu is filled with Chinese dishes, don't chicken out—try the Philippine ones. Portions are not huge, but the food is cheap so it's best to come here in a group and sample a variety of dishes. Three dishes are about right for two people. Rice is included. The rule here, unless you like to live dangerously, is to let the waitress be your guide. They're very friendly and happy to offer suggestions.

The cuisine is different from any we've ever tasted, although there are definite Chinese overtones. Some interesting and distinctive specialties are pork inihaw (thin sliced, barbecued pork and scallions, $3.75); pork or chicken adobo (chunks of meat, marinated and cooked in vinegar and spices, $3.75); and pansit canton gisado (spaghetti-like noodles sauteed with mushrooms, shrimp, and bits of pork, $3.25). Particularly good is the chicken sotanjon, a glazed mixture of thin, transparent sai foon noodles, diced chicken, celery, scallions, and mushrooms ($3.50). There is also a somewhat strange but interesting vegetable dish, pinacbet—okra, eggplant, and tomato cooked in a fish sauce ($3.25).

More familiar are the appetizers, deep fried shrimp ($1.75), and a delicious crisp eggroll that is unmistakably flavored with peanut butter ($1.75).

For purists, there's kari kari, composed of oxtail, tripe, greenbeans, and peanut butter ($3.75) and four bitter melon dishes—pork ($3.75), chicken ($3.75), shrimp ($4.25), and beef ($3.75)—which call for adventurous tastebuds, two years in the Philippines, or both.

Michelle

2568 N. Milwaukee   Daily, 9:00 A.M.–9:00 P.M.
Phone: 384-7882
Parking: Street

Our favorite Polish restaurant is a largely unknown and very authentic place simply called Michelle. It's a plain, almost institutional-looking restaurant, but the warm, pleasant atmosphere makes you feel at home. All the Polish specialties are cooked here—pierogi, nalesniki, bigos, golabki, and kolacky—at prices that would please a Scrooge. Complete dinners, including soup and dessert, cost under $3.50.

It is obvious from the first spoonful that the soups don't come from a can. We especially like their thick barley soup, sprinkled with fresh dill. However, unless you're a czarina (duck blood soup) aficionado, give a pass to Michelle's version. It's unabashedly strong and definitely calls for an acquired taste.

Among the entrees, we recommend the golabki (stuffed cabbage, $3.00), Vienna schnitzel topped with a fried egg ($3.70), a marvelous oxtail stew ($2.65), and the thin, honey-colored pancakes called nalesniki ($3.00). They're filled with a slightly tart cheese that is almost custard-like in consistency and accompanied by a dish of sour cream, which helps to make a good thing even better. The real tour de force, however, is bigos ($3.00), a smoky-flavored casserole of sauerkraut, pork, and sliced Polish sausage. It has the heady, well-integrated flavor of a dish that has to have been cooked for hours, perhaps even days.

Side dishes—cole slaw, creamy cucumber salad, potato salad, or the humble boiled potato—are all tasty. Desserts too are homemade, delicious, and not to be missed. We think Michelle's kolacky is the best in town, especially if you get one fresh from the oven (at lunch you have a better chance). The dough is thin, almost strudel-like, and fillings range from plum to poppyseed. They also make a rich, moist lemon cake and thick, cinnamon-sprinkled rice pudding.

Patria

2011 W. North
Phone: 486-6565
Parking: Street
Full bar

Daily, 11:00 A.M.–10:00 P.M.
Closed Wednesday

A pleasant, unpretentious Polish place that deserves far more play. Prices are a bargain—not much over $3.00 for a complete dinner, and the food is authentic, abundant, and hearty. Included with each meal is a simple salad bar (check out the fresh rolls, and cucumber, green pepper-crunched potato salad), homemade soup, beverage, and dessert.

Soups and many of the entrees rotate each day. Among the latter, crisp pork tenderloin, tongue with horseradish sauce, boiled beef, or pierogi (cheese, ground meat and/or fruit stuffed dumplings), are satisfying.

However, the most fun is their Polish plate ($4.25), crowded with tastes of nearly everything: pierogi, nalesniki (a well-browned, eggy crepe rolled around a cheese or ground meat filling), veal cutlet atop a bed of sauteed onions and mushrooms, another meat (perhaps meatloaf, chicken livers, or boiled beef), peas, carrots, cabbage, and a boiled potato.

Good homemade desserts, too, especially if the cinnamon-swirled sour cream coffee cake is around. Spend the next day working it off at the neighboring Luxor Steambaths.

The Patria's dark, panelled walls are bedecked with a gallery of "for sale" paintings. A tiny bar hugs the front of the dining room, and lighting is rather somber. Waitresses make up for the restaurant's lack of physical charm with an abundance of their own.

Polonia

2210 W. 55th
Phone: 778-9218
Parking: Street
No liquor

Daily, 9:00 A.M.–9:00 P.M.

Not only can you eat here for less than $3.00, but what a meal! Sharing the plate with each entree is a boiled potato topped with buttery fresh mushrooms, sliced tomatoes, green beans (canned), and chewy torpedo-shaped little dumplings. There is also rye bread, a small salad, beverage, and dish of canned fruit.

With all this, entrees seem almost superfluous, but they're way too tasty to ignore. Particularly delicious is the roast chicken ($2.60, served mainly on weekends). Bedded down on a peppery, sausage-like dressing, it literally tastes just like the chicken grandma used to make—if she made good chicken. Equally munificent is the roast duck and dressing ($2.90), though it could have been a bit warmer.

Roast pork ($2.70) comes in medium thin slices, has a fine flavor, and chewy texture. Breaded pork tenderloin ($2.70) and breaded pork chops ($2.70) are two other old reliables, and there's also lamb shanks with cabbage ($2.60), kidney stew with rice ($2.50), and Hungarian goulash ($2.60). If you're searching for lighter fare, try the cheese blintzes ($2.10), light honey-toned envelopes wrapped around tart pot cheese. The pierogi ($2.10) are a little disappointing, as their buttery sauce is too bland and watery.

Good soups too, including a hot sweet beet borscht (35¢) and an unusual creamy dill soup (35¢), flecked with rice, cucumbers, celery, and fresh dill.

The setting is as straightforward and homey as the food. The waitress comes on a little gruff, but we could tell she didn't mean it. She even urged us to hurry up and come back.

Sawa's Old Warsaw

4750 N. Harlem,
  Harwood Heights
Phone: 867-4500
Parking: Lot
Full bar

Tue.-Sat., 11:30 A.M.–10:00 P.M.
Sun., 11:30 A.M.–9:00 P.M.
Closed Monday

Dining at Sawa's is like being at a Polish wedding party minus the music. They really load food on you. It's served buffet style, so be prepared to eat. The price for this pleasant gluttony is $3.95 ($4.55 on weekends; children, $2.65 and $3.15, on weekends).

Start off with the salads: kidney bean, potato, cole slaw, marinated tomatoes and onions, relishes. Meanwhile the waitress has provided an amply-filled basket of rye bread, and several kinds of rolls, including onion.

For a main dish, there's thick, spicy Polish sausage, rather bland stuffed cabbage, and a killer kraut (too strong for us). The juicy kotletai (breaded fried meatballs) are intriguingly seasoned and the tender spare ribs have a sweet, but not cloying, glaze. A dense filling of mashed potatoes help to make the pierogi extra chewy. Douse them with sour cream, and do the same for the thick, semi-sweet nalesniki (rolled cheese-filled pancakes).

If all this fails to fill you, there's plump, crisply-coated fried chicken, excellent ham, and rare roast beef. Not much room is left for dessert, which is just as well, as the apple slice is insipidly doughy and the chocolate cake not the stuff dreams are made of.

The Old Warsaw looks more like new Northwest side— black booths, red velvet drapes, lots of fancy hanging fixtures. Waitresses are personable and there when you need them.

There are two more Sawa's, one at 9200 S. Cermak in Broadview (343-9040) and another at 1504 Miner Street in Des Plaines (298-2210).

Warsaw Restaurant

820 N. Ashland Avenue
Phone: 666-3052
Parking: Street
Full bar (upstairs)

Daily, 6:00 A.M.–11:00 P.M.
Fri. & Sat., 6:00 A.M.–Midnight
Sun., 11:00 A.M.–Midnight

The Warsaw is a tidy neighborhood place with a primarily Polish-speaking clientele. The emphasis here is on simple, well-prepared food served in liberal portions.

The menu features a long lineup of complete dinners, averaging around $3.50, including such Polish specialties as bigos, nalesniki, and pierogi. Try any of them and you'll be satisfied. Bigos ($2.10), or hunter's stew, is a hefty combination of sausage and sauerkraut. The pierogi ($2.60) are sauteed in butter rather than boiled and are filled with your choice of either meat, cabbage, cheese, or fruit (when in season). Our particular favorite is the nalesniki ($3.30), three rich, thin pancakes rolled around a cheese, jelly, or applesauce filling (you can select any combination). They are sauteed to a honey color and give us hunger pangs just thinking about them.

Other menu regulars include boiled beef accompanied by a mild horseradish sauce ($3.50) and tender roast chicken filled with a spicy bread dressing ($3.70). The Warsaw special ($3.90) includes some meats and some sweet. Your plate is filled to capacity with sausage, sauerkraut, stuffed cabbage, pierogi, and nalesniki. They make for strange neighbors, especially when tomato sauce starts moving into pancake territory. If potato pancakes happen to be on the menu, they're marvelous too.

All dinners at the Warsaw come with soup, bread, potato, vegetable, dessert and beverage. Try the czarnina (duck soup), a velvety blend filled with shell noodles, prunes, raisins, and just a hint of cinnamon. Sauerkraut soup is thick with shredded cabbage, and the beet soup brims with cabbage, carrots, onions and, of course, beets.

At the Warsaw you can dine downstairs, coffee-shop style or upstairs in a more lush dining room cum entertainment and a higher-priced menu on weekends.

Edith's Bar-B-Que

1863 N. Clybourn	Mon.-Thur., 10:00 A.M.–11:30 P.M.
Phone: 327-5160	Fri., 10:00 A.M.–2:30 A.M.
Parking: Street	Sat., 3:30 P.M.–3:30 A.M.
No liquor	Closed Sunday

This is the place to find ribs leisurely smoked over hickory logs. The end result is a crisp-edged, minimally fatty, tender slab. The only mishap can be slight overcooking or mismatched quality. Good, mild, syrupy sauce (ask for some on the side). Full slabs go for $4.50; half for $2.50. Soggy fries and Wonder Bread are the regular sidekicks.

A clean, friendly, quiet place with just fast enough service. Carry-outs too.

Glass Dome Hickory Pit

2724 S. Union	Mon.-Fri., 11:00 A.M.–8:30 P.M.
Phone: 842-7600	Sat., 11:00 A.M.–10:00 P.M.
Parking: Street	Sun., 3:00 P.M.–8:30 P.M.
Full bar	

True to its name, the Hickory Pit specializes in ribs with a distinct hickory edge. They're moist rather than dry, tender rather than chewy, and sport an attractive glaze. Sauces, with a choice of either hot or mild, are fairly nondescript with the hot being a little less so. $4.95 buys a nice-sized regular slab plus a side of limp fries. There's also a deluxe order for $6.95.

If anything, the fried chicken ($2.75) surpasses the ribs. It's purely plump, meaty, and topped by a crisp, blistery crust.

The varied crowd displays everything from Gucci bags to U. S. mail bags. Good place to stop before a Sox game or while on tour of the Mayor's turf.

Ribs 'N Bibs

5300 S. Dorchester   Tue.-Thur., & Sun., 4:00 P.M.–1:00 A.M.
Phone: 493-0400   Fri., Sat., 4:00 P.M.–2:00 A.M.
                       Closed Monday

Would you buy a barbecued rib from Linn Burton? The used cars he can keep, but the ribs sold at his Hyde Park "rib shack" have to be among the best in the city.

They're meaty, teeth-sinking chewy, hickory-smoked, and covered with a scrumptious sauce. It even does wonders for the Wonder Bread.

Half slabs go for $3.75 and $4.00, large ends and small ends respectively. A full slab (probably enough for one and a half people) costs $6.75, but portions aren't enormous. They also do a Platonic barbecued pork sandwich ($1.50).

The place is carry-outs only, but the ribs keep their warmth a long ride home.

Twin Anchors

1655 N. Sedgewick   Sun.-Thur., 4:00 P.M.–11:30 P.M.
Phone: 944-9714   Fri., Sat., 4:00 P.M.–12:30 A.M.
Parking: Street
Full bar

Ribs have been packing people into the Twin Anchors as long as we can remember, and for good reason. They still have one of the lower price tags in the city; $4.75 buys a plate-and-a-half-sized slab. They're consistently tender, lean, occasionally a bit dry, and usually quite meaty. A nicely spicy sauce comes in a separate bowl.

Black bread, soft-textured, fresh-tasting fries and an overly mayonnaised slaw fill you further.

The place has the loose ambiance of a Northern Wisconsin bar, the staff can be grumpy unless you're a regular or Frank Sinatra (he eats here when in town), and the crowd's both new and old Old Town. Be sure to grab a number when you walk in.

Little Bucharest

3001 N. Ashland
Phone: 929-8640
Parking: Street
Full bar

Daily, 11:00 A.M.–10:00 P.M.
Sunday, 2:00 P.M.–10:00 P.M.

Generous portions of inexpensive Romanian food are served in Old World surroundings in this friendly bar cum restaurant. Tasty bets include Romanian goulash ($2.50), more like braised beef than a traditional stew, and a robust, fleshy quarter of roast duck complete with orange sauce ($2.95). Both come with gooey-textured dumplings, peas and carrots, and for a bit of overkill, mashed potatoes. Another possibility are the well-stuffed peppers ($2.50), amply filled with a juicy mix of ground beef and rice. Ours were slightly marred by an overflow of soupy gravy, but the flavor was delicious.

Closing out the menu are an excellent thueringer ($2.50), stuffed cabbage ($2.50), fried pork chops ($2.50), roast beef or pork ($3.25), and a bargain-priced 16 oz. T-bone ($4.95).

Be sure to sample the soup (50¢), as Little Bucharest makes some of the best around. We've enjoyed czorba, a rich, peasant-style beef and vegetable brew, and a parsley-flecked meatball soup, thick with carrots, celery, tomato, and onions. Dip in some French bread, and you practically have a meal. However, desserts are another must. Either the walnut or lemon torte ($1.00 each) is a multi-layered, multi-flavored example of Romanian baking skill.

Meals can be enjoyed in a casual, red-checked tablecloth bar or the European-elegant dining room, replete with gold-flocked wallpaper and elaborate chandeliers. The soft-spoken, pleasant Romanian-born waitress services both.

The Half Shell

676 W. Diversey   Daily, 11:00 A.M.–2:00 A.M.
Phone: 549-1773
Parking: Street
Full bar

A narrow, noisy, low-key cellar-restaurant that serves fresh-tasting seafood at refreshing prices. Most everything affordable is deep fried, but batter is lightly applied and nearly greaseless. Service is casual, usually prompt, and much improved from what it was a few years ago.

Start out with the raw oysters ($1.70), as they're properly chilled, silky smooth, and touched by a just-off-the-rocks flavor. They're actually kept on ice in a trough behind the bar, and opened just prior to serving. The tangy horseradish-zapped cocktail sauce is so good, it even does wonders for saltines.

The Half Shell surprised us with an excellent salad (75¢), made up of crunchy romaine dressed in a creamy, mustard-touched vinaigrette.

The entrees range from $2.40 for french fried squid to $5.00 and up for a two-pound Dungeness crab. In between are a literal sea of delights. Try the smelt, as they're crisp, dissolvingly sweet, and at $2.60, a nice cheap meal. The flaky, golden-crusted perch ($3.60) carry nearly as much appeal.

Spending a little more buys eight broiled, shell-intact shrimp plus onions, peppers, and tomatoes ($4.60). All are imbued with a charcoal flavor and firm texture, come served on toast and accompanied by a cup of melted butter. Not quite worth it are the frog legs ($4.60), as they are slightly over-aged. For $5.00, one can feast on the 32 pointer, a sampling of just about everything—smelt, shrimp, perch, oysters, clams, and frog legs. Great tasting, pencil thin fries come with all orders as do a standard cocktail sauce and a zippy, thick, marmelade-like dip.

Portside

3125 W. Montrose   Mon.-Thur., 4:00 P.M.–1:00 A.M.
Phone: 588-9529   Fri., Sat., Sun., 11:00 A.M.–1:00 A.M.
Parking: Street
Full bar

Not too many strokes from the river, the Portside is a dimly lit neighborhood hangout that serves a nice array of seafood. The setting is properly fish-netted, seascaped, and seashelled, and the menu has several good catches. No fancy sauces or exotic preparations, but there's a good range from crabmeat salad to linguini with clam sauce to broiled red snapper. Most everything comes with garlic bread and some of the best french fries this side of MacDonald's. They're hot and sweet, crisp on the outside, soft inside, and cut in various sizes from crisp slivers to long, honey-colored threads.

Dive into a platter of skewered shrimp, peppers, and onions ($4.90). Broiled to a proper charcoal turn, the shrimp are firm, fat, and meaty. Perch ($3.75) and smelt ($2.45) provide two less expensive options. Both are carefully breaded and deep fried to a juicy, delicate consistency.

Frog legs ($4.95), however, seem to have journeyed too far, and we found both the deep fried and sauteed versions soggy and stringy. The linguini with clam sauce ($2.75) also suffers from a bland, watery personality.

Share the french fried squid ($2.55) for an appetizer. Crisply coated and chewy, they come with three different dunking sauces, including a potent fruity one similar to that served at the Half Shell. Clam chowder (90¢) is thick and nicely clammy, but can have a slight metallic aftertaste.

Waitresses vary in experience and interest, the crowd is a neighborhood mix (everything from bouffants to wedges), and some terrific jazz fills the jukebox.

Boca del Rio

3438 W. 26th Street   Daily, 11:00 A.M.–11:00 P.M.
Phone: 762-8748   Closed Wednesday
Parking: Street
No liquor

A closet-sized restaurant that serves good simple seafood with a distinct Latin accent. The few tables are decorated with pink paper flowers, and the walls wear a calendar of the Mexican presidents and a poster of a Christmas tree made from boiled shrimp. The latter is highly appropriate, as the Boca is particularly creative with shrimp.

There's a flavorful soup ($1.00) swimming with baby shrimp, potato cubes, and sprays of fresh cilantro, and an excellent fresh-tasting, tangy shrimp cocktail ($3.25, split it among two people), served in a long-stemmed glass. Garlic-touched butterfly shrimp (camarones al mojo de ajo, $4.00) not only are firm-textured and beautifully flavored, but come garnished with an avocado slice, chunks of lime, a tomato, radish rosette, and a scallion fashioned into a palm tree. However, there are only six shrimp which will probably leave you wanting more. The accompanying tartar sauce and cocktail sauce both taste homemade.

Not as picturesque but equally tasty is the abundant oyster cocktail ($3.00). We counted at least a dozen, and all were very smooth, cool, and briny. Seafood soup ($1.25; $3.50) contains a bit of everything—shrimp, tiny crab claws, fin-intact hunks of fish, corn on the cob, and carrots.

There are several concessions made to non-fish eaters, among them a good pork tostada ($2.50), carne asada (grilled strip steak, $3.75), and carne asada-topped tacos ($2.50).

A very pleasant and homey place. Language may be a slight but not difficult problem.

Ostionera Playa Azul

1516 W. 18th St.   Mon.-Thur., 8:00 A.M.–10:00 P.M.
Phone: None   Fri., Sat., 8:00 A.M.–2:00 A.M.
Parking: Street   Sun., 8:00 A.M.–11:30 P.M.
No liquor

Slightly bigger and more ornate than the Boca del Rio (there's a touchable, life-sized mermaid on one wall and an underwater mural on another), the Ostionera offers similar seafood bargains.

Try any of the fresh seafood cocktails—camaron (shrimp), pulpo (octopus), abulon (abalone), ostion (oyster), or vuelve a la vida (a combination of all four). They're served in large soda glasses and laced with chopped onion, avocado, jalapeño pepper, and fresh cilantro in a tangy cocktail sauce. They're priced from $2.50 to $3.50, which sounds heavy, but quantity and quality are tops. Split one among two people, and then each order an entree.

Choices include five shrimp selections, plus shrimp or crab soup, huachinango (red snapper) served either with garlic or Vera Cruz-style (meaning a tomato, avocado, onion, and cilantro sauce). The highest price is $4.75 for shrimp Vera Cruz-style. The bland, overcooked rice which comes along won't do much for you.

One dish we particularly like is camarones a la plancha ($4.00), consisting of four firm, big shrimp, served in their shells. Their taste carries one right down to a thatched roof shack along the Mexican coast. Another tasty morsel is the crisp fried fish (mojarrita, $3.75) that resembles sunfish and tastes appealingly sweet. Shrimp soup ($2.50) is spicy enough to make an imprint, and further enlivened by carrots, zucchini, tomatoes, and celery.

For sipping, request sidral mundet, a mellow-tasting carbonated apple juice. A very clean, casual, relaxing place. Little English is spoken, but whatever you end up with will probably be good.

SERBIAN

Golden Shell

10063 S. Avenue N   Daily, 6:00 A.M.–Midnight
Phone: 221-9876
Parking: Lot
Full bar

The Golden Shell is not the place to go if you're looking for an intimate evening. On weekends the enormous dining room is usually packed, drinks flow, and a lively combo plays everything from "Spanish Eyes" to Yugoslavian folk tunes. Most people dance—old with young, women with women, and a few couples who seem like recent graduates of the Fred Astaire school. There's food, too—big, rugged Serbian meals. You can probably get by with half-orders, priced from $3.00 to $3.50.

An unusual, three-part salad starts the meal off. Joining the basic lettuce and tomato are an oniony egg salad, and zippy, thinly shredded slaw.

Entrees range from short ribs and sauerkraut to stuffed zucchini to wild rabbit. There's fish, too—smelt, perch, froglegs, catfish, and shrimp. Most everything comes with real-tasting mashed potatoes (they probably are) and vegetable (probably canned).

The zucchini is filled with juicy, mildly spiced ground beef, and lightly sauced with tomato. It's a tasty dish, as is the Golden Shell special, pork chops smothered with onions, tomatoes, and peppers in a sour cream sauce that tastes like a thick farmer's cheese.

Roast pig is served in big hunks, and is both very fatty and very juicy. Veal cutlet comes crisp, tender, and carefully breaded but we found the pepper steak, though topped with good sauteed vegetables, to be tough and overcooked.

Desserts offer a caloric high. Try kempita (50¢), a top and bottom layer of flaky pastry sandwiching at least five inches of whipped cream.

St. Sava Monastery

Route 21, Libertyville   Hours are irregular, call first
Phone: 367-9684
Parking: Lot
Full bar

Dining at a Serbian monastery would be unique even if the food wasn't, but at St. Sava it's a treat too. There is no written menu, so visitors take pot luck, usually a choice from among a few Serbian specialties. Meals are prepared by parishioners, and served in a roomy, summer-camp-like dining room. During the summer, fresh produce from their communal garden augments each meal.

We feasted on sarma (stuffed cabbage), which owed its exceptionally moist texture to a ground pork filling, and cevapcici, a traditional sausage. The latter look like tightly rolled White Owls, and taste mildly spicy, juicy, and coarse-textured. Two hunks of a feta-like cheese, a pepper slice, tomato quarter, and radish add colorful garnish. Prices for a meal are generally in the $3.00-$4.00 range, and include thick-cut, French-style bread and Turkish coffee. Don't be surprised if they offer seconds, and not just of coffee.

The monastery serves as a gathering place for area Serbians, but everyone is treated with the warmth and affection of old friends. There might be a slight language problem, but it doesn't matter. Easily the next best thing to a trip to the Adriatic.

Directions: Take Tri-State Tollway (I-94) to Ill. 120. Go about a mile to Ill. 121. Head south another mile and look for tall spires. The restaurant is in a green frame house across from the church, but be sure to look at the church too.

Gladys' Luncheonette

4527 S. Indiana
Phone: 548-6848
Parking: Street
No liquor

Daily, 24 hours
Closed Monday

The soul food here is some of the best in the city. Filling meals can be had for well under $3.00, sometimes even under $2.00. And the baker has a magic touch—biscuits and corn muffins are the best ever, feather-light and out-of-the-oven fresh.

Besides countless breakfasts and some sandwiches, Gladys' offers about ten dinners which include soup, two side dishes, and biscuits or cornbread. Dessert is extra. Chicken, needless to say, is fantastic. You can have it either fried or smothered in gravy for $1.85. For a truly gigantic meal, try the turkey wing and dressing ($2.85). The meat is so tender that it falls off the bone, the gravy is mellow, and the dressing is delicious—moist, spicy, and crumbly. Other choices can include smothered pork chops ($3.00), chicken livers and rice ($2.00), breaded perch ($2.65), and beef stew ($2.00).

For side dishes, you can stuff yourself on terrific fried corn, steamed cabbage, blackeyed peas, sweet potatoes, strong collard greens, rice, or spaghetti.

You will become nothing but fat and sassy on Gladys' desserts. There are two juicy cobblers, apple and peach (60¢), sweet potato pie (60¢), stewed apples (60¢), and strawberry shortcake (60¢). If you can't find room, be sure and take some home with you. In fact everything at Gladys' can be ordered to carry out and lots of people do just that.

Gladys' is open twenty-four hours, and it's liable to be crowded at any time.

H & H Restaurant

1425 W. 87th   Daily, 24 hours
Phone: 445-4888
Parking: Lot
No liquor

For years H & H Cafe on East 51st Street was one of the most popular restaurants on the South Side. When it burned down a couple of years ago, owner Hubert Maybell decided not to mess around. He moved out to 87th Street and opened up a gigantic restaurant specializing in "soul smorgasbord."

The long table is laid out with a fabulous spread: all kinds of salads (macaroni, three bean, tossed, potato, slaw, pickled corn), candied yams, mashed potatoes, spaghetti, creamed corn, okra, turnip greens, smothered chicken, fried chicken, ham hocks, rib tips, fried catfish, and everyone's favorite—chitterlings. To fill you further, there are flaky biscuits, fantastic buttery corn muffins on a par with Gladys', peach cobbler, apple cobbler, and, sometimes, vanilla tarts. Though everything's good, the sweet-sauced ribs are something else, and the fried chicken's not far behind.

You'll eat till you can't move, and all for prices that are more than kind. The buffet costs $3.10 from 11:00 A.M. until 3:00 P.M. From 3:00 P.M. til 2:00 A.M. it escalates to $3.30. Sunday smorgasbord stays at $4.00 all day. And kids under twelve will set you back only $2.00.

The H & H is spotless, and all the staff is very friendly. You just walk in, grab a plate and fill it up. Carry-outs are available too.

Florida

5551 N. Broadway
Phone: 878-7743
Parking: Street
B.Y.O.

Daily, 11:00 A.M.–Midnight
(Hours may change)

The Florida has to be one of the more ethnically diverse restaurants in the city. Not only do they offer Mexican and Cuban dishes, but smatterings of Ecuadorian, Peruvian, Argentinian, and Chinese. Portions are generally big enough to feed half a soccer team, and prices low enough not to totally crush your wallet. Food seems to be cooked to order, but sometimes comes surprisingly fast and at other times, not so surprisingly slow.

All meals carry salad, bread, and coffee (the salad might be forgotten), and several meals include tasty, soupy black beans, buttery rice, and caramelly, soft, fried bananas. Our advice: skip the more familiar Mexican fare (though the avocado tacos ($2.50) are delicious, as is the onion, tomato, green pepper-sauced steak ranchero ($4.25), in favor of South American/Chinese. Everything is seasoned well, and picturesquely served.

Particularly good is the Cuban boliche asado ($4.50), two fork tender cuts of roast beef soothed by a light, homeytasting gravy. Churrasco ($4.50), a skinny, flat strip of steak, though a bit dry in parts, is flavored with an excellent tangy marinade. The chicken end of arroz con pollo ($4.50) is plump and juicy, and the pepper-studded, moist, yelloworange rice comes piled with abandon.

Rice also dominates the Chinese offerings (look for carne ahumada, etc., $4.75), but this time it's fried, somewhat drier, and even more flavorful. A plate of barbecued smoked pork slices and another of fried wonton (mariposa) come on the side.

The Florida is a quiet place. It hadn't been open too many weeks before our visit, and consequently they didn't have it together yet. A few listed items weren't available, and a few orders got mixed up. Asi es la vida, but what we did receive tasted terrific.

Ann Sather's

(one of our favorites)

925 W. Belmont
Phone: 348-2378
Parking: Street
No liquor

Daily, 11:00 A.M.–8.00 P.M.
Sunday, Noon–7:00 P.M. (Menu
    prices slightly higher)

If your favorite fantasy centers on fresh-baked bread and pyramids of pies and puddings, Ann Sather's will fulfill it. With its immaculate, cheerful, tearoom sort of charm, it is the brightest spot on a dreary stretch of Belmont Avenue, and we love it. Knicknacks are everywhere, and decorations change with the season. Service is exceptionally friendly and fast (especially if you get Maud, Doris, or Betty), food quality is impeccable, and prices remarkably low. Complete dinners include soup, bread, salad, entree, two side dishes, beverage, and dessert.

Bread comes first, and what bread it is—thick, fluffy white bread, banana-nut bread, perhaps a gooey caramel roll, moist fruit bread, or carrot bread. All are freshly made in Ann's kitchen.

For an appetizer, we suggest the Swedish cold fruit soup (fresh and dried fruit in cinnamon-spiced raspberry juice) or any soup of lentil, pea, or vegetable origin.

Entrees vary each day. Try the moist, tender, baked chicken ($3.65), any of the pot pies (around $3.25), or the very tasty Swedish meatballs ($3.10). There's also roast pork or lamb ($4.20), swiss steak ($4.50), or maybe a strawberry or peach omelette ($2.85). Side dishes are very nice: supersweet Swedish brown beans, home-made applesauce, sweet and sour cole slaw, German potato salad, or some great candied squash if it's in season. Meat portions aren't huge, but once you make your way through the side dishes your ability to go on is threatened.

No matter how stuffed you feel, dessert is a must. Sather's makes the best homemade pies ever: strawberry-banana with homemade whipped cream, almond cream, banana cream, apricot-prune, fresh plum, and many more. Puddings, especially the spice with rum sauce, are terrific.

Lunch is equally good here. Try the hot Swedish meatball sandwich ($1.35) or the paper-thin Swedish pancakes with lingonberries ($1.35), or the delicious cheeseburger ($1.15).

Svea

5236 N. Clark
Phone: 334-9619
Parking: Street
No liquor

Mon.-Fri., 7:00 A.M.–8:00 P.M.
Sat., 7:00 A.M.–4:00 P.M.
Closed Sunday

Svea looks like a perfect setup for Hansel and Gretel. Crisp print curtains match the wallpaper, shiny copper pot lids and wooden utensils line the cornflower blue walls, and natural pegged beams intersect the ceiling. With its pots of blooming pussywillows and crocuses, and twinkling cleanliness, Svea can't help but lift the most sagging of spirits.

Of course, the food helps too. Each evening features six regular offerings and at least three specials, plus soup (try clam chowder), orange-spiced limpa bread, salad, beverage, and dessert.

Entrees arrive pristinely hidden by plastic covers. Five Swedish meatballs ($2.75) come to an order, and they're moist, not too spicy, and evenly pink inside. Thick cut brisket ($3.00) brims with juice, but request the oddly yellow-tinted, but tasty, horseradish sauce on the side. A light breading and homey flavor make the fried chicken ($2.95) another worthy choice. The kitchen was also dishing up pork chops, baked ham, filet of sole, and pan biff med lok (hamburger steak with grilled onions), all for under $3.25, the night we visited.

If one could call a boiled potato exquisite, those at Svea definitely are, and the pan fried potatoes reach near golden-crisp perfection. If you've room, skip the complimentary desserts in favor of the cold, thick fruit soup (50¢).

Svea also makes terrific lunches. At noon, try any of the open face sandwiches (95¢-$1.10), Swedish meat pie ($1.95), or pytt and panna ($1.75), a lovely roast beef hash.

The restaurant caters to a neighborhood crowd, composed primarily of older men and women, most as wholesome and neatly attired as the scenery. A word of caution: don't arrive much after 7:00 P.M., or you might find the door locked and lights off.

Svea's

11160 S. Western, Beverly
Phone: 881-9245
Parking: Lot
No liquor

Wed.-Sat., 2:00 P.M.–8:00 P.M.
Sun., 11:00 A.M.–7:00 P.M.
Closed Monday and Tuesday

No relation to its Andersonville namesake, this popular south suburban Swedish retreat serves complete meals at completely affordable prices. Although the food would be more at home in a Norman Rockwell painting than a Bergman setting, it has a nice, solid, unembellished quality. Svea's is populated mostly by gray-haired couples, with a sprinkling of sons and daughters, who undoubtedly appreciate being turned onto a good bargain.

Appetizers are a Swedish-American alliance: cranberry float, tomato juice, pickled herring, yellow pea soup, and cold fruit soup. The latter, packed with prunes, black and yellow raisins, apple slices, and lemon peel, is the most innovative and enjoyable of the bunch. A basket of hot, full-bodied rolls add good company. The mostly iceberg lettuce salad offers no special thrills, but dressings seem to have an extra spark.

Entrees are varied, and the brown-skinned, flaky broiled trout ($3.55) is especially good as is the moist, tender whitefish ($3.55). Fried chicken is another delight—fat, meaty, and crisply battered. Almost as pleasure-inducing are the bubbly-crusted pork chops ($3.50) and the lightly sauteed chicken livers and onions ($3.40). An overly enthusiastic gravy bath mars an otherwise commendable veal cutlet ($3.60), but skip the stuffed cabbage ($3.25), as they're tiny, overcooked, and too salty.

Side dishes might include mashed butternut squash, mixed vegetables, a cabbage wedge, and boiled or mashed potatoes. Desserts are worth the guilt. Choose, if you can, from a wealth of fresh baked pies: tart cherry, cloudlike coconut, strawberry/rhubarb, blueberry, apple, or whatever's in season.

Villa Sweden

5207 N. Clark
Phone: 334-1883
Parking: Street
No liquor

Daily, 11:00 A.M.–8:00 P.M.
Smorgasbord:
Thursday, 4:00 P.M.–8:00 P.M.
Friday, 11:00 A.M.–2:30 P.M.
Sunday, 11:00 A.M.–8:00 P.M.

Located in the Andersonville neighborhood, Villa Sweden offers Scandinavian cooking at its best. With its deep blue and white color scheme, the dining room offers a sedate, restful atmosphere. Waitresses dress in costume and are pleasant and efficient.

The big attraction at Villa Sweden is its elaborate smorgasbord ($4.25 per person; children, $2.50; Friday, $3.00), which, together with Mategrano's, is the best in the city. No one could possibly leave hungry.

Food is artistically arranged, with cold and hot dishes being kept at their proper temperatures. The selections are varied, and the supply seems endless. There are several cold meats and a variety of salads: herring, cucumber salad, pickled beets, Hawaiian fruit salad, thin-sliced ham, salami, delicious corn beef, and hopefully—the true beauty—a whole, poached salmon. There are chafing dishes of roast chicken, Swedish meatballs, sweet brown beans, and a surprisingly tasty spaghetti. A smooth custard with raspberry sauce and fruit compote comprise the dessert selection.

Beverage, limpa bread, and sweet tea bread are served at the table. You're actually encouraged to eat as much as you want, and each time you go up to the buffet table, the waitress clears your old plate. It all reminds you of a good dream.

On non-buffet nights, the complete dinners aren't too hard to take, either. Priced in the $3.00 to $4.75 range, they begin with a choice of soup or juice, and include salad, potato, vegetable, entree, dessert, and beverage. Some recommended offerings are the Swedish meatballs, baked chicken with lingonberries, and the baked ham.

Bangkok House

2544 W. Devon
Phone: 338-5948
Parking: Street
B.Y.O.

Daily, 4:00 P.M.–9:30 P.M.
Fri., 4:00 P.M.–11:00 P.M.
Sat., 4:00 P.M.–11:00 P.M.
Sun., 4:30 P.M.–9:30 P.M.
Closed Tuesday

If you savor hot, fiery food redolent with curry and hot pepper, Thai food is for you and prepared to perfection at Bangkok House. However, Bangkok House also features many dishes similar to and no more potent than those found in Cantonese restaurants. Tell Ms. Limphaibule, the owner and hostess, how adventurous you feel, and she will guide you accordingly.

Ease your way gently by sampling one of the marvelous appetizers: fresh, crisply fried wonton ($1.25), delicious vegetable-stuffed eggroll ($1.25), or chicken or beef satay (skewered grilled meat, served with curry sauce, $1.75).

Particularly recommended among the peppery dishes are chicken with red peppers and cashews ($3.25), beef with hot peppers and green onions ($2.75), and chicken with Thai curry ($2.45). If you like your curry to walk on the mild side, the shrimp curry contains loads of firm shrimp, pineapple, and sauteed onion in a mild, pleasantly spiced sauce ($3.25).

Best of the non-spicy dishes is the savory sauteed chicken with young corn and black mushrooms ($2.95). The chicken shares a subtle sauce with black mushrooms, bamboo shoots, sweet onions, and a real delicacy, miniature corn on the cob. We found the roast duck, Thai-style, unenjoyable ($2.45), as the meat was too fatty and the sauce too salty. The sweet and sour dishes are filled with colorful ingredients, but are neither sweet nor sour enough and come in a tomato-soup-like sauce.

All entrees are accompanied by a large bowl of perfectly cooked rice (at a slight extra charge) and a pot of tea. For dessert, Thai pudding is in the "must try" category. It's an unusual but delectable combination of ground peas, sugar, and coconut milk topped with fried onions. Don't let these ingredients turn you off, because the silky, moist pudding is both refreshing and delicious.

Bangkok Restaurant

3525 N. Halsted
Phone: 327-2870
Parking: Street
B.Y.O.

Daily, 3:00 P.M.–11:00 P.M.
Fri.- Sat., 11:00 A.M.–11:00 P.M.
Closed Monday

One more authentic Thai restaurant which has appeared in the past couple of years is this comfortable corner storefront. Just about everything we've tried has been well-prepared, generous with ingredients, and interestingly seasoned. Prices are low enough to try a variety of dishes. As for the spiciness of the food, this is only one aspect of Thai cooking. There's plenty on the menu that everyone can enjoy.

Among the mild selections are delectably crisp, meat-filled, fried wonton ($1.50), sweet and sour chicken or shrimp (not batter-fried, $2.50), and a light, slightly sweet meatball soup with rice stick ($1.50).

The real jewel of the kitchen is charcoal chicken ($2.50), one of the best renditions of the bird we've ever eaten. Skin is crackly, the meat is moist and plump, and a delicious teriyaki-like marinade permeates all. It is served with a side of sweet apricot sauce. Other mild offerings include moist Korean rice filled with sprouts, chicken, shrimp, egg, peas, parsley, and shredded carrots ($2.75), and Thai barbecued pork ($1.75).

Some slightly hotter dishes worth a try are pan-fried ground beef and rice with mint ($2.00), and shrimp salad ($2.95), peppery charcoaled shrimp served on a bed of shredded lettuce. The hot shrimp soup ($2.50) is no misnomer—it clears out your sinuses and brings on a mild state of euphoria. It boasts firm fresh shrimp, button mushrooms, and a delicious lemony tang, but is absolutely the hottest thing around.

Desserts are unusual, but the ground bean pudding-cake (50¢) has an interesting texture and is quite good. There's a drink called mali (50¢) that's made from a Thai flower and would delight a hummingbird. Service is friendly and fast, but there is a language problem which is bound to improve as the waitresses become more familiar with non-Thai patrons.

Siam Cafe

4654 N. Sheridan   Daily, 11:00 A.M.–11:00 P.M.
Phone: 784-9580
Parking: Street
B.Y.O.

One of our favorite discoveries is this tiny Thai restaurant in Uptown. It is run by an amiable family who offer one of the lowest-priced Asian menus around. Only one item, sweet and sour shrimp at $2.75 is over $2.00. The feeling here is very homey. There's a big stack of Thai magazines near the entrance, and one evening we ate dinner to the accompaniment of *Tora! Tora! Tora!* on the TV.

The cuisine here is primarily Chinese with Thai overtones, making it milder than that found in other Thai restaurants. The exception is the zingy cucumber salad laced with jalapeño peppers which serves as a preliminary to each meal.

The food is priced low enough so that you can experiment with a variety of dishes. Particularly recommended is the Siam Bar B Q ($1.50), a half dozen small skewers of barbecued pork which comes with a dip of creamy peanut sauce (like a homemade peanut butter). The whole thing is slightly oily, but very delicious. There are egg rolls ($1.00), fried wonton ($1.00), and soups: wonton, beef, and ya ka mein (long, curly noodles, pork slices, and bean sprouts in a light broth.) Good-sized bowls cost $1.25.

The roast duck with rice ($2.00) makes an excellent entree. The skin is crisp and glazed with a teriyaki-like sauce, and the meat is succulent and juicy. Tomato-green pepper-beef ($2.00) or beef kai lan (thin strips of beef sauteed with Chinese broccoli and bean sprouts, $1.50) are other possibilities. Barbecued pork and rice ($1.50) is terrific; lean, thin-sliced pork in a semi-sweet red bean sauce. The colorful sweet and sour dishes contain fresh, crisp ingredients, but the meat is not batter-coated, and the sauce could use more zip. The menu also lists bargain-priced beef, chicken, pork, and shrimp chop suey, chow mein, and fried rice.

Try not to dip your fingers in the silver water bowls as we did. The bowls are for drinking.

Thai Cousin

(one of our favorites)

5019 N. Western   Mon., Wed.-Fri., 1:30 P.M.–10:00 P.M.
Phone: 784-9030   Sat., Noon–11:00 P.M.
Parking: Street   Sun., Noon–10:00 P.M.
B.Y.O.   Closed Tuesday

Possibly our favorite Thai restaurant, this filmy-curtained, spotless little place offers a vast array of typically Thai dishes, many of which cannot be found elsewhere. Service is both pleasant and polite, portions aren't enormous, but prices are kind enough to enable you to order a good sampling.

Start out with shrimp eggroll ($1.00), compact, bite-sized tubes that have a sweet, unusual, almost almond flavor. The crisp, rich ha-kern ($2.50) come on like a cross between shrimp toast and pork cracklings. Both can be dipped into sweet, fruity sauces.

The lime-sparked shrimp soup ($2.25, feeds 2 to 3) is a real killer. Plenty of shrimp, scallions, fresh ginger, and hot pepper bits pack the cloudy broth with bite. Squid tom yan ($1.00) offers even more adventure, as the sour broth carries several cut-up squid, fresh cilantro, scallions, a bay leaf, and a special twig-like spice. It's not dull, but definitely not for everyone.

In selecting a favorite entree, it's a toss-up between grilled shrimp with garlic sauce ($2.75) and Bangkok-style noodles (specify the big noodles with no gravy, $1.95). The latter share a sumptuous caramel-like glaze with strips of beef and emerald bok choy. The aroma of the shrimp will lay you flat. Served literally sizzling in an iron pan, the taut, tail-intact shrimp soak up a beautiful garlicky flavor.

Another worthy dish gathers tender abalone, black mushrooms, and bamboo shoots ($3.90) in a muted brandy-touched sauce, and a subtle marinade also pervades the tender grilled pork ($2.25). Not as successful is the waterfall beef salad ($1.95). Although powerfully spiced with chili peppers and lime, the meat is way too tough. The crisp-skinned Peking duck with pineapple ($2.65) would have been better had it not been so fatty.

Thai Little Home Cafe

3125 W. Lawrence   Daily, 11:30 A.M.–9:30 P.M.
Phone: 478-3944
Parking: Street
B.Y.O.

An unassuming family-run corner cafe located in Albany Park. Although the kitchen makes a few nods toward non-native dishes, their Thai food is the reason for being here. Most of it is skillfully seasoned and easy to take for even the most timid taster.

Begin with moo stay ($1.75). Six skewers of drippy, tender barbecued pork co-host a smooth, red pepper-spiked peanut butter sauce and tiny cucumber triangles. Dip the pork in the sauce, then cool off with the crunchy cukes.

None of the entrees, other than the whole fried fish, costs more than $2.50. Ingredients are similar, all come piled on top of rice, which makes each deceivingly filling. Shrimp pud prik ($2.50), a sauteed mass of tender shellfish, fried onions, and bamboo shoots possesses a delectable crunch and bite. Steer clear of the bright green slices of jalapeño pepper, and you're home free.

Beef cooked in coconut milk ($2.15) has a pleasant, non-assertive flavor, with just a hint of sweetness. Bamboo shoots and soft button mushrooms add textual zest. Although cashews replaced the almonds in our chicken with almonds ($2.10), they add a nice crunch to a fairly bland dish. The less indigenous beef, green pepper, and tomato ($1.95) is permeated by a soy-based marinade, and is served in a mammoth portion.

A noodle dish (sen me lud nar), fish cakes Thai-style, beef simmered in coconut milk with red pepper, and sweet and sour pork or shrimp round out the menu.

Service is unhassled and varies in promptness depending on how many people are being served. Customers are mostly young, and reflect the neighborhood's ethnic mix.

Thai Restaurant

5143 N. Clark   Tue., Thur., Sun., 4:00 P.M.–10:00 P.M.
Phone: 334-5757   Fri., Sat., 4:00 P.M.–Midnight
Parking: Street   Closed Monday
Wine and beer

The venerable oldie on the Thai scene, this comfortably converted Clark Street storefront enjoys a steady popularity. Reasons include an abundance of selections, use of good-quality ingredients, skillful flavoring, and attentive service. Food isn't super cheap, so come in a group and share the wealth.

The diminutive, crisp eggroll (3 for $1.50) offer a spicier filling than their Chinese counterparts; fried wonton ($1.50) provide even more intense crackle without the spice.

Several dishes are responsible for our return visits. One of these, Thai curry scampi with pineapple ($4.35) boasts firm shellfish, pineapple, and sauteed onions in a light, slightly sweet sauce. Heady garlic overtones do equally good things for shrimp in garlic cognac sauce ($4.35). We're also particularly fond of Thai Restaurant chicken ($3.95), crisp honey-colored pieces (drumsticks, wings, etc.) sharing a quietly spiced sauce with crunchy glazed onions, cabbage, carrots, green peppers, and bok choy.

Sauteed pork with baby corn ($3.75) and its close relative, sauteed chicken with baby corn and mushrooms ($3.85) both enjoy an active flavor and showering of firm, crisp vegetables. However, the rubbery pork can be a challenge to chew. A dish well below the others is lobster fried rice ($3.25) which we found bland and nearly lobster-less.

Other interesting possibilities abound, such as sauteed abalone with bamboo shoots in cognac sauce ($4.05); grilled duck with vegetables ($4.05); sweet and sour red snapper ($4.75); and fried froglegs with spicy sauce ($4.75). Nothing is really overpoweringly hot or spicy—we promise.

UKRAINIAN

Family Restaurant

2301 W. Chicago   Daily, Noon–8:00 P.M.
Phone: 384-9892
Parking: Street
Full bar

The Ukrainian writing on the window gives a clue to the authenticity inside. Small groups of men in heavy tweed jackets and slouch hats converse in the dimly lit bar. A few families and single men dine in the rear room, where painted murals, yellow tablecloths, and plastic flowers lend color and warmth. The feel is very old country, very cozy.

The brief menu, one side printed in Ukrainian and the other in English, offers two to three evening specials, although it's possible that something altogether different might be on hand. Prices average $3.25 and nothing's over $3.50, even the barbecued ribs.

Our gruff-mannered waitress started us out with a marvelous thick crusted rye and a huge bowl of creamy tomato-rice soup. Entrees follow quickly. Pyrohy (dumplings, $3.00) are light and not too gummy. Half are filled with finely minced meat and half with sour cream-laced mashed potatoes. To add a bit more tang and calories, extra sour cream is served on the side.

A plate-dwarfing slab of liver comes smothered with fried onions ($3.25) and crisp, meaty pork chops ($3.25) are served in an equally generous portion. Flanking the meat are two mounds of mashed potatoes and a feisty, carrot-studded sauerkraut.

On other evenings, such muscle builders as lamb shanks, goulash, Polish sausage, and holubki (stuffed cabbage) might emerge from the kitchen. Beverages include German beer, wine, and buttermilk.

Sophie's

2132 W. Chicago   Daily, Noon–10:00 P.M.
Phone: 252-9625
Parking: Street
No liquor

Sophie's is a simple, immaculate, Mom-and-Pop-run restaurant in the old Ukrainian neighborhood on Chicago Avenue. Everything in the small dining room looks like it's been polished with a toothbrush. Owners Ivan and Sophie have been at their Chicago Avenue location for thirteen years, and still seem to enjoy what they're doing. While offering you a glass of "Lake Michigan Champagne," Ivan usually will get a conversation going about prices, politics, or conditions in Chicago. In the meantime, good things are happening in the kitchen.

All meals include soup, and are super-bargain priced between $2.00 and $2.10. And it's all honest, nothing-fancy cooking. Soups are made from scratch and vary each day. There's a slightly sour sauerkraut soup filled with shredded cabbage, carrots, giblets, and bacon bits, a beet soup, potato soup, mushroom-noodle, or an unusual, refreshing cold apple soup.

The entrees are generally limited to four. If you like dumplings, Pyrohy are usually available, filled with cheese, potatoes, sauerkraut, or blueberries (in season). The beef stew has that homemade touch, and the meat can be cut with a fork. It comes with a mushroom-flavored gravy, boiled potato, salad, and a canned vegetable. The slightly spicy, loaf-shaped meatballs are quite tasty. Pork tenderloin, roast chicken, or perhaps duck ($2.50) may also be among the offerings. All come with vegetable, potato, and salad.

Genesee Depot

3736 N. Broadway
Phone: 528-6990
Parking: Street
B.Y.O.

Wed.-Sun., 5:30 P.M.–9:30 P.M.
Closed Monday and Tuesday

The name is misleading because this charming, plant-and-antique-filled storefront is the farthest thing from a railway station diner that we can imagine. But the evocation of nostalgia is well-intact.

The menu is succinct, limited to only three entrees which rotate on a weekly basis. Meals range between $3.95 and $4.95, and include a basket of superb homemade bread, soup or salad, and vegetables vinaigrette. Although the salad is several carrot curls above average, we recommend the soup, especially if the lentil is around. It's thick and stew-like, amply studded with meat and possessed of a rich, sweet flavor.

Brisket ($3.95) is a standby, and generally our favorite entree. Elevating its stature is a creamy, just-bitey-enough horseradish sauce, and sour cream-topped, nicely light, pierogi-like dumplings. The red snapper creole, served atop a bed of brown rice, also has a nice lingering touch. Other possibilities might be stuffed pork chops, ham with raisin sauce, baked chicken with a sour cream topping, and beef stroganoff.

We'd like to have whomever does the Depot's baking locked permanently in our kitchen. Desserts are without exception, mouth-wateringly marvelous. There's usually a firm, fudgy chocolate cheesecake topped by a thin layer of sour cream, and lined by a crust hinting of chocolate. Or perhaps a refreshing rhubarb-custard tart, extra moist cranberry-orange cake, butterscotch caramel meringue pie, or prune cake with whipped cream.

The restaurant is tiny and because they don't take reservations, expect to wait rather unceremoniously at the door. The food is well worth it.

The Hamburger King

3435 N. Sheffield   Daily, 6:30 A.M.–11:30 P.M.
Phone: 281-4452   Closed Sunday
Parking: Street
No liquor

If you're down to your last dollar and spare change, and in need of a nourishing meal, Hamburger King is the place to go. The food isn't glorious and some things are best left alone, but the price is definitely right.

Hamburger King is a gathering place for locals of all ages and persuasions. The decor is funky, and seating can be had at either a long, curving counter or at a few tables. The Japanese cooks do a commendable short-order job, considering the variety on the menu. All dinners come with soup (served only till 8:00 P.M.), bread, entree, vegetable, and potato or rice. Prices go as low as $1.00 for a cheese omelette and up to $2.30 for the grilled pork chop dinner.

If you happen upon the barley soup, it's fairly rich and quite tasty. Grilled liver and onions ($1.35) are very nice, and the hamburger steak with fried onions isn't bad either. There are a few Chinese dishes on the menu, such as a tasty yet ka mein (noodle soup) and egg foo young. The egg foo young tastes fresh, is heavy on bean sprouts, and three large patties cost only $1.35 on the dinner. Ask them to hold back the gravy because it's not the soy-molasses type, but the same kind used on the regular meat dishes.

Hamburger King is not for the gourmet, but among greasy spoons it has few peers.

Petey's Bungalow

4401 W. 95th, Oak Lawn
Phone: 424-8210
Parking: Lot
Full bar

Tue.-Sat., 4:00 P.M.–1:00 A.M.
  (Dinners till 11:00 P.M.)
Sun., 2:00 P.M.–Midnight
Closed Monday

A warm, friendly place housed in a 50s' style blond brick bungalow that serves multi-course all-American meals buoyed by a slightly Greek touch. It's the kind of spread reminiscent of a Sunday afternoon Iowa farm table. The food's solid and trustworthy, nothing unknown or out of the ordinary, but all of it carefully chosen and prepared.

Meals begin with cool, crunchy relishes (carrot sticks, celery, radishes, peppers, scallions, and olives) and move on to four family-style "salads"—creamy macaroni, marinated green beans, mayonnaise-based slaw, and cottage cheese. The tossed salad which follows is almost unnecessary and not particularly noteworthy, but the soups (perhaps clam chowder or a hearty vegetable) are sure soothers. After a piece or two of garlic bread, the need to proceed any further is questionable.

However, entrees are generally a treat, particularly the house specialty, buttery pan fried chicken ($3.95). Not only did four generously proportioned pieces come to an order, but we were served two breasts and two wings. Lightly breaded, tender boneless perch ($4.75) is another option as are chicken livers, peppers, and onions ($4.75), broiled whitefish ($4.75), and succulently glazed baby back ribs ($5.50, but worth the extra change).

The rest of the menu relies heavily on very tasty steaks, priced beyond our reach but not outrageously so. Good and plentiful cottage fries (or else a baked potato) accompany all. There's also dessert: Try the chocolate-sauced peppermint ice cream or the very cinnamony rice pudding.

The slacks-suited waitresses are the old fashioned kind, given to comforting pats on the shoulder. Drinks are big and cheap, so there's always plenty of action in the bar.

Lakeside Inn

233 W. Rand Rd. (Ill. 120),   Daily, Tues.-Sat.:
   Lakemoor   5:00 P.M.–12 Midnight
Phone: 815-385-2113   Sun., 1:00 A.M.–10:00 P.M.
Parking: Lot   Closed Monday
Full bar

The perfect Sunday afternoon-in-the-country restaurant. The Inn is actually more midwestern roadhouse than gracious New England, and steeped in relaxed casualness.

The sixteen-page menu requires an Evelyn Wood course. It's mostly pure Americana, with a hint of Bavaria and Italy thrown in for flavor. There's a chicken noodle casserole ($3.00), fried cat fish ($3.50), pan fried chicken ($3.00), turkey cutlet with creamed mushroom sauce ($3.00), beef a la deutsch with mushrooms, onions, peppers, and tomatoes ($2.50), sauteed frog legs on toast ($4.00), and lots more.

Good choices include the lightly batter-dipped sweetbreads, slightly marred by an overenthusiastic mushroom gravy ($4.50) or a hunter's casserole of shirred eggs, fried potatoes, thick-cut Canadian bacon, green peppers, and onions ($2.25). Another tempter is "duck in the pond" ($4.50) which comes minus the lily pads but colorfully adorned with sauerkraut, potato dumplings, peas, carrots, a sage-sparked dressing, and spiced crabapple.

And that's not the half of it. Meals also include a zippy kidney bean salad, routine tossed salad, a choice of potatoes (including hashed browns), and basket of feathery biscuits and solid bran muffins. Homemade desserts too, if you have the room.

All this is done by Floyd Lee, an energetic septuagenarian. A great place for the family, especially if they like to eat.

Directions: Take U.S. 12 north to Ill. 120. Go west about two miles. The restaurant is on the south side of the road.

Margarita Club

1566 Oak, Evanston	Lunch: Daily 11:00 A.M.–3:00 P.M.
Phone: 869-2720	Dinner:
(Reservations)	Tue.-Sat., 5:00 P.M.–9:30 P.M.
Parking: Street	Sun., 5:00 P.M.–8:00 P.M.
Full bar	Closed Monday

A lovely dining room with the genteel grace of an earlier era, the walls are painted cadet blue, chandeliers hang from the high ceilings, and white pillars add stateliness. The carnation-decorated tables are placed at spacious intervals, perfect for intimate tête à têtes, but not very conducive for eavesdropping. The young waitpersons have a studied elegance of their own. Even the bread is served with tongs.

The hand-scripted menu lists interesting and imaginative dishes, though a few are priced a bit beyond our budget. However, resting just within it is a breadcrumb-coated sea food casserole ($4.50), containing scallops, a mystery fish, and mushrooms held together by a rich, slightly bland mornay sauce. Porc robert ($4.95) features four could-be-more-tender slices nobly complemented by a light mustard sauce.

Other options are chicken breast in wine sauce ($3.95), beef bourguignon ($4.95), and an international gallery of daily specials such as eggplant parmigiana and pastitsio. A light, finely textured white bread, well-dressed salad, and tasty, buttery rice or dutchess potatoes add companionship. Portions lean more toward the waist-watcher than the wrestler, which is to be expected, given the dignified setting.

For dessert we enjoyed a cool, delicate, blueberry-bombarded cheesecake ($1.00).

R. J. Grunt's

2056 Lincoln Park West
Phone: 929-5363
Parking: Street (difficult)
Full bar

Daily, 11:30 A.M.–Midnight
Fri., 11:30 A.M.–1:00 A.M.

R. J. Grunt's can herd you around like cattle and ply you with expensive, exotic (but delicious) drinks, but we'll keep coming back for more. More, that is, of their lavish salad bar, probably the best in town. For $2.95 you can stuff yourself on herring, excellent chopped liver, caviar, 3-bean salad, tossed lettuce salad, cole slaw, a wheel of cheese, and an incredible array of fresh fruit (pineapple, cantelope, plums, pears, cherries—whatever's in season), and more. It's truly Bacchanalian and not to be missed. The luncheon salad bar costs $1.85, but the offerings are much more limited.

Grunt's gimmicky, complicated menu reads about as easily as a cryptogram. It's geared to please all of the people all of the time. There's sirloin steak ($6.95), steamed shrimp ($4.50), Dungeness crab ($6.95) and a "love omelette" ("sauteed eggplant . . . nestled lovingly into freshly beaten eggs"). All dinners automatically include a trip to the salad bar and a mini-loaf of bread.

Best bets, however, are the sandwiches. Our favorite is the barbecue beef (thin-sliced, juicy brisket) with fried onions and cottage fries, the hamburger or cheeseburger (all $2.35), or a crisp veal cutlet, melted cheese and tomato sauce conglomeration ($2.35). One dollar will buy you salad with your sandwich. But resist the tempting, but we think ripoff-priced, fruit juices (85¢) and milk shakes ($1.25).

There's a singles-bar feel and crush to Grunt's, but the mirrors, high ceiling, and bigger-than-life paintings make the room seem larger than it is. Waitresses are young and generally friendly.

FRITZ THAT'S IT
1615 Chicago Avenue, Evanston
Phone: 866-8506
Son of Grunt's. Same as above, only more so.

St. Regis Hotel

520 N. Clark
Phone: 337-9465
Parking: Street
Full bar

Daily: 6:00 A.M.–2.00 A.M.
Sat., 6:00 A.M.–3:00 A.M.
Sun., Noon–2:00 A.M.

The St. Regis is an offbeat place located on what remains of Clark Street's skid row. You enter the dining room through a bar filled with men who look like extras from *The Man With the Golden Arm.* After the street and the bar, you're not prepared for the dining room. It's quite elaborate with dark panelling, sumptuous booths, red linen tablecloths, and subtle lighting.

One look at the extensive menu, and you can see that the St. Regis offers bargains to rival those of the ethnic restaurants. Complete dinners, including appetizer, beverage, and dessert, average $3.35.

Appetizers range from soup (barley, chicken noodle, vegetable, etc.) to chopped liver or herring. A decent, standard salad is next. Entrees vary daily and might include roast pork loin with dressing ($3.45), fried liver with onions or bacon ($2.75), breaded veal cutlet and spaghetti ($3.25), roast turkey with trimmings ($3.45), and eggplant parmigiana ($3.25). All are tastily prepared, and the tender, crisply fried liver is exceptional. Vegetables and potatoes are served with dinner, including a good quality baked potato with sour cream. There are also several seafood selections (including scallops, oysters, and whitefish) priced under $3.95, all of which come with salad and potatoes.

Desserts go beyond the usual jello and ice cream to a choice of sundaes, layer cakes, pudding, or half a grapefruit.

Though there are no gourmet pretenses about the St. Regis, its kitchen assures you a meal that is both simple and well-prepared.

New Siam

1060 W. Argyle
Phone: 769-2644
Parking: Street
B.Y.O.

Daily, 10:00 A.M.–8:00 P.M.
Closed Sunday

You'd never know this place was a restaurant, let alone a Vietnamese one. It looks like countless other carry-out ice cream parlor/snack shops in the city. Only by looking carefully does one notice a tiny rear dining room. It's a neat little pastel affair, sparsely decorated but cozy.

The menu divides itself between Vietnamese and Thai dishes. Because Vietnamese food is a new one to us, we decided to concentrate our eating energies on it. Nothing costs more than $2.00, so order several dishes and explore. The waitress may not get them exactly correct, but it doesn't really matter.

Start with mo stay ($1.50), juicy skewered pork served with toast, thick, dark, peanut sauce, and cucumbers. It's actually a Thai standard, but hard to avoid, especially since we've become mo stay freaks. Eggrolls ($1.00), filled with transparent noodles and shredded cabbage, are another delicious treat.

Most entrees host nearly a layer of black pepper (which somehow doesn't have a detracting influence) and also possess a mild, sweet flavor. These characteristics are well-evidenced in braised meat with fried wheat noodles ($1.50). Another tasty dish is braised chicken ($1.75). Cut into indefinable pieces and nicely glazed, it tastes splendid, but be careful of splintery bones. Fried rice ($2.00) seems strangely pale, but is abundantly stocked with squid, shrimp, scrambled egg, and scallions.

Be sure to conclude your meal with fresh coconut ice cream (50¢). It's an icy, refreshing, soft concoction that contains not only fresh coconut flakes but kernels of corn.

Balkan at Night

3446 N. Pulaski   Wed.-Fri., & Sun., 5:00 P.M.–4:00 A.M.
Phone: 283-0403   Sat., 5:00 P.M.–5:00 A.M.
Parking: Street   Closed Monday & Tuesday
Full bar

The candlelit tables, thick, deep rose-colored curtains, and massive Oriental rugs on the walls of Balkan at Night create a feeling of mystery and intrigue. But, alas, no Bela Lugosi. Instead an enticing selection of Serbian specialties await you.

Main course, plus salad and bread, averages $4.25. All dishes are beautifully arranged and presented, and portions are large.

Experiment with the delicious cevapcici ($4.00), tiny, grilled homemade sausages with a subtle, spicy flavor. The equally good shish kebab ($4.50) is made of fork-tender chunks of grilled pork tenderloin. A combination plate of cevapcici and shish kebab ($4.25) is a good compromise. Muckalica ($4.75) contains a flavorful, stew-like blend of bite-sized pork tenderloin, mushrooms, onions, green peppers, and tomatoes. Pljeskavica ($4.75) is a somewhat coarse-textured chopped steak containing bits of onion and green pepper. Hungarian beef goulash and liver and onions are also available. Daily specials include an interesting musaka ($4.50) on Wednesdays. It's made of ground beef, veal, and pork, cooked between layers of potatoes and either eggplant or cauliflower. If you have a few extra dollars in your pocket, try the Serbian hot plate ($11.50 for two), a mammoth platter piled with grilled pork chops, veal, liver, cevapcici, lamb chops, and more.

Each entree is served with one of the most interesting and artistically arranged salads around. It includes a tangy marinated cole slaw in addition to tossed greens, tomatoes, feta cheese, and pickled beets.

Desserts are priced rather high at $1.00. The slice of apple strudel is large and looks much better than it tastes.

Splurges

The Blackhawk

139 N. Wabash
Phone: 726-0100
Parking: Free lot at Randolph
and Wabash
Full bar
Credit Cards: American Express, Bank America, Carte
Blanche, Diners Club, Master Charge

Mon.-Fri., 11:00 A.M.–
10:30 P.M.
Sat., 11:00 A.M.–1:00 P.M.
Sun., 3:30 P.M.–10:30 P.M.

When Uncle Joe from Kearney, Nebraska comes to town, head him toward The Blackhawk, downtown Chicago's most reliable restaurant. The place is sure to please for its smoothly professional service (with an added bit of flourish), comfortable seating, and fine quality, all-American fare. The menu is weighted with beef and portions are lavish.

All meals begin with garlic-buttered, toasty party rye, which proves to be habit-forming and inevitably vanishes quickly. The restaurant's tour de force, the Blackhawk salad, is next. The legend of the spinning salad bowl is right up there among the best, and we never tire of the waiter's recitation as he tosses the salad "just six times so as not to bruise the tender greens." Its fame is justified as it's one of the best salads around—an enormous, tangy medley of crisp lettuce, chopped eggs, bleu cheese, "secret" Blackhawk dressing, herbs, and optional anchovies.

For an entree, the carved to order roast prime rib ($8.95) is the house specialty. The meat could win a contest on its looks alone, and, happily, its appearance is not deceiving. It's as succulent and flavorful as any beef we've ever eaten. Be sure to request the delicious whipped cream-horseradish sauce to go along with it.

Although prime rib is as important to The Blackhawk as Mikita is to the Blackhawks, you can also count on an excellent steak ($8.25 to $9.50). If you feel like deviating further, try the scrod. It's shipped in each day from a Boston fish market, and it's exceedingly fresh and sweet. Baked potato with sour cream and chives and delectable creamed spinach are perfect accompaniments to the entrees.

Cajun House

3048 W. Diversey
Phone: 772-1230 (reservations)
Parking: Street
B.Y.O. (corkage, 50¢ per person)
No credit cards

Tue.-Thur., 5:00 P.M.–
  10:00 P.M.
Fri., Sat., 5:00 P.M.–
  11:00 P.M.
Closed Sunday, Monday

Although the Creole House has gone Cajun under new ownership, much remains the same. One still has to ring the bell to get in, and the Victorian setting still emits a feel of faded but genteel aristocracy. The sounds of New Orleans jazz add an appropriate background. Service is leisurely, though at times could be more together. The menu, offering complete dinners priced from $8.75 to $10.50, features several Creole and Cajun specialties.

Meals begin with a superb shrimp paté, accompanied by a pungent remoulade sauce. Follow with either the thick, creamy peanut soup, a well-stocked seafood gumbo, or, if it's available, a marvelous, meaty Bayou chili. Cajun House salad comes next. At this point, we usually can't resist an order of sweet, slightly thick, rice fritters (95¢) or crisp hushpuppies and honey (95¢).

Entrees feature a chicken jambalaya ($8.75), sparked with chicken, shrimp, and ham. Served casserole-style, mixed with rice and vegetables, it's topped by a melt of cheddar cheese. There's also luscious chicken pontalba ($9.25), sauteed boneless chicken spread upon a bed of diced potatoes, ham, mushrooms, and scallions. Cajun House prawns ($10.50), served shell-intact and perfumed with garlic and spices, can be delicious if not overcooked. The humble catfish ($9.95) is puffy and moist, but avoid the eggplant creole ($9.95), as it is mushy-textured and unevenly spiced.

Desserts are gloriously tempting, especially a brandy-sauced bread pudding that's the best north of New Orleans. There also might be a pecan tart, pecan parfait, mocha mousse, and cranberry nut sundae. Chicory coffee provides a perfect backdrop.

The Casbah

514 W. Diversey
Phone: 935-7570
Free garage parking
Full bar
Credit Cards: Bank of Amerca, Carte Blanche, Diners Club, Master Charge

Mon.-Thur., 5:30 P.M.–11:30 P.M.
Fri.-Sat., 5:30 P.M.–Midnight
Sun., 5:30 P.M.–10:30 P.M.
Reservations necessary

The Casbah with its dramatic, soft lighting, murals of veiled women and palm trees, ornate hanging lanterns, and carved arches, is the most exotic of our splurges. It conjures visions of Charles Boyer and Hedy Lamarr among the minarets. The food, while less theatrical, is nonetheless unusual and delicious.

Dinners cost between $5.50 and $7.20 and include appetizer, egg-lemon soup, salad, entree, and either American or Turkish coffee. While both of the dinner appetizers—hommos (ground chick pea spread) and djadic (a tart mix of cucumbers, yogurt, and mint) are excellent, be sure to try the beorak (70¢ extra). It's a combination of cheese, parsley and onions baked sizzling hot in a parchment-thin strudel dough.

Among the Armenian entrees are four variations on the shish kabab, with the Armenian kabab ($7.20) being our preference. Tender marinated lamb is alternately skewered between eggplant, green pepper, tomatoes, and onions. Rice pilaf is served with all of the kababs. Two other top choices are meat beorak, chopped meat, onions, and tomatoes wrapped in strudel dough ($6.50) and maglube, a tasty casserole of well-seasoned rice, lamb cubes, cauliflower, and pinenuts ($6.00, served only on weekends). Kibbe (deep fried balls of cracked wheat, ground lamb, onions, and walnuts, $6.00) and sarma (stuffed grape leaves, $6.00) are two other possibilities.

For dessert, baklava (80¢) is fresh and syrupy sweet, and the Turkish coffee makes a fittingly rich accompaniment.

Cape Cod Room

140 E. Walton (at Michigan Ave.)   Daily, Noon–Midnight
  in the Drake Hotel   Reservations necessary
Phone: 787-2200
Parking: Street, garages, or doorman
Full bar
Credit Cards: American Express
Coat required

For years the Cape Cod Room has enjoyed the reputation as Chicago's best seafood house, and despite several worthy challengers, on a clear day, it is still king of the sea. What's impressive is not just the staggering variety of fresh and saltwater fish and shellfish offered, but the number of ways in which each is prepared. For example, lobster comes as newburg, thermidor, parisienne, and mornay, in addition to steamed or boiled. The standard repertoire is further augmented by seasonal specials, such as soft shell crabs, mahimahi, and grouper.

As the menu is a la carte, you won't escape without a noticeable dent in your pocketbook; however, the value is generally excellent.

Begin your meal with the Cape Cod's justifiably renowned Bookbinder soup ($1.35), chunky with red snapper and further perked with a vial of sherry. There are also cherrystone or little neck clams ($2.50) and a tangy, fresh-tasting shrimp cocktail ($2.95).

From the stream of entrees, we especially like the delicate sole amandine ($6.95), tender sauteed Cape Cod scallops ($8.75), and either lobster or crab newburg ($9.75 or $8.75). We found the pompano en papillote (cooked in parchment, along with lobster, mushrooms and red wine ($9.00), beautifully served but too strong-tasting.

The accompanying salad or cole slaw is tasty, but we have been disappointed by the somewhat gummy, bland au gratin potatoes. There is also a selective and agreeably priced wine list.

The cozy, rustic New England Inn atmosphere is delightful. Although Cape Cod has long had a reputation for snobby service, the staff seems to have mellowed considerably in recent years.

L'epuisette

21 W. Goethe

Phone: 944-2288

Parking: Street or garage

Full bar

Credit cards: all accepted

Coat and Tie

Tue.-Sun., 5:00 P.M.–

11:00 P.M.

Closed Monday

Reservations

A combination of glorious seafood, gracious service, and a good deal makes us always happy with L'epuisette. Even though the price tag goes from $9.00 to $12.00, there's much to be had for the money. Food is carefully prepared, and portions are more than ample.

A choice from several appetizers—a generous slice of melon, a mostly citrus fruit cup, red snapper soup, or Boston clam chowder—is included with the dinner. The snapper comes across too spicy and brackish, but the chowder is chunky and well-flavored. For an extra 95¢, one can dine on marvelous caper and chopped egg-decorated sardines, which rest atop a beefsteak tomato. Hot French bread precedes the salad course, which includes a fresh, crisp, flavorfully-dressed Caesar.

Easily our favorite entree is their inimitable crabmeat-stuffed trout meunière ($9.95). Beautifully browned, rich, and flaky, ingredients blend to mouth-melting perfection. Almost as delectable is the soft-shell crab amandine ($9.15), unusually sweet and firm, and gilded with a profuse showering of buttery almonds. Another rich offering is crabmeat au vin blanc ($9.75), a creamy casserole topped with breadcrumbs and braced with shallots and mushrooms. Other possibilities include filet of Dover sole Marguery, shrimp creole or de jonghe, and froglegs meunière.

Desserts, although almost unnecessary, are uniformly excellent. There's a wonderful chocolate-sauced snowball or porfiterole (try either with coffee ice cream) and a fine cheesecake.

L'epuisette is housed in a muted, wormwood panelled dining room. Service, by the primarily Latino staff, is friendly and proficient without being pretentious.

L'escargot

2925 N. Halsted
Phone: 525-5525
Parking: Street
Full bar
Credit cards:
  Bank of America,
  Master Charge

Mon.-Thur., 5:00 P.M.–9:30 P.M.
Fri.-Sat., 5:00 P.M.–10:30 P.M.
Closed Sunday
Reservations

Pastel-stained walls, baskets of fresh fruit at each setting, and a display table of mouth-watering desserts give L'escargot a charming country ambience. The narrow bar, with its navy and white polka dot cloth-covered tables, offers limited but more intimate seating. Cooking is that of the French provinces, devotedly prepared. Complete dinners, often including a complimentary cold vegetable dish like ratatouille, range from $9.50 to $12.50.

For openers, try the celeri remoulade, the delicious but salty smoked filet of herring, or the superb sausage en croute. Soups, with the exception of the spritely watercress, are not particularly unusual. The simple, but perfectly-flavored salad which follows is composed of tender Boston lettuce tossed with a tangy vinaigrette dressing.

The eight or so entrees vary, and among those we like best are the roast duck with either orange or cherry sauce and any of the fish. The fresh poached trout, stuffed with pureed mushrooms and topped by a light cream sauce, is particularly good. So are the coq au vin (which boasts a rich yet subtle sauce) and the goose, lamb, pork and bean-filled cassoulet.

Among the fabulous desserts at L'escargot, the fruit tarte (especially strawberry-apricot) is perfection itself—a blend of flaky pastry, plump fruit, and delicate custard. There is an ample wine list too, and the service is generally excellent (though, like anywhere, you can hit upon an off-night).

Also, from 5:00 to 6:30 P.M., a petit diner is served, which includes an hors d'oeuvre or soup, a choice from three to four entrees, salad, dessert, and coffee, all for $5.50.

La Fontaine

2442 N. Clark
Phone: 525-1800
Parking: Free, in garage
  across street
Full bar
Credit Cards: Bank of America,
  Master Charge
Jackets are preferred for men

Mon.-Sat., 5:30 P.M.–
  10:30 P.M.
Lunch, Tue.-Fri.,
  11:30 A.M.–2:30 P.M.
Reservations necessary

Both the cooking and the setting are exquisite at La Fontaine, one of Chicago's coziest French restaurants, located in an attractively refurbished brownstone.

The $12.50 prix fixe dinner begins with a flourish, as the appetizers are pure pleasure. Highly recommended are la coquille Deauvilloise (hot seafood and mushrooms in a creamy champagne sauce) or le delice de La Fontaine (a blend of ham, fresh mushrooms, and melted cheese served over a toasted crouton). Also excellent are the light, puffy quiche lorraine or the smooth salmon mousse with a green mayonnaise sauce.

Each of the three soups—the cheesey onion, St. Germain (pea soup with croutons), and vichyssoise—is deftly prepared and subtly flavored. Good French bread and unsalted butter make a fine accompaniment. However, we found the Boston lettuce salad slightly watery and lacking flavor.

This disappointment is soon forgotten when the entrees appear. The crisp duck, thickly glazed with orange sauce and peaches, is a marvel (served for two). There are three inventive fish selections: trout soufflé with champagne sauce, sea bass flamed in pernod (served for two), and poached turbot with hollandaise. Filet mignon with Bearnaise sauce and sirloin sauteed with shallots are excellent, but the thin-sliced veal sauteed with mushrooms, applejack, and cream sauce is served in a rather small portion. Marvelous soufflé potatoes and creamed spinach or a fresh vegetable with hollandaise sauce go along beautifully.

Desserts, though not spectacular, include a rich chocolate mousse and a splendid cream caramel. The wine list is fairly extensive and can be expensive.

Gene and Georgetti's

500 N. Franklin
Phone: 527-3718
Parking: Lot
Full bar
Credit Cards: American
  Express, Diners Club

Daily, 11:30 A.M.–12:30 A.M.
Closed Sunday
Reservations necessary

Gene and Georgetti's is an unpretentious steak house but we doubt you'll find a more gorgeous piece of beef in Chicago. They range in price from a good-sized "small" sirloin for $9.95 up to $13.50 for an enormous, 28-ounce T-bone. The meat is of excellent quality, charred to perfection on the outside and tender and juicy inside.

If you prefer your meat embellished, give the pepper steak a try—big chunks of butter-tender sirloin are cooked in a savory wine sauce along with green peppers, onions, and mushrooms. Lamb chops ($11.50) are large and thick, and the liver ($6.75) is good too, although it is thick-sliced rather than thin. The menu also sports several less expensive pasta dishes.

All entrees include a platter of crisp cottage fries and either a salad or cole slaw. The slaw is fresh tasting, though heavy on scallions, but the salad is nothing special.

If possible, reserve a table in the main first floor dining room (the restaurant has several rooms on two floors). Although somewhat noisy, this location offers the most attractive setting, less surly waiters, and an excellent spot to absorb the action. Gene and Georgetti's has always enjoyed a popular following among businessmen, both legitimate and otherwise, and it's fun to watch and listen to the wheeling and dealing. However, if nothing's shaking, the steaks will more than hold your attention.

ITALIAN (SICILIAN)

Mama Lena's Italian Kitchen

24 E. Chicago
Phone: 337-4050
Parking: Street or pay lot
   next door
B.Y.O.
No Credit Cards

Daily, Seating at 6:00 P.M.
   and 8:30 P.M. only
Closed Sunday
Reservations necessary

Mama Lena's is more like an Italian home than a restaurant. There's no menu to order from. Instead, guests are treated to whatever Sicilian specialty Mama's been cooking in her kitchen. Dinners are served twice nightly, and the complete five course meal costs $10.50 per person.

Mama Lena seems to lavish the same kind of love and care on her patrons as she did in cooking for her family of nine children. She is ably assisted by two of the nine, Sal and Carl, who are raucous, good humored, and always ready to trade quips with the customers. One evening when we had requested water, they obliged with a length of hose hooked up from the kitchen. Sound crazy? It is, but, before the evening's over, a good-natured, familial camaraderie exists between proprietors and patrons.

The food doesn't take second billing as it's generally quite delicious. Mama Lena has a repertoire of thirty-six meals, among them linguine with clam sauce, canneloni, braccioli, and several veal and chicken dishes.

Each dinner begins with a good-sized antipasto salad—crisp greens, cherry tomatoes, Italian olives, provolone, salami—all sprinkled with a slightly salty oil and vinegar dressing. It is served with some heavenly oregano-spiced tomato bread. A pasta dish follows, perhaps a large plateful of fafalli (bow-noodles) topped by a delicate sauce concocted from fresh tomatoes, ricotta, and romano cheese, peas and onions. Very light and exquisite. Next comes the main course. On a recent visit we were treated to a ground sirloin-eggplant melange which also featured fresh mushrooms, tomatoes, and mozzarella. Dessert (somewhat ordinary cannoli) and excellent coffee round out the meal.

El Piqueo

5427 N. Clark
Phone: 769-0455
Parking: Street
B.Y.O. (25¢ charge for glassware)
Credit Cards: American Express,
    Carte Blanche, Diners Club

Tues.-Sat., 5:00 P.M.–
    10:30 P.M.
Closed Sunday & Monday
Reservations

While Piqueo may not be the most well known of our "splurges," a surprising number of people consider it their favorite Chicago restaurant. The distinctive Peruvian cuisine is delicious and shows obvious signs of painstaking care. Moises Asturrizaga serves as host while his sister, Juana, devotes her talent to the food. There is no written menu. Each night they serve a special five-course dinner at a fixed price that has recently gone up to $10.00.

A typical evening's meal might begin with escaveche, bite-sized pieces of raw turbot marinated in lemon and lime juice spiced with onions and a touch of cayenne. It's delicate, spicy and refreshing. For the next course you might luck upon copa, a divine blend of shrimp and broccoli in a spicy, egg-based cream sauce. Soup's next and ranges from a gentle beef noodle to a hearty shrimp-vegetable.

Beef, prepared one of several ways, is generally the evening's entree. It might come grilled on a skewer, as a beautifully flavored stew or as filete en cebolla (beef sauteed with onions). If you call in a day in advance, Juana will prepare her specialty, duck a la pericuoli ($9.50). We've never put in the call yet, but hear it's fantastic. Papas huancaina, boiled potatoes in a piquant cheese sauce, are an excellent accompaniment to the meat.

A demitasse of coffee and a light, creamy flan close the meal. Service is as unobtrusive and smooth as the flan. Señor Asturrizaga usually wends his way among the tables in order to explain various dishes or just to converse.

The decor at Piqueo is as unique as the cuisine—lush llama rugs and colorful native weaving decorate the walls. Lighting is subdued, seating is comfortable, and an intimate, relaxing atmosphere prevails.

Peking Duckling House

2045 W. Howard
Phone: 338-2016
Parking: Street
Full bar
Credit Cards:
American Express

Tue.-Thur., 11:00 A.M.–10:00 P.M.
Fri., 11:00 A.M.–Midnight
Sat., 5:00 P.M.–Midnight
Sun., 5:00 P.M.–10:00 P.M.

For anyone who hasn't tried Mandarin cooking, the Peking Duckling House is an excellent place to start. We feel that it consistently offers the city's best Northern Chinese cuisine, one that is characterized by a spicy yet subtle flavor and complex preparation. The extensive, eight-page menu alone takes at least ten minutes to savor.

A complete dinner of soup, appetizer, main dish, rice, dessert, and tea costs at least $6.00 per person, as everything is priced a la carte. You can definitely eat more cheaply by foregoing one of the courses, though we don't suggest it.

We recommend opening your assault with either the sizzling rice soup (in which hot crisp rice cakes are ladled into a broth rich with black mushrooms, bamboo shoots, peppers, and carrots, $1.75 for two) or the thick, unusually flavored sour and hot soup ($1.75 for two). For an appetizer, we like the light crisp green onion cakes ($1.60, serves two or three) that practically disintegrate at first bite.

Outstanding among the entrees are Moo-shu pork ($4.25), a shredded meat, vegetable, and egg combination that you eat wrapped in thin pancakes, or the spicy Szechuan beef ($4.25), crunchy with bamboo shoots, celery, and green pepper. Two excellent dishes with a slight bite are chicken or shrimp with peanuts ($3.85 and $4.25). A mild alternative is chicken and vegetables served on a crisp bed of sizzling rice ($3.85). Duck should not be ignored, particularly the deep-fried, tea-smoked duck ($5.90), served with steamed buns and plum sauce, or the pressed duck ($4.95).

For dessert, be sure to try apple or banana fritters ($1.40 for two). They're not the hard candy-coated version found in most Mandarin restaurants, but have a light, puffy batter. They're flamed in a brandy-honey sauce, and help finish your evening with a flourish.

Lunches

Ireland's

500 N. LaSalle   Daily, 11:00 A.M.–11:00 P.M.
Phone: 337-2020
Parking: Street
Full bar

An attractive spot for good fish soups, ordered by the cup
(75¢) or crock ($1.95). The very best is their oyster stew—
big on oysters in a mild, milky broth. There's also both kinds
of clam chowder, turtle soup, and a creamy, very fishy fish
chowder. A hot loaf of delicious sourdough rye comes along.

They also do up excellent smelt ($2.25, when in season)
and one of the finer salad bars around: tons of fresh fruit, two
kinds of herring, German potato salad, corn relish, crisp vegetables, homemade croutons—and everything's easy to get at.
It costs $2.85, but comes at no charge with the smelt.

Fast service and lots of office shop talk.

San Pedro

(one of our favorites)

In Plaza del Lago Shopping
Center (just off Sheridan
Road, in Wilmette)
Phone: 251-6621
Parking: Lot
B.Y.O.

Daily, 11:00 A.M.–3:00 P.M.
(lunch)
3:00 P.M.–5:00 P.M.
(tea)
5:15 P.M.–9:30 P.M.
(dinner)
Sun., 11:00 A.M.–7:30 P.M.

San Pedro is a blissful place for lunch. Despite its name,
only the architecture and handsome decor are Spanish. The
food is strictly American tearoom with a slight French accent.

Just one glance at the menu is a Pavlovian experience. It's
one of the most mouthwatering we've ever read. There's an
omelette with fresh strawberries and sour cream ($3.50),
quiche lorraine ($3.50), and cheddar cheese souffle ($3.50).
Our special favorite is mushrooms polonaise ($3.50), a flaky
pastry shell filled with fresh mushrooms in a delicate sour
cream-flavored sauce. An unusual and appealing dish is the
pecan loaf with mushroom sauce ($3.50). It tastes something
like bread dressing for turkey, and is really quite delicious.
Don't overlook the more mundane but excellent roast beef
hash, topped by a poached egg and velvety tomato sauce
($3.50). A variety of luncheon salads and sandwiches is
available, too.

Most lunches include a small salad (the white asparagus-
pineapple-watercress combination is exquisite), a good and
gooey homemade caramel roll and either soup or dessert.
However, if you are able to resist the alluring desserts—fudge
pie a la mode, rhubarb-strawberry pie, banana cream pie—
you deserve a citation from Dr. Stillman.

Expect a wait at San Pedro. The restaurant rivals back-
gammon in popularity among the suburban set.

National Self Service Cafeteria

68 W. Van Buren   6:30 A.M.–8:00 P.M.
Phone: 427-0290
Parking: Difficult
No liquor

A big, spacious, workingman's cafeteria that's like a trip back in time. Food is serve-yourself, steam table-style, and expectedly cheap. The menu varies daily, but dishes worth checking out are the homey, tender roast chicken and potatoes (the potatoes have really soaked up the juice, $1.75); swiss steak and noodles (a little greasy, but good flavor, $1.75); and the lamb shank and potatoes ($1.85).

There are sandwiches, including either a salmon or tuna salad (85¢), made-from-scratch soups, and side orders of corn bread (20¢) and bran muffins (40¢). Homemade pies for dessert; they're nothing glorious but definitely substantial.

The customers are 95 percent men, most of whom sit alone eating, and reading the day's happenings in the newspaper.

Sayat Nova

157 E. Ohio   Mon.-Sat., 11:30 A.M.–Midnight
Phone: 644-9159   Sunday, 2:00 P.M.–10:00 P.M.
Parking: Street (difficult)
Full bar

Not only an intimate, atmospheric setting but a meal that will lift one far beyond the burger and BLT blues. Try either of the two combination plates. Each costs $2.50, and all of the dishes are well-chosen and tasty. The first combo features a moist ground meat-stuffed eggplant, bean salad, oil and vinegar-dressed lettuce, pita bread, and beoreg, creamy smooth cheese wrapped in a delicate, flaky pastry.

Stuffed eggplant and stuffed grape leaves plus salad, pita, and taboule, a marvelous cracked wheat salad, sparked with bits of tomato, onion, sweet pepper, oil, lemon, and mint highlight the second combination.

Other possibilities include an Armenian stew, a charcoal grilled lulla kebab (similar to meatballs) sandwich, and kibbee, a crisp, spicy sphere fashioned of ground meat, cracked wheat, and pine nuts. Delicious appetizers, too, and a rich, syrupy baklava for dessert.

A great place for lunch, especially if you're anywhere around Michigan Avenue.

Magic Pan

60. E. Walton
Phone: 943-2456
Old Orchard Shopping
    Center
Phone: 677-2110
Parking: Walton (street)
    Old Orchard (parking lot)
Full bar

Mon.-Thur., 11:00 A.M.–
    Midnight
Fri., Sat., 11:00 A.M.–
    1.00 A.M.
Sun., 11:00 A.M.–9:00 P.M.

Magic Pans are sunny, cheerfully-decorated restaurants that serve a tantalizing variety of crepes. Lunches are a good bet price-wise, as a crepe and salad duo costs under $3.00, while dinners generally run $4.50-$5.75. The scrumptious dessert crepes are extra.

Some of our favorite choices are the light spinach soufflé crepe or the curried chicken with a coconut-spiced apple topping. The ham and cheese combination consists of two crisp, deep-fried crepes, one filled with thin-sliced ham and the other with a sizzling melted cheese. Portions are deceivingly more filling than they look, though one can easily make room for dessert.

The crepe a la mode ($1.75) is an indecently rich concoction, an ice cream-filled crepe topped by a dark chocolate sauce. There's an apple crepe ($1.50), a banana crepe garnished with brown sugar sauce, whipped cream, and almonds ($1.85). For an all-out splurge, order the Beignets—bow-shaped, deep-fried crepes that are incredibly crisp and light. They are sprinkled with cinnamon and powdered sugar, and come with a dip of either brandied chocolate or apricot sauce. At $2.95, they're expensive, but the portion is immense, and if there was ever a time for being free with the bills, this is it.

Dining at the Magic Pan is a visual as well as a taste treat. There are several nice touches: fresh flowers on the table, hanging plants, sugar cubes in little wire baskets, and an abundance of fresh, spring colors.

Recently new Magic Pans have opened in the Woodfield Shopping Center, Oakbrook Mall, and Hawthorne Center.

ECLECTIC

Great Gritzbe's Flying Food Show

25 E. Chestnut
Phone: 642-3460
Parking: Street
Full bar

Daily, opens at 11:30 A.M.
(Sunday brunch from
10:00 A.M.–2:30 P.M.)

Gritzbe's will be packed, but if you have the time, the wait among the free cheese spreads (they're all homemade, and one even includes chocolate chips) is worth it.

The menu is equally creative. There's a French Toast Connection (deep fried, egg-coated bread, stuffed with chicken salad and cheese, served with pineapple jam, $2.35) and a Monte Gritzbe (another french fried concoction, this time with ham and turkey tagged with a side of strawberry jam and sour cream, $2.75). Skinny shoe string fries come along.

Good salads: a creamy, anchovy-touched "soggy" salad, $1.35; a martini salad (the brew comes in a separate pitcher, vegetables and dips on the side, though who knows what could happen by the end, $3.25); and, our favorite, hot, teriyaki-sauced fresh vegetables including corn on the cob, mushrooms, cauliflower, brussel sprouts for $1.95.

Lots more, like "strawberry fields forever," an all-you-can-eat dessert spread ($2.50 alone, or $1.50 with sandwich or salad) which we're not as crazy about as most people.

A trendy, sophisticated, space-age place done in muted grays, mirrors, and sweeping curves.

Rosemarie's

2445 Ridge, Lansing,
   Illinois
Phone: 875-9789
Parking: Street
No liquor

Tue.-Sat., 11:30 A.M.–2:30 P.M.;
   5:00 P.M.–9:00 P.M.
Sun., Noon–6:00 P.M.
Closed Monday

Straight out of a picture book with its billowy white curtains, vases filled with sprays of straw and cloth flowers, and working cuckoo clock, Rosemarie's serves wonderfully charming lunches. Such things as delicate chicken a la king in a buttery puff pastry ($1.95), two small, crusty "European" hamburgers, seasoned with onions and parsley ($1.75), and, on most days, golden crisp potato pancakes ($1.35).

Good pea soup and lightly-touched, airy desserts. Try the multi-layered, moist dobosh torte or flaky apple slice. Imported ciders, iced tea, and lemonade to drink.

Epicurean

316 S. Wabash
Phone: 939-2190
Parking: Take the bus
Full bar

Mon.-Fri., 11:00 A.M.–9:00 P.M.
Sat., 11:00 A.M.–Midnight
Closed Sunday

If you have to eat lunch downtown, you're generally better off bringing your own. Bright spots, budget-food wise, are few and far between. However, skip the salami sandwich one day, and try the Epicurean. It offers fine Hungarian cooking at reasonable prices and has long enjoyed a reputation for its homemade strudel.

Entrees are generally priced from $2.25 to $3.00. Some traditional favorites include Szekely goulash with noodles ($2.50), chicken paprikash ($2.50), Hungarian stuffed cabbage ($2.40), and Hungarian stuffed peppers ($2.40). If you're into something sweet, there's a fantastic apple-strawberry pancake ($2.25) as well as the special light Hungarian crepe, palascinta ($2.25), filled with either cheese or jelly.

All entrees come with a small dish of pickled, whole baby beets and a basket of rolls. The strudel (75¢) rightly deserves its fame; the leaves are paper thin and flaky, and the filling is fresh, abundant, and not overly sweet. It is served warm, dusted with powdered sugar.

The Epicurean is run as a good downtown restaurant should be. Service is prompt and efficient, but not unduly rushed. It's definitely a pleasant place to unwind.

Dinners here are higher-priced, and include a complete meal. One compensation is that the best strudel of them all—cherry—is served only at night.

Mallers Building Coffee Shop

5 S. Wabash, 3rd Floor
Phone: 263-7696
Parking: Take the "el"
No liquor

Mon.-Fri., 6:00 A.M.–5:00 P.M.
Sat., 7:00 A.M.–2:30 P.M.
Closed Sunday

Mallers is Chicago's hidden deli, located on the third floor of that famous downtown landmark, the Mallers Building. It's one of the Loop's best lunch spots and even boasts a picturesque view of the Wabash "el." A crowd gathers here at noon, and the scene is sometimes nothing short of frantic. The cooks are yelling in the kitchen, secretaries line up for carry-outs, and everyone else sits contentedly munching on chopped liver or corned beef omelettes.

The menu features most delicatessen standards. The corned beef sandwich ($1.80) is usually moist and flavorful, served in an adequate, though not overpowering, portion. The coarsely chopped liver has a nice texture and taste. There's a good combination plate for $2.30 that offers chopped liver, a cheese blintz, farmer's chop suey (fresh salad vegetables and sour cream), and fruit salad (which turns out to be canned fruit cocktail). The blintzes are delicious—delicate and crisp, with a sweet, mild cheese filling. There's also a lox and cream cheese plate, as well as an appealing chopped liver and potato pancake duo ($2.60).

Chocolate phosphates are good. So's the rye bread. The waitresses are true pros, so the service is short-order swift. It's a fun place to eat and sure beats Toffenetti's.

Manny's

(one of our favorites)

1139 S. Jefferson
  (off Roosevelt Road)
Phone: 939-2855
Parking: Rear lot and street
No liquor

Daily, 5:00 A.M.–5:30 P.M.
Closed Sunday

You'd almost think they were giving food away at Manny's, the way the crowd gathers at noon. You'll never see a broader cross-section of people eating in one restaurant. There are Roosevelt Road merchants, firemen from the nearby academy, hardhats, students, shoppers, etc., all converging on Manny's for the same reason: speedy service, low prices, and the most appealing and varied cafeteria-style food in the city.

There are about a dozen hot dishes offered daily at an inflation-fighting average of $2.20. Roast veal breast ($2.20), brisket ($2.20), short ribs ($2.45), chicken pot pie ($1.80), spaghetti and meatballs ($2.15), gefilte fish ($1.90), oxtail stew ($2.15), corned beef and cabbage ($2.20), and prune tzimmes ($2.40) are just a sampling. They all are tasty and served in truck-driver portions. Potato and vegetable are included.

Manny's makes a great-looking, great-tasting corned beef sandwich, served on rye or an onion roll. There's also brisket, tongue, ham, pastrami, and roast beef. All cost $1.65 and are served with a potato pancake and kosher pickle.

The side dishes are terrific, with the Jewish big "K's" being well represented. There's kishke, knish, kreplach and kasha (the latter two come in chicken soup). Each costs 55¢, and the meat-filled knish is particularly delish.

Desserts are almost as varied as the entrees. Priced from 40¢ to 50¢, there are cream pies, rice pudding, cherry squares, canned figs, sugarless baked apples, and Napoleons.

Club Lago

331 W. Superior
Phone: 337-9444
Parking: Street
Full bar

Mon.-Sat., 8:00 A.M.–8:30 P.M.
Closed Sunday

If it's lunchtime and you're really hungry, this is the place. Monster-sized portions of Italian regulars like mostaccioli ($2.05) and spaghetti and meatballs ($2.45) are prepared with a deft and generous hand. Particularly worthy of the calories are green noodles al forno, baked casserole-style and topped with a rich blanket of melted cheese ($2.05), and veal parmigiana ($2.75), a crusty, plump patty bathed with cheese and tossed with parsley. There might also be an Italian sausage omelette ($1.85), a sausage and pepper plate ($2.75), or eggplant parmigiana ($2.65).

The setting's strictly Chicago tavern and well-packed with white collars. Service is fast, no one's afraid to eat, and the no-nonsense but motherly waitresses will do their best to encourage more.

F & T Restaurant

1182 N. Milwaukee   Daily, 5:30 A.M.–7:00 P.M.
Phone: 252-1150
Parking: Street
Full bar

A step inside the F & T takes you back in time. The restaurant retains its old world atmosphere, with dark panelling, ornate ceiling, its old comfortable booths, and a scattering of bentwood coat racks. Food is prepared from scratch and served cafeteria-style.

Main courses, priced between $1.50 and $2.25 might include stuffed cabbage, roast chicken, Polish sausage, meat loaf, oxtail stew, spare ribs, duck (Saturdays only), and baked steak smothered with vegetables (Sundays only). Also, carved-to-order sandwiches, rugged soups, and prune or cheese blintzes for dessert.

SOUPS & SANDWICHES

The Bowl and Roll

1246 N. Wells   Daily, 11:30 A.M.–10:30 P.M.
Phone: 943-1437   Fri.-Sat., 11:30 A.M.–Midnight
Parking: Street (difficult)   Sun., 11:30 A.M.–10:00 P.M.
Full bar   Closed Monday

The snug, cavern-like Bowl and Roll is a super little soup house. The menu features three kinds of meal-in-itself soups, all beautifully prepared and served with hot, crusty Toscana bread. The chicken soup (¼ chicken, $2.00; ½ chicken $2.75) is a fresh, light medley of garden vegetables, noodles, and tender whole pieces of chicken. Goulash soup ($3.00) is a heavier affair—rich, thick with big chunks of meat, a weighty dumpling, and vegetables. Hungarian sausage soup ($3.00) rounds out the triumverate. There are also three sandwiches: a tasty chopped liver, Hungarian sausage, and cheese. For dessert, have a pecan brownie (55¢).

The Loophole

59 E. Randolph   Daily, 10:30 A.M.–7:30 P.M.
Phone: 236-6243   Closed Sunday
Parking: Take the "el"
Wine

A handsome new "fast food" spot in the loop, run by the Blackhawk people. Good quality abounds: fresh and generous ingredients, good recipes, nice portions. Help yourself to soups and sandwiches, and for a piece of each action, try the "soup and a half" (bowl of soup with half a sandwich, $1.85).

Excellent chunky goulash soup and a slightly too tart gazpacho are available every day, plus such specials as lentil with sausage, beef and barley, potato/cheddar cheese, etc. Our favorite sandwich is the shrimp-studded egg salad served on either an onion roll, rye, or crusty Toscana bread. Superb chili ($1.00) and cheesecake (65¢) too. Carry-outs available.

SWEDISH

House of Sweden

5314 N. Clark   Daily, 11:00 A.M.–8:00 P.M.
Phone: 334-8757   Closed Wednesday
Parking: Street
No liquor

Their lunch menu features such Swedish delights as an open-face egg and anchovy sandwich ($1.65), hot Swedish meatballs and gravy on limpa bread (request it, $1.45), and Swedish pancakes with lingonberries ($1.60), or rolled pancakes with strawberries and whipped cream ($1.25).

There's also an allspice-spiced hamburger smothered with fried onions (pannbiff, $1.80), and another burger topped with a fried egg, which includes a side of diced fried potatoes (pariser sandwich, $1.95). A good ham sandwich, too ($1.45).

Finish with one of their delicate, homebaked pies. With any luck, the coconut cream will be around.

Brunches

Effendi

1525 E. 53rd   Sunday brunch: 11:00 A.M.–2:30 P.M.
Phone: 955-5151
Parking: Street
Full bar

A Turkish-style, do-it-yourself brunch ($4.00 per person) that combines the ethnic with the everyday. There are some intriguing cold dishes: delicious marinated kidney beans; bulghur spiked with chives and scallions; soft chunks of eggplant, tomato, and dill in a smooth vinaigrette; an oniony potato salad; and a fresh whole fish.

On the hot side are tender, sauteed chicken livers, fluffier-than-usual scrambled eggs, and flaky, strudel leaf-covered spinach beorek. There's also jam-filled crepes, a variety of cakes and cookies, and complimentary champagne.

Service can be confused, but the setting's lovely: a spacious, pillared and beamed, high-ceilinged room, outfitted with big plants and brass, and located atop the Hyde Park Bank building.

Lee's Canton Cafe

2300 S. Wentworth
Phone: 225-4838
Parking: Street
B.Y.O.

Sunday dim sum brunch:
11:00 A.M.–2:00 P.M.

On Sundays, Chinese and non-Chinese families alike gather at Lee's for a Sunday brunch unlike any other. It features at least thirteen different varieties of dim sum. What are they? —an unusual array of steamed or fried dumplings and pastries filled with meat, fish, vegetables, or sweets. Most are dainty, snack-like morsels, costing about 65¢-75¢ for two to three pieces.

You have to get here early to try the egg puff, a sweet, melt-in-your-mouth, sugar-sprinkled cruller. They're delicate and delicious, and so popular that Lee's is liable to run out. If so, don't despair. There are other goodies, including a large, pork-filled bun called cha shu bow; woo gok, crisp, deep-fried, meat-filled potatoes, and sui mi, steamed wonton-like dough filled with chopped meat. There's also a tasty deep-fried bean cake containing egg, green onion and minced meat.

Unlike New York where they pass the dim-sum tray around so that customers can point and pick, at Lee's you'll have to take a chance. Ask your waiter for advice, and, after a few meals, you'll become a pro.

Lee's is good for other occasions, too, and makes delicious noodle soups and fantastic fried rice.

Mr. Ricky's

9300 N. Skokie, Skokie
Phone: 674-9300
Parking: Lot
No liquor

Sunday brunch,
10:00 A.M.–2:00 P.M.

Mr. Ricky's has one of the better brunch deals in town, especially if your idea of paradise is an unlimited supply of lox (both Nova and salted), two other kinds of smoked fish, pickled herring, cream cheese, four types of bagels (rye, plain, onion, and poppyseed), kaiser and onion rolls, tomatoes, cucumbers, onions, noodle pudding, and deliciously sweet fried smelts. There's also orange juice, your choice of either fried or scrambled eggs (cooked to order), and doughnuts or sweet rolls. $4.25 for adults, $2.95 for kids under six.

The Original Pancake House

(one of our favorites)

153 Greenbay Road, Wilmette
Phone: 251-6000
1517 E. Hyde Park, Chicago
Also: 2021 N. Lincoln Pk.
   10437 S. Western
   621 E. St. Charles Rd.
Parking: Lot or street
No liquor

Daily (including Sunday),
   7:00 A.M.–10:00 P.M.
Fri., 7:00 A.M.–11:00 P.M.
Sat., 7:00 A.M.–1:00 A.M.

The ultimate of pancake houses! The most voluptuous offering is the apple pancake, an incredibly rich, puffy, baked pancake filled with fresh sauteed apples and topped by cinnamon-caramel glaze ($2.75). If you're not up to the apple, there's a more delicate baked German pancake sprinkled with powdered sugar and served with fresh lemon wedges ($2.75).

The rolled crepes—mandarin orange ($2.25), cherry kijafa ($2.25), lingonberry ($2.00), and strawberry ($2.25)—are great. And if you're in the mood for something less flamboyant, there are buttermilk ($1.30) and wheat germ pancakes ($1.40), plus a good plain waffle ($1.35). Great coffee!

Ratso's

2464 N. Lincoln   Sunday brunch: 11:30 A.M.–3:30 P.M.
Phone: 935-1505
Parking: Street
Full bar

Ratso's gets a fine brunch together—eggs benedict, lox, bagels and cream cheese, chicken teriyaki, potato and smoked sausage casserole, and tomato quiche. Abundantly stocked vegetable salads include broccoli in garlic-flavored sour cream; delicious creamy cauliflower; marinated cherry tomatoes, zucchini, and onions; soy-doused bean sprouts and scallions, etc. Terrific banana-raisin- (maybe it's yogurt) sour cream-brown sugar tossed crepes for "dessert."

The only hassle is dodging the crowd; everyone knows what's good and makes a rush for it. But there's plenty, and it goes for $3.50 ($2.95 with a coupon from the *Reader.*) Coffee's 50¢ more, and if there's entertainment, another 50¢.

2¢ Plain

Hintz & Buffalo Grove Rd.,
  Wheeling
Phone: 394-0084
Parking: Lot
No liquor

Sunday brunch:
9:30 A.M.–3:00 P.M.

This has to be the best of the buffet brunch bunch. For $3.95, it's all you can eat, and they really mean it. Included in the spread are two kinds of lox, three types of smoked fish, chive cream cheese, bagels, kaiser rolls, and thick slices of challah. There's a whole (real) turkey, scrambled eggs, french toast, hollowed-out watermelon filled with fresh strawberries and fresh pineapple (in season), cantaloupe slices, and chocolate eclairs. Hopefully their generosity and good quality won't change. The setting's strictly deli, but it's spacious, not too noisy, and unrushed.

More Brunch and Breakfast Ideas:

The Bagel's amazing scrambled omelettes. Also R.J. Grunt's really outdoes itself with its $3.50 brunch-buffet. Burt's Coffee Shop at 2800 W. Foster makes good lox and onion omelettes ($2.10), fried matzoh ($1.65), and marvelously crusty French toast made from thick sliced challe ($1.45). The Victoria Restaurant, a raunchy diner just west of the Belmont "el" (953 W. Belmont) dishes up some delicious buttery, vanilla-flavored French toast for 75¢. The pancakes at Steak 'n Eggers (2100 N. Clark, 2737 N. Clark, 1174 W. Cermak, 1106 W. 95th) are generally reliable. Also the Swedish pancakes at Svea's on Clark, the Maggie's kippers and eggs, Irish sausage, and fried tomatoes, and any of the Korean grills (ask for pool gogi and eggs).

If you're really broke, the Hamburger King serves two eggs, hash browns, and toast for 45¢, and Sammy A's Razorback Restaurant, 2618 N. Halsted, dishes up three eggs, grits, and toast for only 50¢.

Sandwiches

Corned Beef

You can certainly find a decent corned beef sandwich in Chicago. With prices going up, you may not be able to afford one, but it's still comforting to know that they are out there. The following are among the best and, fortunately, are not too outrageously priced.

Braverman's

1604 W. Chicago
Phone: 421-3979

Daily, 10:00 A.M.–8:00 P.M.
Closed Sunday

Chicago's most popular place for corned beef. Why?— because they're big, though definitely not what they once were. Your $2.10 buys a near-whopping mound of juicy, thin-sliced, good quality meat piled between two fresh slices of rye (or an onion roll or, maybe, a kaiser roll). A crisp kosher dill is the lone companion.

Braverman's is primarily serve-yourself, which is fine because the skillful men who carve the meat are interesting to watch. They cut delicious brisket sandwiches ($2.10) too. And if you're strong of stomach, good kishke (40¢) and greasy potato pancakes (40¢) can be hard to resist.

Big stampede around noon. Cross-section crowd. A fun place.

Jerry's Food and Liquors

215 E. Grand
Phone: 337-2500

Daily, 6:30 A.M.–6:30 P.M.
Sat., 7:00 A.M.–4:00 P.M.
Closed Sunday

A noisy workingman's sandwich shop where the name of the game is crunch the customer. If you're not ready to bark out your order when the counterman calls on you, watch out. Not for the timid or indecisive, at least during the noon crush. A better-than-average corned beef sandwich—lean, meaty, succulent ($1.75). Also good pastrami ($1.75), boiled ham ($1.60), and better egg salad (95¢) than you could make at home.

Eating is done at counters. Carry-outs available. Much calmer during off-hours, but you miss some of the atmosphere.

S & S Deli (Goldie's Pump Room)

(one of our favorites)

594 Roger Williams,
    Highland Park
Phone: 432-0775

Daily, 6:00 A.M.–8:00 P.M.
Saturday, 6:00 A.M.–7:30 P.M.
Sunday, 6:00 A.M.–7:00 P.M.

A little grocery/candy store cum deli run by Mildred and Aaron Goldstein. Terrific lean corned beef sandwiches—thick, fresh, and made by Goldie himself. Not only great-tasting but cheap ($1.50). Also more of the same with excellent roast beef ($1.50). Not to mention the super-rich and thick chive cream cheese.

Goldie is a character, and his place has an old-time, personal feel. People come from near (and far).

Directions: Take Edens Expressway to Clavey Road turn-off, east to Greenbay. Turn north on Greenbay to Roger Williams and east a block or so.

Gyros and Souvlaki

The gyros craze has definitely passed its peak, although you're liable to see one spinning in almost every restaurant you pass. Just in case you've spent the last two years exploring the Nile or North Dakota, gyros is a mixture of spicy lamb and beef pressed into a loaf and then broiled on a vertically spinning rotisserie. The browned meat is sliced thin, then piled onto pancake-sized grilled pita bread along with sliced tomatoes, onions, and perhaps parsley, oregano, paprika, and a yogurt-sour cream sauce.

How can you spot a good one? The meat should be crusty yet juicy, not too greasy, well-seasoned without being overpowering, and laid on thick. Pita is best grilled till golden and puffy and just brushed with oil, rather than bathed in it.

Don't overlook souvlaki (shish kabob), as either it or gyros still makes a terrific snack ($1.45–$1.50).

Angie's

1971 N. Lincoln
Phone: 929-8300

Daily, 6:00 A.M.–2:00 A.M.

More spread out and diversified (fried chicken, pizza) than other gyroterias, Angie's still gets together a commendable gyros. It's juicy, crispy, and spicy with a tart, lemon-garlic flavor. Moist yet well-cooked pita, yogurt sauce, and lots of tomatoes combine to make Angie's gyros a fine all-arounder. Cold, flaky baklava (60¢) is excellent here.

Athenian Room

807 W. Webster   Daily, 7:30 A.M.–12:30 A.M.
Phone: 348-5155   Fri., Sat., 7:30 A.M.–2:00 A.M.

Gyros with a difference. The meat is more ground-beef textured than usual and red barbecue sauce or white wine sauce (in place of yogurt) are possible toppings. Terrific, very tender souvlaki. And great, thick Greek french fries, sprinkled with lemon juice and oregano.

This friendly, hang-loose place adjoins Glasgott's Groggery, and the twain often does meet.

Elihniko Souvlaki

(one of our favorites)

2602½ W. Lawrence   Daily, 11:00 A.M.–11:00 P.M.
Phone: 334-8601

A tiny, funky, hole-in-the-wall in Greektown that serves great souvlaki (no gyros). Big, juicy chunks of lamb served on crisp, honey-colored pita. The whole thing's sprinkled with lemon juice, paprika, oregano, an optional yogurt-cucumber sauce, and, of course, tomatoes and onions. Very potent. Very authentic.

Gyros King

3152 N. Broadway   Daily, 11:00 A.M.–2:00 A.M.
Phone: 472-4300

Big, heaping portion of well-seasoned gyros, lots of onions and tomatoes and nicely grilled, not too oily, pita. One complaint, the meat isn't always cut crisp enough. You used to have to request sour cream-yogurt sauce, but now they put it on automatically (so say something if you don't want it.) Gyros King is where we tried our first gyros, and it really flipped us. Though we no longer cartwheel, it's still a mighty good sandwich.

Olympos Gyros

2665 N. Clark
Phone: 871-2810

Daily, 11:00 A.M.–Midnight
Fri., Sat., Sun., 11:00 A.M.–1:00 A.M.

Lean, crisp, but still juicy gyros. Served with ample onions and sauce, but skimpy with the tomatoes. Pita is well browned, but not greasy. Souvlaki doesn't fare as well. The lamb cubes are good-sized, but they're usually kind of tough. Fresh tasting, flaky baklava (55¢) prepared by owner's mother.

Samiramis

(one of our favorites)

5253 N. Clark
Phone: 784-8616

Daily, 11:00 A.M.–11:00 P.M.
Fri.-Sat., 11:00 A.M.–2:00 A.M.

Tucked in between restaurants proffering limpa bread and Swedish meat balls, Samiramis remains strictly Greek. Not even a hint of cardamom in the gyros. And they do make a great one here. Well-packed, lots of meat, and nicely crusty (the cook is careful to let the meat brown.) Excellent lemon-flavored shish kabob (souvlaki). A gyros-shish kabob combo ($1.65) is also available. Marvelous, syrupy, cinnamon-flavored baklava (50¢).

Sparta Gyros

3202 N. Broadway
Phone: 549-4210

Daily, 11:00 A.M.–2:00 A.M.
Sat., 11:00 A.M.–3:00 A.M.

The most unassuming-looking of the Broadway gyros line-up. Not only do they make an excellent, potent, very meaty gyros, but one of the cooks is a treat to watch for his efficient (we should say, spartan) assembling of a sandwich. The souvlaki has a nice tangy flavor, but the sandwich could be heftier. A polished, spotless place.

Hamburgers

We're a nation of hamburger eaters. Unfortunately many people have settled for a pre-packaged, anemic slab disguised with extras and served on a bleached-out bun that now passes for a hamburger. If you're looking for the real thing—all beef, thick, juicy, cooked to order and served on dark rye or maybe a good kaiser roll—do not despair. The following restaurants do the hamburger proper justice.

Acorn on Oak

Phone: 944-6835   Daily, 11:30 A.M.–11:00 P.M.

A dark, pub-like place that serves an unusual hamburger. It's called the gourmet burger—a fat, three-quarter pounder spiced up with chopped green peppers and onions (they're inside the burger). Nice charred edges, juicy insides, and good, if not the most stomach-soothing, taste. Thick fries too. All this pleasure for a fairly stiff $3.25.

Chicago Claim Company

2314 N. Clark
Phone: 871-1770

Mon., 5:00 P.M.–11:30 P.M.
Tue.-Thur., 11:30 A.M.–3:00 P.M.;
    5:00 P.M.–11:30 P.M.
Fri., 5:00 P.M.–12:30 A.M.
Sat., 11:30 A.M.–4:00 P.M.;
    5:00 P.M.–12:30 A.M.
Sun., 3:30 P.M.–10:30 P.M.

The Claim Company does let you add garnishes to your hamburger, and good ones like sauteed mushrooms, french fried onions, swiss cheese, and teriyaki sauce. However, underneath it all, there's juicy, succulent meat to be found. Their lavish burger, crisp cottage fries, and excellent all-you-can-eat salad (fresh mushrooms, cherry tomatoes, etc.), make for a fabulous feast. The whole thing costs $3.60 and we think you get your money's worth.

There's more to the menu than the hamburger, most of it priced beyond our reach. All is served in a setting cleverly and expensively designed around a gold mining theme. (One major drawback: The place is literally a gold mine and a wait for a table is inevitable as there are no reservations.)

Cooper and Cooper

4748 N. Kimball
Phone: 539-3968

Daily, 24 hours

Some night when you're in the mood for an old-time hamburger, sizzled while you watch and dripping with fried onions, head for Cooper and Cooper. Their meat is fresh ground (not pre-wrapped in patties), and the burger comes out properly juicy (a little greasy, maybe, but really juicy). The bun is grilled too, and the whole affair meshes perfectly. And it costs 60¢ (70¢ with cheese).

Goldstein's

7308 Circle, Forest Park   Daily, 5:00 P.M.–1:00 A.M.
(1 block west of Harlem;   Closed Sunday
  1 block south of Lake St.)

A local, timeless sort of lounge that serves a fantastic half-pound "Goldyburger." The striking thing about the burger is that it tastes so good. We don't quite know why, it just does. You can have your Goldyburger plain ($1.75) or fancy. Try the Hawaiian (topped with pineapple and crisp bacon, $2.25) or the Royal burger (with bacon and cheese, $2.25). Only the mushroom burger ($2.15) is a disappointment, as the mushrooms are neither sauteed nor fresh.

Standard french fries come with (don't bother with the potato pancakes), and you can include a good, heaping tossed salad ($1.00). Service is friendly.

Hackney's

(one of our favorites)

Harm's Road (south of
Lake Avenue), Glenview
Phone: 724-5577
Lake Avenue (east of Wau-
kegan Road), Glenview
Phone: 724-7171
Milwaukee Avenue (south
of Dundee), Wheeling
Phone: 537-2100
Route 12 (1 mile north of
Route 22), Lake Zurich
Phone: 438-2103

Daily, 11:15 A.M.–10:15 P.M.
Fri., 11:15 A.M.–11:15 P.M.
Sat., 11:15 A.M.–1:15 P.M.
Sun., 12 Noon–10:30 P.M.

For some people, Hackney's has the "only" hamburger. We remember when it was 95¢. Others can go further back. Now the Hackneyburger's up to $2.40 (and the size seems to be getting smaller.) Fortunately, quality and taste are still excellent. Perfectly cooked, super-juicy, and served on fresh dark rye. And it's pure ambrosia when the coarse-grained rye soaks in the meat juices.

A platter of terrific, very crisp french fries and a cup of tart, creamy cole slaw are included. But don't forget Hackney's french fried onions ($2.10)—they're another institution. Served in a loaf, they're thin-sliced, crisp, coated with the featheriest of batters, slightly greasy, and great. In fact, we've tasted none better. The best turkey sandwich in town, too. Always crowded.

MacDuff's

(one of our favorites)

4035 W. Fullerton　　　　　　　　Daily, 11:30 A.M.–8:00 P.M.
Phone: 235-0408

A friendly, boisterous local bar serving Chicago's true Big Mac—a gigantic beefburger ("hamburger" is a forbidden word) weighing in at over three-quarters of a pound. The lean, succulent burger costs $2.65 and is made from prime ground round. No extra trimmings, but it's served on your choice of black bread, rye, or an onion roll. Mediocre french fried onions, french fries, and a good dill pickle come along. Colorfully presided over by Ogden, Bookie and Billy MacDuff, a father-sons team, their beefburger tends to put others to shame, and they're mighty proud of it.

Otto's

2024 N. Halsted　　　　　　　　Daily, 4:00 P.M.–2:00 A.M.
Phone: 528-2230　　　　　　　　Sat., 11:00 A.M.–3:00 A.M.
　　　　　　　　　　　　　　　　Sun., 11:00 A.M.–2:00 A.M.

Otto's makes a fine hamburger—chunky, moist, and filling. No special frills, but good quality meat and a chewy kaiser-type roll. It comes with fries and costs $2.35 ($2.50 with cheese).

There are tempting side dishes like corn on the cob (75¢), but don't be beguiled by the onion rings ($1.00), as they're disguised beneath breading. Otto's also makes good home-made soups ($1.00 for a big bowl) and chili with burgundy wine ($1.25).

Cozy pub atmosphere and pleasant summer beer garden. Mainly a young crowd.

Sauer's

311 E. 23rd Street
Phone: 225-6171

Daily, 11:00 A.M.–7:30 P.M.
Closed Sunday

A fat, round, perfectly charred hamburger wedged between two slices of rye! Excellent taste. The $2.25 price includes french fries and slaw. Good, potent barbecue sauce served on the side. The menu also includes a fine roast beef sandwich ($1.95) and an inexpensive daily special like Tuesday's pot roast, red cabbage, and potato dumplings ($2.10).

Everything's done smoothly in this mammoth, reconverted warehouse. Very popular for lunch, and just a few blocks from McCormick Place.

Set Back North Lounge

7228 Circle Ave.,
   Forest Park
Phone: 366-0805

Sun.-Thur., 10:00 A.M.–11:30 P.M.
Fri., Sat., 10:00 A.M.–12:30 A.M.

A knotty pine panelled tavern with a folksy small town feel. The hamburger they serve is their own special creation. Called Andy's Poor Boy, it's juicy ground sirloin topped with a layer of melted Swiss cheese, and sandwiched between garlic-buttered French bread. The taste is great and makes for a nice change. Its $3.25 price includes crinkle cut fries and a creamy slaw.

They also do a good Italian sausageburger ($2.95); it's crisp, chewy, and also served on French bread.

Topnotch Beefburger Shop

1822 W. 95th	Mon., Thur., Fri., 10:00 A.M.–8:00 P.M.
Phone: 447-7218	Tue., Wed., Sat., 10:00 A.M.–7:00 P.M.
	Closed Sunday

A really good, old-fashioned burger—juicy, unpretentious, no glitter (maybe, order some grilled onions and tomatoes), and made from roundsteak they grind right in their own kitchen. The cost is $1.75 for a king size (two thinnish, big patties) and 90¢ for a regular.

Be sure to get fries. They're done the old way, and taste just like the kind we used to gorge on after high school. And there's also a terrific homemade cubesteak, served on a buttery French roll ($1.30).

Hotdogs

Sorry, we had to draw the line somewhere. Though we know it's un-American, we just don't like hotdogs. We thought about having someone do our "research" for us, but ...

Anyway, if we do get the urge, we head for a beach refreshment stand (the hotdog's nothing special, but what great brown mustard) or a pushcart vendor (try the one at 32nd and Normal). Some true fans swear by Fluky's (6740 N. Western), Terry's (2721 W. Touhy), and Wolfy's (2734 W. Peterson). And we've got to admit that Chicago does make a superlative rendition—try getting one with celery salt and tomatoes in Oshkosh.

Italian Beef

Italian beef stands are a Chicago institution. They rank right behind taverns, funeral parlors, and hot dog stands in number. Beef places can usually be recognized by their seediness, garishness, or both. However, there are times when nothing tastes better than a juicy, dripping beef sandwich on soft French bread.

Beef stands offer three basics: plain beef sandwiches, Italian sausage sandwiches, and the real masterpiece, a beef and sausage combination, always referred to as a "combo." Also there is the option of adding sweet green peppers and/or a spoonful of hot pepper salad. The pepper salad can usually be found on the counter and is only for the iron-mouthed.

How can you recognize a superior sandwich? Look for juicy, paper-thin, sliced beef piled with abandon atop fresh bread. It should become soggier as you eat until it almost collapses. A good one always requires at least three napkins. The best sausage is barbecued rather than steamed, so that the outside skin is crisp and the meat spicy and succulent.

The following are some of the most pure Chicago:

Al's Bar BQ

1075 W. Taylor

Daily, 10:00 A.M.–1:00 A.M.
Fri., Sat., 10:00 A.M.–2:00 A.M.

Always crowded, open-air place (moves indoors in winter) across from Italian lemonade stand. Good, big, soggy sandwich. Huge, crisp, charcoal-broiled sausage. Lively place, lots of action. Beautiful example of pre-Circle Campus Taylor Street atmosphere.

Beef or Sausage: 85¢
Combo: $1.40

Carm's Bar-B-Q

804 S. Cicero   Daily, 7:00 A.M.–6:00 P.M.
Phone: 287-3930   Fri.-Sat., 8:00 A.M.–8:00 P.M.

Was for many years "the" beef stand—the one you traveled miles to get to at 11:00 on a Saturday night. Still a good sandwich. Not too spicy—lots of meat. Charcoaled sausage. Big, roomy, air conditioned. Classic beef stand atmosphere.
  Beef or sausage sandwich: 95¢
  Combo: $1.20
There's also Carm's #2 at 7101 W. Roosevelt in Berwyn, open until midnight every evening.

Margie's Bar-B-Q

1324 N. Cicero   Daily, 10:30 A.M.–12:45 A.M.
Phone: 378-9733   Fri., Sat., 10:30 A.M.–1:45 A.M.

One of the best beefs around. Very juicy—oodles of beef. Recently a few complaints about over-fatty meat, but the bread's chewy and just soggy enough. Charcoaled sausage. Cramped, no seating indoors, but nice, tree-shaded picnic tables outside.
  Beef or sausage: 90¢-95¢ (with peppers)
  Combo: $1.15-$1.20 (with peppers)

Mr. Beef

666 N. Orleans
Phone: 337-8500

Daily, 7:00 A.M.–6:00 P.M.
Fri., 7:00 A.M.–8:00 P.M.
Sat., 10:00 A.M.–2:00 P.M.

Best beef near the Loop; swamped at lunch. Peppery beef. Bread soaks in juice nicely. Clean, shiny, stand-up counter. Also enclosed picnic tables outside with good view of factories and traffic.

Beef: $1.25
Sausage: $1.00
Combo: $1.60

Napolitano Snack Shop

640 N. Damen
Phone: 226-9271

Hours vary, but not open evenings

More for meatball or sausage sandwiches than strictly beef. Sausage is barbecued crisp and topped by a light lather of tomato sauce. Fresh bread brought in daily from neighboring Gonnella bakery. Homemade hot pepper salad and lots of friendly conversation.

Beef or Sausage: $1.00
Meatball: $1.00

Roma's

(one of our favorites)

6161 N. Milwaukee
No phone

Daily, 11:00 A.M.–Midnight
Fri.-Sat., 11:00 A.M.–2:00 A.M.

Huge meat portions make this the biggest beef sandwich around. Also a generous slice of charcoal-broiled sausage. Moderately spicy. Excellent hot pepper salad, which is also for sale by the jar. Only beef stand with booths plus counter. Air-conditioned.

Beef or Sausage: $1.10
Combo: $1.40

Submarines

Submarine sandwiches range from the great and bountiful to those that should remain permanently submerged.

Among the former:

Capt'n Nemo's

7367 N. Clark
Phone: 973-0570

Daily, 11:00 A.M.–9:00 P.M.
Closed Sunday

A friendly, family-run operation. Everything's out on display, making it easy to select what looks good. The "Sea Farer's" our choice—scrumptious tuna salad, brick cheese, hard boiled egg, tomato and lettuce on French bread (two sizes: $1.15 and $1.70). Two other good ones: "Super cheese" with American, Swiss, brick, muenster and provolone ($1.50 and $2.30) and "Italian Swiss," mainly Italian hard salami and Swiss cheese ($1.50 and $2.90).

A different homemade soup each day and desserts, including eclairs and homemade cheesecake. Bright colors. Nautical look. A thoroughly nice place.

Fontano Brothers Super Mart

(one of our favorites)

1058 W. Polk St.
Phone: 226-8815

Mon.-Fri., 8:00 A.M.–7:00 P.M.
Sat., 8:00 A.M.–6:00 P.M.
Closed Sunday

In the back room of this busy Italian grocery, subs are laid out with a passion and flavor that rivals the best of Philadelphia's hoagie hangouts. Sink your teeth into the proscuittini, capicolla, provolone combine ($1.65). Meat is sliced just thin enough, everything's piled on thick, and all is topped by a spicy, marinated pepper/celery salad. The moist tuna and cheese ($1.40; $1.75) is no slouch either.

Heavy on local atmosphere—family photos, hanging cheeses, sacks of candy, and lots of yelling.

Grand Daddy Sandwich Shop

1324 W. Grand
Phone: 226-9648

Daily, 7:00 A.M.–4:00 P.M.
Sat., 8:00 A.M.–4:00 P.M.
Closed Sunday

Look for the painting of Popeye on the window to locate this fine sub stand. Fresh ingredients: lots of ham plus salami, swiss cheese, tomatoes, lettuce (shredded, but not the stringy kind), oregano, and oil. Excellent flavor, and prices are good too. Subs come in three sizes, priced at $1.00, $1.15, $1.50 and up. Run by a pleasant couple, their place also doubles as a small grocery store. A few tables. Brisk, fast-moving lunch business.

Jimmy's Sub Station

1203 W. Bryn Mawr   Daily, 10:00 A.M.–Midnight
Phone: 784-9151

Jimmy's bills itself as offering the "king of submarine sandwiches." While we wouldn't go that far, they do make a decent one. The main pluses: lots of meat, fresh bread, and herbs. Try the "little king sub" (ham, mortadella, salami, American cheese, and fine shredded lettuce, 95¢ and $1.60).

Mario's

1629 W. Grand   Daily, 8:00 A.M.–4:30 P.M.
Phone: 243-8695   Sat., 8:00 A.M.–4:00 P.M.
                                  Closed Sunday

Mario's is filled with dark booths, hanging coconut heads, pictures of the Blackhawks, and a poster depicting every one of Rocky Marciano's fights. A club-like and very Italian place.

The food may take second place, but not by much. A great sub is the "Mario special," stuffed with ham, mortadella, salami, provolone, lettuce, and tomato ($1.85). Also, spicy meatball sandwiches (95¢ and $1.55), Italian sausage (95¢ and $1.55), and on Fridays, pepper and egg ($1.10 and $1.60).

Millie's Sugar Bowl

1473 W. Grand Ave. Mon.-Sat., 8:00 A.M.–5:00 P.M.
Phone: 738-2274   Closed Sunday

Millie's should be a Chicago landmark. Spry, diminuitive, eighty-year-old Millie still handles all the slicing herself, mainly because she doesn't trust anyone else to do it. The going is slow, but the results are worth it. $1.15 buys three kinds of meat, provolone, a healthy sprinkling of oil and oregano, all piled compactly on fresh French bread. Subs go as low as 40¢ for a minced ham and American cheese.

While you wait, check out the goodies in Millie's combination grocery/school store—everything from jujubees to jacks to jumpropes.

Plumper's

3336 W. Bryn Mawr Daily, 11:00 A.M.–9:00 P.M.
Phone: 478-9440   Sat., 11:00 A.M.–7:30 P.M.
       Closed Sunday

Fresh-tasting, firmly-packed subs. We like the "Italian cold cuts" ($1.00; $1.95), three kinds of meat and provolone. Pluses: hollowing out of the sesame-studded bread, and lots of good options like brown mustard, horseradish, mouth-puckering pickles. Minuses: stringy, excelsior-like lettuce, and unpleasant-tasting tuna salad.

Run by graduates of neighboring Northeastern U. Very clean and spacious.

Vittori's

1132 W. Taylor
Phone: 733-6232
421-0194

Mon.-Sat., 8:00 A.M.–4:00 P.M.
Closed Sunday

Strictly carry-outs in this bustling family-run sandwich shop. Try the Burt special, an ample stack of Italian salami, ham, peppery proscuittini, provolone, romaine, lettuce, tomatoes, oil, and oregano, all stuffed into squeezably fresh bread. The whole thing goes for $1.30, and is easily one of the better subs around.

Muffuletta

The muffuletta is a New Orleans import closely related to the sub. What makes it different is the use of a round loaf of sesame-sprinkled bread, and a seasoning of marinated olive salad in place of lettuce, tomatoes, and oregano. Delicious stuff.

Vieux Carre

2271 N. Lincoln
Phone: 929-5220

Mon.-Thur., 11:00 A.M.–9:00 P.M.
Fri., Sat., 11:00 A.M.–11:00 P.M.

Vast variety of ingredients (regular ham, prosciutto, salami, swiss cheese, provolone, and olive salad), and a weighty price ($2.85), but one sandwich can easily feed two. Spicy, moist, and flavorful. Terrific bread from the Italian and French Bakery.

A few small tables where one can eat, relax, and watch the Lincoln Avenue parade.

Yellow Submarine

5971 N. Clark
Phone: 334-4339

Mon.-Sat., 11:00 A.M.–9:00 P.M.
Sun., 11:00 A.M.–8:00 P.M.

Fewer ingredients (ham, salami, provolone, olive salad), but they lay it on multi-layered and thick. The olive salad's crunchy and pungently spiced. Very filling and tasty. Sold by the whole ($2.30) and in halves ($1.20). Carry-outs only.

Tacos

The best and most authentic tacos can usually be found in corner groceries or small, funky snack shops, the kind with orange vinyl chairs and day-glo juke box. Possibilities for the filling are endless, everything from goat meat to guacamole. Tortilla shells are lightly tossed in oil rather than fried crisp. Drippiness, even downright greasiness, are part of their charm.

Armi-Day Foods
(one of our favorites)

835 W. Armitage
Phone: 549-9410

Daily, 9:30 A.M.–8:00 P.M.
Sun., 9:30 A.M.–5:00 P.M.

In our opinion, this little neighborhood grocery serves the best taco in town. All kinds of varieties from a 50¢ bean, on up. Try the super taco (90¢), two soft tortillas wrapped around a mountainous pile of beans, ground beef, onions, tomato, lettuce, cheese, hot sauce, and scrumptious guacamole. No way to eat one without having half of it drip out.

Azteca Tacos

1850 S. Blue Island

Hours vary

A tiny outdoor stand that hands out warm, beautifully sloppy tacos. A big plus is that the meat is shredded with a cleaver just prior to serving. Having one with "everything" means onions and hot sauce. The real thing, and only 55¢.

Azteca Tacos

1836 S. Blue Island   Sun.-Thur., 7:00 A.M.–11:00 P.M.
Phone: 666-3799   Fri., Sat., 24 hours

A full-service restaurant a few doors north of the like-named carry-out stand. All kinds of tacos, from cabeza (beef head) to chicharron (crackly pork rind) to chicken. Try the pastor, a pork/beef combine that is formed into a gyros-like loaf, charred crisp on a rotating grill, and then sliced. Perfectly juicy, greasy, and good.

A big, roomy place not unlike a Mexican bus station restaurant. Friendly staff. Tacos priced from 65¢ to 70¢.

Birria Tepatitlan

1832 S. Blue Island   Daily, 7:00 A.M.–9:00 P.M.
Phone: 733-4480

All types of tacos, but the specialty is birria, or goat meat. It tastes similar to lamb, is very moist, and need we say, unusual. Small dishes of hot sauce, chopped onions, and lime wedges are placed on tables for optional garnish. Tacos go for 70¢. No English is spoken.

Miscellaneous Sandwiches

Bungalow Inn

2835 N. Racine
Phone: 281-9829

Daily, 11:30 A.M.–10:00 P.M.
Closed Sunday

A pine-panelled German bar specializing in sausages and neat, open-face sandwiches. Good, thin-sliced, rare roast beef on rye ($1.85). Sausage sandwiches are $1.25 or you can have a bratwurst, knackwurst, or thueringer plate with sauerkraut and either a boiled potato or German potato salad ($2.10).

The B.A.R. Association

1224 W. Webster
Phone: 871-1440

Daily: 11:00 A.M.–1:00 A.M.

An intimate, romantic spot for sipping, sandwiches, and whatever else comes to mind. Excellent, though high-priced, is the cheese steak sandwich ($3.85) which combines slivered slices of tender beef, sauteed mushrooms, onions, and melted cheese on a French roll. Equally tasty is the tomato surprise ($2.95), a bubbly hot meld of tuna, tomato, mushrooms, and cheese. Good thick hamburgers too. All sandwiches come with an ample mound of deep fried, skin-intact potato chunks.

During the summer, all can be enjoyed in a pleasant, plant-laden outdoor patio.

Carlson's Deli

2113 W. Touhy
Phone: 761-1002

Mon.-Fri., 9:00 A.M.–7:00 P.M.
Sat., 9:00 A.M.–6:00 P.M.
Sun., 10:00 A.M.–6:00 P.M.

A whistle-clean Swedish deli that has to serve the best carry-out ham and cheese in town. Mild, thin-sliced ham is placed between thick layers of cheese, and spliced between two fresh slabs of rye. The result is at least six inches thick, just moist enough, and goes for $1.05.

While you wait, browse through neatly displayed boxes of Swedish pancake mix and blueberry soup mix, tinned sardines, and cloudberry preserves. Last time here a blond, blue-eyed little girl carefully dusted the shelves with a broom fashioned from twigs.

Continental Delight

3757 W. Fullerton
Phone: 277-4646

Mon.-Sat., 9:00 A.M.–8:00 P.M.
Sun., 9:00 A.M.–2:00 P.M.

A sunny, cheerful deli that must be a haven for every kind of sausage ever made. Many can be ordered and eaten sandwich style in an adjoining room. Particularly delectable is the thick, juicy knackwurst ($1.65). There's also thueringer, Polish sausage and kraut, and ham and cheese. Nice salads, too, including a tart coleslaw and an unusual-tasting German potato salad. Good fresh rye bread, and fresh-baked pastries, for dessert.

The Falafel King
(one of our favorites)*

4507 W. Oakton, Skokie
Phone: 679-9219

Daily, 11:00 A.M.–10:00 P.M.
Closed from Friday at sundown
until Saturday at sundown

An Israeli answer to Burger King. Crisp falafel balls (deep-fried, mashed chick peas and spices) are stuffed into hollowed-out pita bread along with lettuce, tomato, and tahini (sesame) sauce. It tastes great and is nutritious besides. Cost is $1.10 for a regular falafel and 65¢ for a mini-version. Also shish kabob ($1.50), shawirma (similar to gyros, $1.50), and kifti kabob (ground spiced meat, $1.15). The owner grinds his own meat and everything tastes fresh.

Garden Gyros

2621 N. Clark
Phone: 935-3100

Daily, 11:00 A.M.–Midnight
Fri.-Sat., 11:00 A.M.–2:00 A.M.

Although everybody's making gyros, Garden Gyros does that and more. Their menu includes a variety of Mediterranean sandwiches, all served in pocketed pita bread. There's falafel ($1.45), oregano-spiced kifta kabob ($2.00), and a good hamburger covered with sauteed onions, mushrooms, and green peppers ($2.35).

The owner is Turkish and his repertoire also includes home-made yogurt and a good, gooey baklava.

Hemingway's Moveable Feast

1825 N. Lincoln
Phone: 943-6225

Mon.-Fri., 10:00 A.M.–11:00 P.M.
Sat., 8:30 A.M.–11:00 P.M.
Sun., 8:30 A.M.–9:00 P.M.

Chicago's longest list of carry-out sandwiches—127 different kinds. Quality varies, and the place could be cleaner. Try good, hefty #66—lox, chive cream cheese, onion, and tomato on a bagel ($1.75) and #67, gefilte fish, horseradish (watch out), tomato, and onion on an onion roll ($1.50). And if you'd like smoked shark meat and cream cheese on whole wheat ($2.45), they've got it. Rattlesnake, too.

Link's Family Circle Deli

5157 W. Addison
Phone: 777-4777

Daily, 10:00 A.M.–6:00 P.M.
Sun., 10:00 A.M.–5:00 P.M.

A gorgeous, gleaming grocery/deli that serves a variety of hot and cold sandwiches. Cold is better (the hot are liable not to be hot enough), especially the ham ($1.25) or roast beef ($1.25) on chewy Rosen's rye.

Choice of several good side salads (19¢ each), including a tangy German potato salad and a firm, fresh cole slaw.

There's one long table on which to park everything. Free coffee, and occasionally, cheese spreads.

Muencher Hof

3700 N. Clark   Sun., Tue.-Thur., Noon–Midnight
Phone: 248-1624   Fri., Noon–2:00 A.M.
                       Sat., 11:00 A.M.–3:00 A.M.

A soulful, family-run German tavern that serves hearty snacks and sandwiches. Try the juicy, crisp-crusted German hamburger ($2.50). It comes breadless, topped with fried onions, and served with sides of red cabbage and German potato salad. There's also thueringer or knackwurst with kraut (each $2.50).

On the sandwich side are an excellent ham and cheese on rye ($1.95) and Hungarian salami ($1.95).

New York Style Pizza

5047 N. Lincoln   Lincoln Ave. hours:
Phone: 334-4499   Tue.-Thur., 11:00 A.M.–Midnight
914½ Noyes, Evanston   Fri.-Sat., 11:00 A.M.–1:00 A.M.
Phone: 864-9400   Sun., 4:00 P.M.–Midnight
                       Closed Monday
                       Evanston hours:
                       Tues.-Thur., 4:00 P.M.–Midnight
                       Fri., Sat., Sun., 11:00 A.M.–
                           Midnight

New York Style brags about making the world's worst pizza (it doesn't), but it might just make the world's best "wedge." Mainly, because we've never tasted another. A wedge tastes something like grilled pizza on French bread and is in reality a grilled submarine. Try the "vegetarian" (mushrooms, onions, peppers, tomatoes, cheese, and tomato sauce) or the "sundance" (sausage, pepperoni, onions, peppers, and cheese). Good eating for $1.40.

Note: A wedge by any other name (at least in Chicago) is a grinder and delicious versions can be found at Eastern Style Pizza p. 221 and Chicago Pizza and Oven Grinder p. 220.

Resi's Bierstube

(one of our favorites)

2034 W. Irving Park
Phone: 472-1749

Daily, 2:00 P.M.–2:00 A.M.
Sat., 2:00 P.M.–3:00 A.M.
Closed Monday

A cozy German bar serving fantastic sandwiches and sausages. Open face ham and Swiss cheese on delicious "Cicero" rye ($1.45) can't be beat. Fattest, juiciest thueringer ever, plus German fries ($2.25). Good bratwurst too ($2.25). Dark German mustard and horseradish are the condiments.

On weekends, however, the most popular dish is hackepeter (raw ground sirloin, topped with chopped onions, $1.95). One night the man next to us ate five orders.

Steins of Dortmunder for 55¢, and soft pretzels (25¢). Very friendly. Very German. Outdoor beer garden.

Richard's

7505 W. Madison,
Forest Park
Phone: 366-4977

Mon.-Fri., 11:30 A.M.–1:00 A.M.
Sat., 11:30 A.M.–2:00 A.M.
Closed Sunday

Over twenty sandwiches offered, including eleven varieties of cheese (this is the place to get limburger).

A good meaty choice is the Snoopy Le Baron de Beef ($2.00), similar to a reuben, but with roast beef and cole slaw rather than corned beef and kraut. Also tasty is the Monte-Cristo-like grilled ham and cheese ($1.95) and a hamburger smothered with baked beans and cheese ($2.10). Crisp, tasty, crinkle-cut fries accompany all.

Sarah's

(one of our favorites)

447 W. 26th   Tue.-Sat., 7:00 A.M.–6:00 P.M. or 6:30 P.M.
  (at Canal)   Closed Sunday & Monday
No phone

The best place in town for a breaded steak sandwich (a juicy, crisp-around-the-edges, tender cutlet) lathered with tomato sauce and peppers, and served on french bread. It's $1.50 and worth every bite. 50¢ less will buy a golden, crackly eggplant sandwich. There are pizza slices (30¢) too, if you get there early enough; and sometimes there are delicious, deep-fried, sugar-sprinkled crullers formed from pizza dough.

What's even better is the atmosphere. Friendly camaraderie, lots of talk, and loads of warmth.

La Victoria

2557 N. Milwaukee   Daily, 8:30 A.M.–8:00 P.M.
Phone: 489-5171   Sun., 9:00 A.M.–4:00 P.M.

A nice little grocery that serves Cuban sandwiches (cubanos, $1.00). Gonella bread is sliced at an angle, filled with paper thin layers of ham, pork, and Swiss cheese, then pressed on a grill. The result is toasty bread and a just barely warm filling. A mild and tasty snack.

Snacks

Chili

What better to sink into on a chilly afternoon or evening than a hot, spicy bowl of chili. The following offer an excellent warm-up:

Bishop's Chili Hut

1958 W. 18th   Mon.-Sat., 9:00 A.M.–7:30 P.M.
Phone: 829-6345   Closed Sunday
7220 W. Roosevelt   Mon.-Sat., 9:00 A.M.–1:00 A.M.
Phone: 366-4421   Sun., Noon–9:00 P.M.
20 W. Cass, Westmont   Mon.-Thur., 9:00 A.M.–10:00 P.M.
Phone: 852-5974   Fri., Sat., 9:00 A.M.–Midnight
                                 Sun., Noon–9:00 P.M.

The place to go for chili and chili mac. 90¢ a bowl, and lots of oyster crackers and hot pepper sauce on the side, though the chili's pretty peppy on its own. Wash it down with a stein of beer. Casual, friendly places. Also, chili to go (fresh or frozen).

RR Western Restaurant and Lounge

56 W. Madison   Daily, 11:00 A.M.–3:00 A.M.
Phone: 263-8207

Something different. A cowboy bar in downtown Chicago featuring country music (after 8:00 P.M.) and thirty variations of chili and chili-based sandwiches. It's darker than a side street inside, but once you adjust there's much to see—a vast gun display, bleached steerskulls, ten gallon hats, etc.

The basic chili ($1.00) and chili mac ($1.19) are thick and spicy, and there are also more far-flung variations like chili mac cheese tamale ($2.25) and chili perch (ugh!).

Bucket of Suds

(one of our favorites)

3123 N. Cicero   Daily, 11:00 A.M.–1:00 P.M.;
Phone: 283-9485   4:00 P.M.–1:00 A.M.

One of our all-timers, the Bucket not only displays a staggering collection of liquor (over 600 different kinds) but is presided over by Joe Danno, easily one of our town's more unique characters. Good-humored and friendly, with a voice something like W.C. Fields, he quotes Euripides, has a phenomenal knowledge of jazz, and will concoct a special drink to fit either your mood or personality.

Food is incidental, but it's good, especially the smooth-tasting chili. Robust, filling, and not overly spicy, it can be fired up further with his own special hot sauce. Delicious, thin-crust pizza and bountiful cheese plates too.

A funky place, and always fun!

Sheehan's Chili Bowl

1065 W. Argyle   Daily, 10:30 A.M.–6:00 P.M.
Phone: 334-5333   Sat., 11:00 A.M.–8:00 P.M.
                                                 Closed Sunday

Grandchild of the original downtown Sheehan's which goes back to the 1890s. Present owner is a third generation chili man, and uses the original family recipe. It's good, spicy stuff, more soupy than thick, and very cheap and filling. Three versions—plain, chili mac, and chili tamale—go for 75¢. Refills are 50¢. Peppery and potent.

Fish Houses

Chicago may not have the fresh oyster and clam bars or the outdoor crabmeat cocktail stands of coastal cities (wouldn't it be nice), but we do have some good little places to get seafood. These fisheries range from riverfront shacks to the big and shiny. Besides selling fish (fresh, frozen, and smoked) for home-eating, many offer short-order carry-out snacks, primarily deep-fried fish chips and shrimp.

Ben's Shrimp House

(Around) 1049 W. North Ave.
Phone: 337-0263

Tue.-Thur., 11:00 A.M.–
   10:30 P.M.
Fri., 11:00 A.M.–Midnight
Sat., 11:00 A.M.–2:30 A.M.
Sun., Noon–11:30 P.M.

A good little riverfront place serving sizzling hot, nugget-sized fish chips in a brown paper bag. Fresh taste; not too heavy breading.

Fish chips—$2.20 (per lb.)
Shrimp—$5.00 (per lb.)

The Fish House

530 N. Wells
Phone: 642-4158

Daily, 8:00 A.M.–6:00 P.M.
Fri., 8:00 A.M.–7:00 P.M.
Closed Sunday

You need a number here around lunchtime. The place can be packed. Fish chips are nice and crisp, but the coating is a little heavy. For a bargain lunch, try the perch sandwich on a french roll (75¢). The french fried mushrooms (50¢) are an added treat literally exploding in your mouth. Good shrimp too.

Fish chips—$2.10 (per lb.)
Shrimp—$4.40 (per lb.)

J. K. Anderson & Son Fish

2701 S. Ashland
Phone: 847-9386

Mon., Tue., 9:00 A.M.–Midnight
Wed.-Sat., 9:00 A.M.–2.00 A.M.
Sun., Noon–Midnight

A nice little southside fish shack perched along the river, which offers crisp, nearly greaseless nuggets of bargain-priced french fried shrimp. Fish chips vary from flaky to over-soft. Try the mild barbecue-like sauce—it's really good.

Fish chips—$1.90 (per lb.)
Shrimp—$3.60 (per lb.)

Joe's Fisheries

1438 W. Cortland
Phone: 278-8990

Mon.-Thur., 7:00 A.M.–Midnight
Fri.-Sun.: Open continuously till
midnight Sunday

Another riverfront hideaway serving some of the best, meatiest shrimp around. They're medium-sized, and you get a generous amount. Fairly light breading, not greasy. Good, big fish chips too. A popular late-hours place.

Joe's is kind of hard to find. Cortland runs parallel to Armitage (1900 north.)

Fish chips—$2.20 (per lb.)
Shrimp—$4.50 (per lb.)

Lawrence Fisheries

2120 S. Canal
Phone: 225-2113

Daily, 24 hrs.
Closed holidays

A big, clean carry-out place picturesquely perched beside factories, railroad tracks, and the river. A versatile menu: fish chips, oysters, shrimp, clams, and froglegs. The oysters are especially delicious and cooked to order. Excellent fish chips too.

Fish chips—$2.10 (per lb.)
Shrimp—$4.10 (per lb.)
Oysters—$3.40 (per lb.)
Froglegs—$3.30 (per lb.)
Clams—(prepackaged—$1.35 for a box dinner with french fries, slaw, and roll)

Juice Bars

Getting juiced is not too difficult as the city has some fine fruit juice bars, some as convenient as your local commuter train station or local grocery store.

Garden Food Products

Illinois Central Station   Mon.-Sat., 7:30 A.M.–9:15 P.M.
  (Michigan and Randolph)   Sun., 10:00 A.M.–7:00 P.M.

A hidden oasis for commuters and shoppers. Nestled inconspicuously in the IC station, Garden Food Products offers a staggering variety of juices. Twenty-one flavors in all: guava, mango, black cherry, coconut, passion fruit, apricot, raspberry, strawberry, and more. Exotic combinations too, like Bango Bongo (coconut, mango, and strawberry) and Ol' Smoothie (banana and red cherry). Prices are also smooth. 30¢ for 5 oz.; 40¢ for 8 oz.; and 50¢ for 10 oz. A great place.

Kramer's Health Food

31 W. Adams   Mon.-Sat., 9:30 A.M.–6:30 P.M.
Phone: 922-0077   Closed Sunday

A bustling downtown health food store that has a tiny juice bar and a grumpy waitress. But soothe yourself anyway by sipping raspberry juice (60¢), coconut milk (60¢), a Tahiti cream (coconut milk and banana juice, 95¢), or a Velvet Nectar (raspberry juice, coconut milk, and ice cream, 95¢). There's even a Van Johnson—fresh bananas, pineapple juice, wheat germ oil, tiger's milk, egg, and honey—for $1.50; and guaranteed to give you freckles.

Punch Bowl

Marshall Field and Co.   Daily, 11:00 A.M.–5:30 P.M.
Randolph and State   Closed Sunday

The waiting room is no more, but luckily the Punch Bowl remains. There are only six flavors offered, but the raspberry-coconut milk combination (45¢) can't be beat.

Sherwyn's Health Food Shop

642½ W. Diversey   Mon.-Sat., 9:00 A.M.–8:00 P.M.
Phone: None   Sun., 9:00 A.M.–2:00 P.M.
  (at this writing)

A new and welcome New Town juice bar. Possibilities include combos like carrot and celery; apple and strawberry; and pineapple and coconut. Prices range from 45¢ for a small apple juice up to $1.80 for a Power Lifter (apple juice, wheat germ, lecithin, protein powder, egg, and honey.)

Sandwiches too, such as avocado and alfalfa sprouts on whole wheat or carrots, cukes, and zucchini on soy/millet bread. No gyros!

Treasure Island Food Marts

1639 N. Wells
Phone: 642-1105
3460 N. Broadway
Phone: 327-3880
5221 N. Broadway
Phone: 769-3536
2540 W. Lawrence
Phone: 271-8711

Mon.-Fri., 8:00 A.M.–9:00 P.M.
Sat., 8:00 A.M.–7:00 P.M.
Sun., 9:00 A.M.–5:00 P.M.

Treasure Island does have everything, including a natural fruit juice bar. A great boost for the harried and relaxed shopper alike. The papaya juice is delicious, and you can concoct your own blend, perhaps strawberry and banana. Cost is 53¢ for a 7 oz. glass and 63¢ for a 9 oz. glass.

Ice Cream Parlors

Despite the popularity of fast service, multiflavor franchises, Chicago still has a fine sampling of old fashioned ice cream parlors. Filled with nostalgia, some of these places haven't changed much since the days of Dobie Gillis, Oogie Pringle, and Judy. Often run by the same family for generations, everything just seems to taste better and richer in these parlors. Probably because most of them still make their own ice cream, toppings, and, sometimes, even whipped cream.

Hopefully, the "real" ice cream parlor will be around for a long time. Here are some great places to indulge:

The Buffalo

4000 W. Irving Park
Phone: 725-9488

Daily, 10:30 A.M.–Midnight
Fri., Sat., 10:30 A.M.–1:00 A.M.
Sun., 11:00 A.M.–Midnight

Nearly another casualty of the oil crisis, The Buffalo was almost doomed to be replaced by a Shell station. Luckily, good sense and community action prevailed and the Buffalo stands, unmolested. At least for another three years.

It's such a grand looking place: heavy wooden booths, mirrors, stained glass, tile floor, and flowery murals of frolicking cherubs. The ice cream is as rich as the decor. Sundaes come with at least two big scoops, a lavish dollop of hand-beaten whipped cream, and Nabiscos. Some add chopped nuts and bananas.

Try a hot fudge with the works (pecans and bananas, $1.35), a caramel walnut sundae ($1.35), or a hot fudge marshmallow ($1.35). Also good are the fresh (frozen) strawberry or raspberry sundaes (95¢). Very chocolately chocolate sodas (90¢) and thick shakes and malts (85¢).

A great place for ice cream, but expect to wait in line and maybe sit in the modern adjoining room, especially in the summer.

A second Buffalo opened recently at 6000 W. Dempster, Morton Grove (Phone: 966-2426).

Crystal Palace

Marshall Field & Co. Tue., Wed., Fri., Sat., 11:30 A.M.–
Randolph & State   5:30 P.M.
              Mon. & Thur., 11:30 A.M.–6:30 P.M.
              Closed Sunday

Although we truly miss all the ladies with their shopping bags, the loungers, the weirdos, and everyone else who liked to hang out at Field's third floor waiting room, the ice cream parlor that has usurped its place is certainly a beauty. It's pure 1890s fantasy: muted cotton candy walls, mirrors, stained glass, plants.

The ice cream manages to equal the setting's lavish opulence. Try any of the frango mint concoctions—sundae ($1.10), soda, malt or milkshake ($1.20 each). They're scrumptious. Or better yet, have hot fudge over frango mint ice cream ($1.10). The sundae's small but it packs power: smooth creamy ice cream and fudge thick enough to hold up a spoon.

Almost as self-indulgent is the English toffee pice (95¢), toffee ice cream folded into a graham cracker crust, sprinkled with a crunchy brittle of almonds and crumbled toffee.

Dr. Jazz

1607 W. Montrose
Phone: 525-9560

Summer hours:
(June-Sept.)
    Daily, 7:00 P.M.–Midnight
    Fri., 4:00 P.M.–1:00 A.M.
    Sat., 1:00 P.M.–1:00 A.M.
    Sun., 1:00 P.M.–Midnight
Non-summer hours:
    Daily, 7:00 P.M.—11:00 P.M.
    Fri.-Sat., 7:00 P.M.–1:00 A.M.
    Sun., 1:00 A.M.–11:00 P.M.

Success has spoiled Dr. Jazz somewhat, but it's still a dazzler—combination fun house, antique store, and fantasy trip. The booths are candy apple red, hanging ceiling fans whir, antique toys, and amusement park games are everywhere, not to mention two musical marvels (a machine, the PianOrchestrion, that plays thirteen instruments at once and another, the violano, that is an amazing marriage of violin and piano.) Silent movies too, at 8:00, 9:00, and 10:00 P.M.

With all this, who needs ice cream? But it's here and excellent (not homemade, even though prices are far from old-fashioned. Terrific sodas ($1.10), big sundaes ($1.45), and the best peanut butter milk shake ($1.25) in town. Green River floats (99¢) and a fresh orange cream (fresh orange juice blended with ice cream, $1.10) too.

Really packed on weekends. And there's a second Dr. Jazz at 1913 Chicago in Evanston.

Gayety Ice Cream Parlor

(one of our favorites)

9207 S. Commercial
Phone: 734-8867

Daily, 9:00 A.M.–10:00 P.M.

The days of hanging out at the soda shop after school are long gone, but the Gayety still looks like the place where it happened. Even though most of their business is now carry-out, the flavor isn't gone—especially of the ice cream. It's homemade, so are the toppings and even the whipped cream.

Sundaes, among them a fresh-tasting raspberry, maplenut, and caramel nut are 95¢. Sodas and shakes (try a banana shake) are 95¢ and a hot fudge split is $1.15. Ice cream cones are 25¢.

The owner barks orders at his young workers, who should be applauded for dishing out fantastic concoctions in the smallest work space imaginable. Carry-out orders are huge and slightly higher-priced.

Ideal Candy Shop

(one of our favorites)

3311 N. Clark
Phone: 327-2880

Mon.-Sat., 11:00 A.M.–9:30 P.M.
Sun., 11:00 A.M.–5:00 P.M.
Closed Tuesday

Located at the same Clark Street address for some forty years, Ideal still retains the appearance and personal feeling of the past. Elaborately wrapped, rainbow-colored boxes of candy, all-day suckers, neat rows of rich chocolates, and stuffed toys hold reign. But you can still dig into ice cream at the tiny counter in the back. Good homemade hot fudge and hot butterscotch splits (85¢). Although Ideal doesn't make its own ice cream, good, creamy Highlanders is used. Regular sundaes are 60¢ and sodas are 55¢. Malts and milk shakes come in three sizes—heavy, extra heavy, and super heavy (60¢–90¢–$1.10). They also make the best caramel apples (30¢) around, sticky with thick homemade caramel, and a fantastic nut brittle.

It's a neat little place, with memories enough to carry you right back to the summer of '36.

Gertie's Ice Cream Parlor

(one of our favorites)

5858 S. Kedzie
Phone: 737-7634

Daily, 10:30 A.M.–11:00 P.M.
Fri.-Sat., 10:30 A.M.–11:30 P.M.

The oldest of our ice cream parlors (1901) and a great one. Quality is superlative. In season, they make a fresh strawberry soda that is the real thing—lots of big, fresh strawberry halves ($1.00). A great strawberry sundae ($1.10) too.

Regular sundaes and sodas are $1.00, but we like to splurge a little with a caramel or banana milkshake ($1.10), hot fudge sundae with pecans ($1.25), or tin roof sundae (Dutch chocolate sauce and peanuts, $1.35). Also, there are fancier sundaes with valentine names like Lover's Delight ($1.25) and Sweet Sixteen ($1.25).

An old time, comfortable place with plush, purple-cushioned booths and some of the biggest, gaudiest stuffed animals this side of Riverview. The owner can be a little gruff, but his homemade ice cream is wonderful. It's available for carry-out at $1.15 a quart, and flavors include fresh banana, peppermint, and maple-walnut.

Margie's Candies

(one of our favorites)

Corner of Armitage & Western   Daily, 7:00 A.M.–1:30 A.M.
Phone: 384-1035

Run by a pleasantly eccentric woman, Margie's makes what have to be the most generous hot fudge and hot caramel sundaes around. The superb homemade sauces are served separately in silver containers, and there's not only enough topping to thoroughly cover your ice cream, but some left over to eat by itself. A luxury for 95¢.

Fruit sundaes, peach, raspberry, and banana, cost 95¢, and so do Boston sodas. Margie also claims the world's largest sundae ($5.00). Ice cream's from Highlander, but the whipped cream is homemade.

Margie's is filled with a profusion of stuffed animals, plastic flowers, and plants, and has stood on the same corner since 1925. It's not a beauty, but what fantastic sundaes!

Peacock's Dairy Bar

626 Davis, Evanston   Daily: 11:00 A.M.–Mid-
Phone: 864-4904   night
100 Skokie Boulevard, Wilmette   Sat., 11:00 A.M.–
Phone: 251-4141   12:30 A.M.

Peacock's makes eighteen flavors (including green mint, cinnamon, chocolate almond, coconut, and, in summer, a fabulous fresh peach) of incredibly rich ice cream. Any flavor may be used in their sodas ($1.35) and sundaes ($1.35). A good place for a coffee soda with coffee ice cream. There are creme de menthe, black raspberry, and burgundy cherry sundaes, as well as a very generous hot fudge. Cooling raspberry or pineapple fruit freezes for $1.05.

Peacock's is big, bright, and airy, and serves sandwiches too.

Italian Lemonade

When the discomfort index starts moving above 80°, there's not much to do besides moan, sit in a bathtub, air-conditioned closet, or have an Italian lemonade. If you opt for the latter, it's a slushy mixture of fresh chopped lemon (peels and all), smoothly crushed ice, and sugar. Good lemonade is made on the spot in a special Italian lemonade machine (although as the old machines break down, places are switching to soft ice cream machines, with good results).

Lemonade stands open and close with the robins and the Cubs. You can generally count on finding at least one in business from early April til early October. Prices of lemonade go up according to size, and can range from 10¢ to $2.75 for a gallon (to keep in the freezer for emergencies.)

Lemonade stands generally open at around ten in the morning and stay open til at least ten at night (later, if weather's hot.) Although there aren't many real lemonade stands left, here are a few good ones:

Carm's

1057 W. Polk

Good, very smooth lemonade at this little Taylor Street-area stand. They also dish out beef sandwiches and subs. They'll stay open at least til midnight if it's good and hot out. Usually crowded on a summer evening.

Mario and Donna's
(one of our favorites)

1068 W. Taylor

Not far from Carm's, this tiny stand is a classic. They only serve lemonade and sno-cones. Very icy-textured lemonade made in an old machine. They add flavors here and the lemonade with fresh watermelon, peach, or cantaloupe chunks is indescribably good. Interesting street scene and tortilla factory next door.

Mattioli Brothers

206 W. 15th, Chicago Heights

A smooth, more solid fruit-ice-like lemonade that fulfills all flavor fantasies. The list is endless—blueberry, peach, watermelon, mango, strawberry, raspberry, apple-cinnamon, pistachio, coconut, rum-raisin. Pieces of real fruit are used and it tastes it. Even better, they're open all year!

ITALIAN LEMONADE

Romano's

(one of our favorites)

1136 W. Armitage

Great lemonade—smooth, usually lots of lemon chunks, good flavor. Romano's is probably our favorite. Recently switched to the new machine, but the product is just as good. They also sell Italian beef sandwiches, etc.

Tito's

1901 S. California

In a hidden corner of Chicago (underneath some railroad tracks)—a family-run trio of businesses: lemonade stand, beef and sausage stand, and open-air fresh fruit set-up. Picnic tables too. If the lemonade were bad (and it isn't), this place would be worth coming to for atmosphere alone. It's neighborhood Chicago at its best.

Pastry and Coffee

Cafe Pergolisi

3404 N. Halsted
Phone: 472-8602

Mon., 5:00 P.M.–1:00 A.M.
Fri.-Sat., 5:00 P.M.–2:00 A.M.
Sunday brunch: 10:00 A.M.–3:00 P.M.
Closed Tue., Wed., and Thur.

Among the last of a vanishing breed. A subdued coffee house in the classic tradition—espresso machines, chess sets, lots of conversation, and classical music. A place to relax and enjoy.

Coffee (espresso, cappuccino, mocha, anise, etc.), tea (fourteen different kinds, including gunpowder and sassafras), and delicious hot chocolate (try the mint chocolate for a real treat). Also, cinnamon cider, lemonade, tamarindo with lemon, and more. Prices range from 40¢ to a $1.00.

The primary pastry is a good, sticky cheesecake ($1.00). Interesting, but doll-sized sundaes ($1.20-$1.50). But where else could you find kumquat sauce?

Cafe Bellini

2913 N. Clark
Phone: 935-8010

Daily, 5:00 P.M.–1:00 A.M.

A very European, very romantic refuge for elaborate coffee and pastry. Waiters wear tuxedos, and lush plants and opera fill the room.

Splurge on such multi-caloric highs as a twelve-layer dobosh torte ($1.00), chocolate rum torte ($1.00), or baba a rum ($1.00). Some sound more extravagant than they taste, but sip along caffe chocolaccino (espresso, creme de cacao, milk, and a cinnamon stick, $1.30) or caffe mocha java (flavored with rum, marshmallow, and cocoa, $1.30), and you'll scarcely notice.

There's also a secluded outdoor garden. A perfect place for an affair, or to fantasize about one.

Kenessey Gourmet Internationale

403 W. Belmont
Phone: 929-7500
Parking: Free with
   doorman at Belmont Hotel

Daily, 11:00 A.M.–11:00 P.M.
Sat., 11:00 A.M.–Midnight
Sun., Noon–9:00 P.M.

Display case stocked with dark chocolate tortes (65¢), eclairs filled with either custard or whipped cream (85¢), cherry, cheese, poppyseed, and apple strudels (85¢), lemon cream rolls (95¢), apricot turnovers (55¢), almond crescents (85¢), and much more. A beautiful sight. Delicious eating. Excellent coffee (45¢), espresso (75¢), cappuccino ($1.00), hot chocolate with whipped cream (70¢), and Kenessey's special (coffee with brandy or rum, $2.50).

Small tables set up so you can leisurely savor it all. No place for a diet; but a great spot to break one. Carry-outs, also.

Downstairs is a gourmet grocery, cheese, and wine cellar. Good, but slightly expensive, open-face sandwiches. Taste their special whipped Hungarian cream cheese.

Lutz's

2454 W. Montrose
Phone: 478-7785

Tues.-Sun., 11:00 A.M.–10:00 P.M.
Closed Monday

A most proper German cafe, serving very exuberant pastries. 75¢ will buy a lovely light whipped cream torte: rich chocolate dobosh, sacher, schwarzwalder cherry, brandy trifle, etc. Our favorites, however, are the fruit kuchens, especially the fresh plum (available in fall only). The rich dough is loaded with fruit, and tastes unbelievably good.

Expensive sandwiches and fancy sundaes also available. In summer, dine outdoors in a beautiful flowered patio.

Don't plan on Lutz's unless you have nothing to lose, because even the coffee's served with whipped cream.

Carry-outs available, in bustling front room.

Pizza

We think Chicago has the best pizza in the United States. In fact we've never had a pizza outside these environs that could even compare with Chicago's second rate places. And being pizza freaks, don't think we haven't tried. In recent years, thick crust pizza in the pan has more or less taken over thin crust turf. The following list, though far from exclusive, includes the best of both. Because of a variety of sizes and ingredients, prices given, where applicable, are for large cheese and sausage pizza.

Chicago Pizza and Oven Grinder Co.

2121 N. Clark
Phone: 248-2570

Daily, 4:00 P.M.–Midnight
Fri., 4:00 P.M.–2:00 A.M.
Sat., Noon–2:00 A.M.
Sun., Noon–Midnight

Not a pizza for purists—more like a pot pie. Pizza sold by the pound at $3.25 per pound (a one-pounder feeds one person but a two-pounder feeds two to three). Excellent sauce made with plum tomatoes, lots of mild cheese, sausage, peppers, onions, and whole fresh mushrooms. Good crust, good quality, but keeps getting higher-priced. Fantastic grinders ($3.50)—glorified baked submarine sandwiches featuring meatballs, sausage, ham, or salami with tomato sauce, melted cheese, and trimmings. Also great mountainous salads. Several Italian wines available. Somewhat pretentious but attractive place, catering to a young crowd. Often a wait. No carry-outs.

Eastern Style Pizza

2911 W. Touhy
Phone: 761-4070
465-9659

Daily, 11:30 A.M.–Midnight
Fri.-Sat., 11:30 A.M.–1:00 A.M.
Sunday, 4:00 P.M.–Midnight

This is the home of the pizza with everything. Your $3.20 will buy a super pizza (serves 2) that has to be eaten to be understood. A medium-thick, crisp crust is showered with pepperoni, sausage, salami, bacon, meatballs, shrimp, mushrooms, peppers, onions, anchovies (optional), and, of course, cheese. If this doesn't sound intriguing you can always opt for a plain mushroom, sausage, or any of the above ($2.20). Also home of the original grinders. They also make a terrific tuna fish sub. Carry-outs only.

There's also an Eastern Style in Niles at the Golf Mill Shopping Center (827-0193).

Gino's East
(one of our favorites)

160 E. Superior
Phone: 943-1127 (upstairs)
943-1124 (downstairs)

Daily, 11:00 A.M.–1:00 A.M.
Fri., 11:00 A.M.–1:30 A.M.
Sat., 11:00 A.M.–3:00 A.M.
Sun., 4:00 P.M.–1:30 A.M.

There's good pizza in the pan right off Michigan Ave. Best thing about Gino's offering is the outstanding crust—flaky, crisp, never doughy, delicious. The extra ingredients (like the sausage) are chopped fine, so that the whole topping kind of melts in together. $6.10 for a large cheese and sausage. Carry-outs available. Tasty.

Two places to indulge: upstairs—plush, chandeliered, and filled with businessmen; downstairs—dark and collegiate, lots of young medical students. Apt to be crowded, even during the day.

Giordano's

(one of our favorites)

6253 S. California
Phone: 436-2969

Mon., Wed., Thur., Fri., 4:00 P.M.–
12:30 A.M.
Fri., Sat., 4:00 P.M.–1:30 A.M.
Closed Tuesday

A spectacular pizza. It's almost like a souffle—high, puffy, and cheesy. The crust is crisp; nothing overpowers anything else and each bite tastes as good as the one before it. A medium cheese and sausage goes for $5.50, and it's big.

The setting's kind of close and grim, but the waitress is nice, and once the pizza comes, you won't notice anything else.

Family Corner

2901 W. Devon
Phone: 262-2854

Sun.-Thur., 11:00 A.M.–11:00 P.M.
Fri., Sat., 11:00 A.M.–1:00 A.M.

Would you believe Indian pizza? It's actually very tasty, curry- rather than oregano-spiced, and an answer to a vegetarian's prayers. Possible toppings include broccoli, cauliflower, bean sprouts, mushrooms, eggplant, green pepper, onions, bamboo shoots, peas, potatoes, and water chestnuts.

The thin, fluted crust has a delicate texture reminiscent of nan, a flat Indian bread. Vegetables have a clear, crunchy flavor, although there could be more of them. The tomato sauce is light; the cheese abundant. For $4.95 (a large), it's definitely worth a try. Extra vegetables cost 50¢ to 95¢ extra. Spiced tea (50¢) goes with nicely.

Golden Crust Pizzeria

4620 N. Kedzie
Phone: 539-5860

Daily, 11:00 A.M.–1:00 A.M.
Fri., 11:00 A.M.–2:00 A.M.
Sat., 4:00 P.M.–2:00 A.M.
Sun., 2:00 P.M.–Midnight

An old-fashioned neighborhood pizza parlor where they still move pizzas in and out of the oven with flat wooden paddles. The result—a crisp, thinnish—and yes—golden crust. It's heavier on cheese and extras than on tomatoes, and very fresh-tasting.

Medium cheese and sausage costs $3.95, but with the extra large ($8.10), you get a free pitcher of beer.

Home Run Inn

(one of our favorites)

4254 W. 31st
Phone: 247-9696
247-9475

Daily, 11:00 A.M.–1:30 A.M.
Sat., 11:00 A.M.–2:30 A.M.
Sun., Noon–Midnight

South Side's most popular pizza place and best thin crust pizza in the city. Busy, bustling, down-home kind of place. Thin, rich-crusted pizza that's piled with mushrooms, peppers, onions, or whatever extras you fancy. Cheesy, gooey, slightly oily—it's good old fifties pizza parlor style. Two rooms—one slick and modern; the other older and funkier with long bar and great "dogs at a dance" wallpaper. Large cheese and sausage is $5.45. Carry-outs available.

Nancy's

7309 W. Lawrence,   Mon.-Thur., 10:00 A.M.–Midnight
  Harwood Heights   Fri.-Sun., 10:00 A.M.–2:00 A.M.
Phone: 867-4641

Home of the stuffed pizza, a truly illicit affair! It's huge, rich, and oozing with cheese. First comes the crust, then the filling (sausage is good but could be more generous), a thick melt of cheese, some more crust, all topped by a spicy frosting of oregano-doused tomato sauce. When it's good, it's very good. However on an off-night, the crust can taste like shirt cardboard.

Service is pizza parlor slow, but it's possible to call ahead. A medium cheese and sausage goes for $7.00 and will easily serve three. Brisk carry-out business.

Nite n' Gale

346 Waukegan, Highwood   Daily, 11:00 A.M.–3:00 P.M.;
Phone: 432-9744   4:00 P.M.–Midnight
                  Fri., Sat., 4:00 P.M.–1:00 A.M.
                  Sun., 4:00 P.M.–Midnight

For years had a well-deserved reputation for its excellent thin crust pizza. Recently made the switch to fat crust with equally successful results. Fresh-tasting crisp crust (occasionally it can be *too* thick), subtle tomato sauce with tomato bits, and a magnificent mass of melted cheese. When it's good, it's really good. Large cheese and sausage, $5.75. Carry-outs available.

Nite n' Gale is housed in large pseudo-medieval English dining rooms. Also serves tasty ribs and a good half-pound hamburger on rye ($2.25).

Directions: Take Edens Expressway to Route 22 (Half Day Rd.). Go east to dead end. Turn left. Go one block and turn right, cross train tracks and then turn left ½ block to Nite n' Gale. Good luck.

Pizzeria Uno

29 E. Ohio
Phone: 321-1000

Mon.-Sat., 11:30 A.M.–1:20 A.M.
Closed Sunday and Monday

One of Chicago's two sister pizza emporiums, and in our opinion, it's now the better of the two. Also much homier, more casual, less crowded. One of the originators of pan pizza, they naturally do a terrific job. Crisp, thinnish crust topped with tomato bits, loads of cheese, and spicy sausage. Rich but worth it. Large cheese and sausage is $6.50. Carry-outs available.

Ria's

(one of our favorites)

3943 N. Lincoln
Phone: 281-8812

Daily: 4:00 P.M.–Midnight
Fri., 4:00 P.M.–1:00 A.M.
Sat., 4:00 P.M.–2:00 A.M.
Closed Monday

Ria's makes a fabulous pizza, which we generally concede to be our favorite. It's mainly the sausage. They lay it on thick, it's homemade and pleasantly spicy with just a hint of orange peel. The crust is medium thick, rich, and flaky. Sauce contains pieces of tomato, a healthy helping of oregano and a fine amount of melted cheese. All works together in producing a pizza that one inevitably dreams about at one in the morning on the road in the middle of Wyoming.

Ria's has full bar service and looks unmistakably like countless other restaurant-lounges throughout America. Large cheese and sausage, $5.55. Carry-outs and delivery available, within a reasonable distance.

Ricobene's

250 W. 26th
Phone: 225-9811

Daily, 11:00 A.M.–12:30 P.M.
Fri.-Sat., 11:00 A.M.–2:00 P.M.
Sun., 5:00 P.M.–Midnight

Located in the shadow of a hulking expressway, Ricobene's must be Chicago's noisiest pizza place. It also does a nonstop business because the pizza's terrific. It's thin-crusted, has cheese that won't quit and fat chunks of mild, good quality sausage. This is strictly an open air carry-out operation, so you might want to call in your order ahead of time. Interesting neighborhood scene. For a surreal experience, try eating in the playground across the street, directly under the freeway. Large cheese and sausage, $3.90.

Directions: Located a half block west of Wentworth, just south of Chinatown.

Salerno's

6633 W. 16th, Berwyn
Phone: 484-3400

Daily, 10:00 A.M.–1:00 A.M.
Sat., 10:00 A.M.–2:00 A.M.
Sun., Noon–Midnight

Big, popular, multi-roomed Berwyn pizza parlor (and restaurant.) They serve a medium thick-crusted pizza. One of the cheesiest we've come across—enough cheese to strangle you. Mildly spicy. Pizzas range in size from a baby to an extra-large, and they're not kidding. Large cheese and sausage, $6.00. Carry-outs available.

Pizza by the Slice

Chicago has several places where you can snack on a slice (or two or three) of pizza. Pizza slices can be bought primarily in bakeries, though some restaurants and sandwich shops also sell it. Here are a few:

De Leo's Bakery

1119 W. Taylor St.   Go in the morning
Phone: 421-9352   Closed Monday

Much like a pizzabread—rich and tomato sauced. Not for cheese freaks. They cut each slice with a scissors. 50¢ a slice.

Italian and French Bakery

1124 W. Grand   Daily, 8:00 A.M.–6:00 P.M.
Phone: 733-5456   Sunday, 8:00 A.M.–1:00 P.M.

Thick, blistery, chewy pizza laid out on trays at this tiny, great-smelling neighborhood bakery. The real thing! Plain tomato costs 45¢ and sausage adds another dime.

John's Jumbo Sandwich Shop

1959 W. Grand   Daily, 10:00 A.M.–11:30 P.M.
Phone: 421-9814   Closed Sunday

A workingman's sandwich shop that's recently been moved and modernized. Crowded at lunch when everyone feasts on beef, sausage, meatball sandwiches, spaghetti, etc. But you can also get a warm slice of pizza to snack on. 40¢ a slice.

The Original Sicilian Bakery

3962 W. Grand   Daily, 9:00 A.M.–7:00 P.M.
Phone: 252-9186   Sundays, 9:00 A.M.–2:00 P.M.

Authentic little bakery, selling a moderately spicy, fine slice of pizza (20¢ apiece). Also delicious cannoli with candied fruit and chocolate chips hidden in the filling (30¢).

Scafuri Bakery

1337 W. Taylor   Go in the morning
Phone: 733-8881   Closed Monday

Very similar to de Leo's. Tomato predominates in this breadlike pizza. Best to get here early when pizza's warm, and they're sure to have some. $1.55 for half a pizza.

Miscellaneous Snacks

If you're looking for something different, perhaps exotica like Chinese dim sum or merely a good bowl of chili, Chicago's got it. Scan this list, and maybe you'll hit upon something you've had a craving for.

Garrett Popcorn Shop
(one of our favorites)

10 W. Madison
Phone: 263-8466

Daily, 9:30 A.M.–Midnight
Sun., Noon–10:00 P.M.

Garrett's starts your mouth watering as soon as you enter the door. Could a rose smell as sweet as freshly popped caramel corn? Prices range from 15¢ for a small bag up to $1.90 for a twenty-ounce sack. Also fresh popcorn, cheese popcorn, popcorn balls, and fudge.

Happy Garden Bakery

2358 S. Wentworth
Phone: 225-2730

Daily, 9:00 A.M.–7:00 P.M.
Closed Tuesday

Located at the far south end of Chinatown, this little bakery specializes in fresh baked dim sum (Chinese tea pastries). Good smells. Some unusual tastes. Especially nice are the soft buns filled with coconut and peanut butter. Also cha shu bow (buns filled with barbecued pork), ham and egg filled buns, a flaky pastry containing curried chicken, and almond cookies.

House of Eggroll

3303 N. Marshfield
Phone: 281-7888

Daily, 11:00 A.M.–10:00 P.M.

It's hard to pass up a place called House of Eggroll. Six different varieties are offered, including chicken, ham, beef, barbecued pork, shrimp and pork, and vegetable, priced from 60¢ to 75¢. They're good sized, crisp-skinned, and make a great snack. Also on the menu, bite-sized, steamed, open-topped wonton (three pieces for 65¢) and fried chicken (!).

Matina's

4020½ S. California
Phone: 254-2849

Daily, 10:00 A.M.–7:00 P.M.
Sunday, 10:00 A.M.–5:00 P.M.

Would you believe chocolate-covered watermelon? Matina's makes up a batch each summer, if the price of watermelon isn't up too high. If it is, they also sell good chocolate-dipped bananas, homemade caramel apples, candied orange slices, spearmint leaves, big gumdrops, and red juju coins in this tiny, charming little candy shop.

In a Class of Their Own

Maxwell Street

1300 South at Halsted   Sundays only: Anywhere from
                                    5:00 A.M.–Noon

The food is gone from Maxwell Street, and so ends some of the best out-and-out street snacking around, though the guy selling home canned fruit that looks like it was left over from the Civil War may still be around. There are still loads of colorful characters, however. Great music too. And if you need some used nuts and bolts, shoelaces, snake oil . . .

Chicago Folk Fair

Held at Navy Pier, usually the first weekend in November

The ethnic eating extravaganza of the year. A tribute to Chicago's melting pot diversity. Food, crafts, and folk dancing are on display. The food section alone stretches for a good half-mile. Edibles from dozens of nationalities are represented, much of it prepared while you watch. What a feast! There's Ghanian peanut stew, Pakistani roast lamb with rice pilaf, Native American fried bread and pumpkin pudding, Norwegian open face sandwiches, Latvian apple fritters, and a mind-boggling amount of strudels, breads, and assorted pastry. One year Chef Louis of The Bakery was even preparing Hungarian palascinta (crepes) for 20¢ each. Prices for everything are minimal and furthermore, admission is free. A must!

A Few Bites More

ALICIA #2, 852 N. Ashland (421-9798)
Tiny place with elaborate decor and authentic Mexican food. Delicious, messy tostadas de carnitas (thin-sliced pork). Good pork stew with salsa verde (green sauce).

LAS AMERICAS, 3723 N. Southport (477-2990)
Neighborhood Mexican restaurant serving delicious juicy tacos and really hot guacamole. Clean and nice.

ARVEY'S, 7041 W. Oakton, Niles (967-9790)
Great place for a Wednesday night bash. Dinners include saganaki (flaming cheese pie), egg-lemon soup, and a big helping of Caesar salad. Mostly Greek entrees, but there's also an inexpensive steak Diane ($3.95) and a broiled skirt steak ($3.95).

LA BELLA SORRENTO, 2800 E. 93rd (374-0030)
Down home local atmosphere (lots of teenagers, drinkers, cops), friendly waitresses, and big portions of Italian specialties. Excellent cheese- or ground beef-stuffed manicotti.

BLUE PEACOCK, 2340 W. Devon (761-5050)
Large, interesting Chinese menu. Try delicate crab rangoon appetizer. Excellent sweet and sour wonton, hong sue chicken, and pepper beef.

BOHEMIA, 6026 W. Cermak, Cicero (863-9297)
Yet another low-priced neighborhood Bohemian restaurant. Old-fashioned ambience. Most dinners under $3.00, including incredibly juicy, crisp roast duck.

BUSY BEE, 1546 N. Damen (384-8775)
Lives up to its name, especially at lunch. Good Polish food in an old-fashioned setting. Delicious thueringer and knackwurst with kraut ($1.80).

CHARLIE'S, 2201 W. Montrose (588-9470)

A typical corner coffee shop that you'd never guess served Middle Eastern food. But they do, and it's good, especially the homemade yogurt. Falafel, kibbi, too. Ask for the special menu.

CHARLIE CHAN'S, 3805 N. Clark (929-3969)

It doesn't take much sleuthing to pick out a good Mandarin meal here. Try princess prawns, moo shu pork, and Birmingham Brown's spicy braised beef. Excellent candied bananas for dessert.

CROATIAN VILLAGE, 551 W. 31st (326-3823)

Menu lists only one or two Croatian specialties, but the spicy, peppery cevapcici (sausage) are very tasty.

THE DUMPLING HOUSE, 4109 S. Harlem, Stickney (484-9633)

Bohemian families on a night out. Big meals under $3.00. Crisp pork tenderloin and smoky-flavored sauerkraut.

GARE ST. LAZARE, 858 W. Armitage (871-0062)

Dark, intimate little bistro featuring a la carte, mostly French meals. Excellent poulet aux fines herbes (chicken marinated and basted with wine, lemon, and herbs) and boudin aux pommes (soft sausage sauteed with apples and raisins). Crepes too. Slow service. Reservations on weekends.

GLENWAY INN, 1401 W. Devon (743-2208)

The best corned beef and cabbage in town (Thursdays only). Also good, sweet-glazed ribs and pan-fried chicken. If you're looking for action, try the place on St. Patrick's Day.

HARRIS RESTAURANT, 3148 W. Irving Park (539-2357)

A sterile coffee shop complete with muzak where the food is actually good. Homey-tasting roast chicken. And they bake their own hot apple pie, strawberry cheesecake, strawberry tart, etc. Open twenty-four hours.

HEARTLAND, 7000 N. Glenwood (465-8005)
Recently-opened Rogers Park health food spot. Cheap,
filling meals usually include three daily specials (try the stir-
fried vegetables and rice). Casual, communal spirit.

HOTSPURS, 7 W. Division (787-8141)
Sleek, plant-filled Rush St. area hotspot that makes a good,
thick, juicy cheeseburger. Several other sandwiches and
omelettes.

HUNGARIAN DELIGHTS, 3510 W. Irving (463-9875)
Cozy, cheerfully-decorated storefront that lives up to its
name. Try the liver dumpling soup, beef or szekely goulash.
Four kinds of strudel (apple, cheese, cherry, and cabbage)
and two types of palascinta (apricot or cheese) available for
dessert.

ICHIBAN, 3155 N. Broadway (935-3636)
A serene, lovely setting for some off-and-on Japanese food.
Best bets are tempura and chicken teriyaki.

INDIAN TRAIL, 507 Chestnut, Winnetka (446-1703)
Gracious restaurant with tearoom overtones. Wonderful
soups, rolls, salad dressings. Mouthwatering desserts: apricot
or raspberry tarts, toasted almond layer cake, sour cream
apple-raisin pie, blueberry crisp a la mode, and boysenberry
sundaes.

ING'S, 5868 N. Lincoln (878-6642)
Decent Chinese food at terrific bargain prices. A mammoth
"dinner for four" goes for a mere $11.00. Good, crisp egg roll.

KAI KAI, 2218 S. Wentworth (225-1952)
Chinatown restaurant popular with local Chinese residents.
Very cheap. Delicious fried rice.

KATEY'S, 3326 N. Lincoln (no phone)
A tiny, hidden Hungarian luncheonette housed in a building that looks perfect for Sam Spade. Try the 40¢ palascinta (a delicate Hungarian crepe).

KIBBUTZ, 2817 W. Touhy (262-7868)
Brisk, no-nonsense, non-dairy Israeli restaurant. Crisp falafel, smooth hommos. Other specialties include brisket, goulash, roast chicken, and kishke.

LIBERTY, 4915 W. 14th, Cicero (863-9371)
Small, family-run, neighborhood diner serving plain but substantial Lithuanian meals. Homemade soups, thick rye, cheese blintzes.

LUCITA'S, 1440 E. 57th (955-0888)
Cozy setting, fast service, and nicely-priced Mexican meals. Enchiladas and burritos are best bets.

MAMA SUE'S, 1402 W. Taylor (942-1082)
Taylor Street newcomer serving mammoth portions of pasta. Homemade tagliatelle and cavatelli. Pizza looked and smelled great too.

MAN CHUN HOUSE, 239 Pulaski, Calumet City (891-5300)
Murky, atmospheric place serving good-quality Cantonese. Try shrimp cashew ding, beef wing young, and soom goo gai kow (chicken with three kinds of mushrooms).

MARGE'S, 1758 N. Sedgwick (944-9775)
Laid back neighborhood tap that serves a fine hamburger —crisp-edged, thick, meaty, juicy. Homemade soups, chili, and excellent ham and cheese, too. Good jukebox.

MARY'S, 1123 N. California (486-9749)
A friendly worker/caseworker-filled diner featuring cheap, filling Polish meals. Terrific soups, especially the cabbage, and fat, tasty, homemade pierogi (the sweet cheese or cabbage are delicious).

MEL MARKON'S, 2150 Lincoln Park West (525-5550)
Probably the best cabbage soup in the city.

EL MEXICANO, 2627 N. Clark (528-2131)
An offshoot of a bowling alley. Potent chile rellenos and good enchiladas, especially the cheesy enchiladas suizas. Dependable, unpretentious.

MEXICAN INN, 95th and Ewing (737-8957)
One of the all-time bargain Mexican meals. Juicy, fresh-tasting tacos. Family-run and usually packed.

MEXICO TAQUERIA, 1350 S. Halsted (733-9295) or 7604 N. Ashland (338-1473)
Some of the cheapest Mexican food in town. Especially tasty tostadas suizas, garnachas (tortilla chips covered with beans and melted cheese), and combination plates. Open twenty-four hours.

MI CASA, SU CASA, 2525 N. Southport (525-5028)
Prices are up, but quality hasn't kept pace. Still make sumptuous, cheesey enchiladas, and tasty sopes (fat, hand-patted tortillas topped with ground beef, beans, lettuce, tomatoes, and cheese).

MONGOLIAN HOUSE, 3410 N. Clark (935-1110)
Some of the nicest-priced Mandarin food around. Big portions too. Don't miss the moo shu pork and Mongolian beef.

MUSHROOM & SONS LTD., 1825 Second St., Highland Park (432-0824)
Greenery galore. Twenty different salad combinations with a choice of homemade dressings. Try the fresh mushroom, raw cauliflower, or fruit. Some fine hot dishes too, particularly brown rice and vegetables. Also "health" sandwiches and deli-type selections.

NEW CHINA, 3710 W. Dempster, Skokie (674-3426)
Standard Cantonese fare with a few standouts—young chew wonton, and fun shee, a black mushroom, shrimp, pork, peapod, cellophane noodle extravaganza.

NEW LITTLE BOHEMIA, 2700 S. Cristiana (762-9537)
Casual neighborhood restaurant/bar featuring big Bohemian meals—roast pork, duck, capon, pickled beef, etc., and all the trimmings. Sometimes there's even pickled wild rabbit in sour cream gravy.

NICK'S LA CANTINA, 1062 Lee, Des Plaines (824-4230)
Friendly, sprawling Italian restaurant. Delicious veal parmigiana, escarole soup, green noodles. Good fried chicken and barbecued ribs too.

OLD POLONIA, 10 N. Clark (263-0663)
Old fashioned basement hideaway filled with steam table offerings & lawyers. Friday's a good bet for cheese blintzes and potato pancakes.

PALANGA, 6918 S. Western (476-9758)
Friendly neighborhood Lithuanian restaurant. Robust soups, superb bread, and crisp duck ($3.00).

LA POSADA, 2601 S. Ridgeway (762-9818)
Popular with Mexican families. Homemade flour tortillas kept in a warmer at your table. Spicy mole sauce, juicy tacos. Big portions, low prices.

PEACOCK'S HILLTOP RESTAURANT, 79 E. 103rd (821-6315)
Lively soul food restaurant. Super cheap. Three side dishes with entree. Sweet peach cobbler for dessert.

SHALIMAR, 2650 N. Clark (750-2322)
Intimate Indian restaurant. Varied menu. Tandoori specialties and good vegetables dishes. Carry-outs available.

SORDANG ASIAN CAFE, 3961 N. Ashland (no phone)
Very authentic Thai cooking. Try the shrimp rolls, crisp candied noodles (mee krob), and steamed crab.

SUMAVA, 2959 W. 63rd (476-4133)
Another Bohemian bargain. Delicious soup to strudel spreads, most for under $3.00. Try either the roast chicken or the duck.

TERESA'S POLISH RESTAURANT, 3031 N. Milwaukee (252-9300).
Plenty of homecooked food at easy-to take prices. Pierogi, homemade soups, blintzes. The works!

UNCLE JOHN'S, 3801 W. Fullerton (252-6464)
Big, neighborhood restaurant-lounge featuring Italian meals. Veal parmigiana is especially good (on Tuesdays it's a $3.00 special). There's usually a combo playing and don't be surprised if people get up from the "audience" to sing.

WESLEY'S POLISH RESTAURANT, 6690 Northwest Highway (631-1161)
Inexpensive meals in a family-run, old-fashioned setting. The crisp salisbury steak, beef with dill sauce, and apple or cheese blintzes are good choices.

WELTY'S, 130 S. Clark (332-0477)
If you're downtown on a Friday, stop in for their superb red snapper soup.

YORIKO CHAN, 5449 N. Clark (275-6215)
A friendly, family-run restaurant that carries a huge Japanese/Chinese menu. Check out the egg roll and sinju chow foon.

Location Index

Loop & Near North

Mid North

Far North

Northwest

Near West

West

South

Southwest

French Kitchen, 34
Gertie's Ice Cream Parlor, 213
Giordano's, 222
Home Run Inn, 223
Matina's, 230
Middle East, 94
Neringa, 82
New Little Bohemia, 237
Palanga, 237

La Posada, 237
Polonia, 99
Ramune, 83
Ruta, 84
Stehlik's, 12
Sumava, 238
Toscano's, 63
Tulpe, 85
Villa Marconi, 65

Suburbs & Beyond

North

Falafel King (Skokie), 193
Fritz, That's It (Evanston), 131
Golden Crown (Northbrook), 19
Indian Trail (Winnetka), 234
Magic Pan (Old Orchard Shopping Center), 152
Margarita Club (Evanston), 130
Mediterranean House (Skokie), 93
Mr. Ricky's (Skokie), 164
Mushroom & Sons (Highland Park), 236
New China (Skokie), 237
New York Style Pizza (Evanston), 195
Nite 'n Gale (Highwood), 224
Original Pancake House (Wilmette), 164
Peacock's Dairy Bar (Evanston, Wilmette), 214
S & S Deli (Highland Park), 169

San Pedro (Wilmette), 149

Northwest

Arvey's (Niles), 232
Bimbo's (Palatine), 56
Buffalo (Morton Grove), 208
Eastern Style Pizza (Golf Mill, Niles), 221
Hackney's (Glenview, Lake Zurich, Wheeling), 176
El Jarocho (Palatine), 88
Lakeside Inn (Lakemoor), 129
Magic Pan (Hawthorne Shopping Center; Woodfield Shopping Center), 152
Nancy's (Harwood Heights), 224
Nick's La Cantina (Des Plaines), 237
La Poele D'or (Arlington Heights), 28
St. Sava Monastery (Libertyville), 110
Sawa's Old Warsaw (Harwood Heights), 100
2¢ Plain (Wheeling), 166
El Zarape (Elgin), 92

West

South & Southwest

Alphabetical Index

248

Dear Reader

If you think that we've left any good restaurants out, or included some that you feel should be omitted in the future, let us know. We'd really appreciate it. Just fill in the postcard and drop it in the mail.

Please include:

Name of restaurant _____
Address _____
Type of food served _____
Favorite dish _____
Price range _____
Other comments _____
_____
_____
_____

Next time Forget About:

Name of restaurant _____
Comments _____
_____
_____
_____

Mail to: The Good But Cheap Chicago Restaurant
          Book
          P.O. Box A3963
          Chicago, Illinois 60690